C000218305

Autho

There are many people to whom I am very thankful for their help and support during the writing of this book. First and foremost, my sincere thanks to the governing board of Moore Theological College for granting me six months of study leave to work on this volume.

Thank you to everyone at SPCK/IVP, especially to senior commissioning editor Philip Duce for his help during the writing process, and to NSBT series editor Don Carson for his input and for agreeing to include this book in the series. Many thanks as well to Eldo Barkhuizen for his very capable copy-editing.

Two people in particular have had a profound impact on my theological formation: Mark Thompson and Peter O'Brien. I would like to thank Mark – friend, colleague and principal of Moore College – for his unfailingly kind support and warm friendship over many years and particularly his encouragement during this period of writing. I am also very grateful to the Lord for Peter and his friendship, mentoring and godly Christian example over many years. This study had its genesis in a final-year project that Peter patiently supervised.

My colleagues on the faculty have been a wonderful support during this project in different ways. I want especially to thank my friends and colleagues in the New Testament department – Lionel Windsor, Will Timmins, Pete Tong and Philip Kern. Philip as well as being a good friend, colleague and department head is a wonderful model of godly, careful teaching. Thanks too to Simon Gillham, Chase Kuhn and Dan Wu for their friendship and frequent encouragement while I wrote this book.

Portions of this book have appeared in expanded form in my earlier work *Christ Absent and Present* published by Mohr Siebeck Tübingen in their WUNT series. I am extremely thankful to Mohr Siebeck for granting me the permission to reuse this material in its current form.

A number of people have very kindly read portions of this book or helped with its production in other ways. Thank you to Andrew Court, Jack Hamer, Kate Hamer, Pat O'Keeffe, Paul Searle, Andrew West, Mark Woodhouse and Paul Young. Thanks to the students of Moore

College for their encouragement while writing – particularly the lunch-time cricketers.

Thanks to the wonderful church family at All Saints Petersham. I also want to thank a number of friends who have, in different ways, given particular encouragement or support during this writing process and for whom I am very thankful to God: Andrew and Kath Bruce; Leo and Vicky Davison; Ben and Sara Gray; Russ and Aimee Grinter; Luke and Anna Jackson; Andrew and Michelle Price; Mark and Sarah Rainbow; and Ross and Megan Walker.

Thank you to my family; to my sister Susannah Orr for her love and support; to my sons Ben, Ollie, Jonny and Daniel for helping me to take my mind off writing as we read stories, played basketball, watched water polo and listened to podcasts about exploding whales. I pray that you will understand the content of this book one day. To my wife, Emma: there is not enough space to write everything for which I am thankful to the delight of my life.

Finally, to the dedicatees of this book my mum and dad. Thank you for everything. I hope this one is more readable.

Soli Deo Gloria!
Peter Orr
Sydney

Abbreviations

AB	Anchor Bible
AcT	*Acta Theologica*
AGJU	Arbeiten zur Geschichte des antiken Judentums und des Urchristentums
AnBib	Analecta biblica
ArBib	The Aramaic Bible
AUSS	*Andrews University Seminary Studies*
AV	Authorized (King James) Version
BBR	*Bulletin for Biblical Research*
BDAG	W. Bauer, F. W. Danker, W. F. Arndt and F. W. Gingrich, *Greek–English Lexicon of the New Testament and Other Early Christian Literature*, 3d edn, Chicago: University of Chicago Press, 1999
BECNT	Baker Exegetical Commentary on the New Testament
BI	*Biblical Illustrator*
Bib	*Biblica*
BNTC	Black's New Testament Commentaries
BTB	*Biblical Theology Bulletin*
BTCP	The Biblical Theology for Christian Proclamation Commentary Series
BZ	*Biblische Zeitschrift*
BZNW	Beihefte zur Zeitschrift für die neutestamentliche Wissenschaft
CBQ	*Catholic Biblical Quarterly*
ESV	English Standard Version
ETL	*Ephemerides theologicae lovanienses*
FAT	Forschungen zum Alten Testament
FRLANT	Forschungen zur Religion und Literatur des Alten und Neuen Testaments
HCSB	Holman Christian Standard Bible
HTKNT	Herders theologischer Kommentar zum Neuen Testament
HTR	*Harvard Theological Review*

HUT	Hermeneutische Untersuchungen zur Theologie
ICC	International Critical Commentary
IJST	*International Journal of Systematic Theology*
Int	*Interpretation: A Journal of Bible and Theology*
JBL	*Journal of Biblical Literature*
JCTS	*Jewish and Christian Text Series*
JETS	*Journal of the Evangelical Theological Society*
JSNT	*Journal for the Study of the New Testament*
JSNTSup	Journal for the Study of the New Testament: Supplement Series
JSOTSup	Journal for the Study of the Old Testament: Supplement Series
JTS	*Journal of Theological Studies*
KEK	Kritisch-exegetischer Kommentar über das Neue Testament (Meyer-Kommentar)
LNTS	Library of New Testament Studies
LXX	Septuagint
MT	Masoretic Text
NASB	New American Standard Bible
NICNT	New International Commentary on the New Testament
NIGTC	New International Greek Testament Commentary
NIV	New International Version (2011)
NovT	*Novum Testamentum*
NovTSup	Novum Testamentum Supplements
NRSV	New Revised Standard Version
NSBT	New Studies in Biblical Theology
NT	New Testament
NTA	New Testament Abstracts
NTL	New Testament Library
NTOA	Novum Testamentum et Orbis Antiquus
NTS	*New Testament Studies*
OT	Old Testament
PL	Patrologia latina [= Patrologiae cursus completus: Series latina]. Edited by J.-P. Migne, 217 vols., Paris, 1844–64
PNTC	Pillar New Testament Commentaries
RB	*Revue biblique*
RSR	*Recherches de science religieuse*
RSV	Revised Standard Version
RTR	*Reformed Theological Review*

SBLDS	Society of Biblical Literature Dissertation Series
SBT	Studies in Biblical Theology
SNTSMS	Society for New Testament Studies Monograph Series
SP	Sacra pagina
SUNT	Studien zur Umwelt des Neuen Testaments
SwJT	*Southwestern Journal of Theology*
TDNT	*Theological Dictionary of the New Testament*, ed. J. Botterweck and H. Ringgren, translated by John T. Willis et al., 8 vols., Grand Rapids: Eerdmans, 1974–2006
T. Levi	*Testament of Levi*
tr.	Translation, translated by
TynB	*Tyndale Bulletin*
WBC	Word Biblical Commentary
WUNT	Wissenschaftliche Untersuchungen zum Neuen Testament
ZECNT	Zondervan Exegetical Commentary on the New Testament
ZNW	*Zeitschrift für die neutestamentliche Wissenschaft und die Kunde der älteren Kirche*

Chapter One

Introduction

Why this book?

This is a book about Jesus as he is now. In some ways, then, it is an extended application of and meditation on Colossians 3:1–2: 'If then you have been raised with Christ, seek the things that are above, where Christ is, seated at the right hand of God. Set your minds on things that are above, not on things that are on earth.'[1]

Generally speaking, Christians have tended to focus their attention on what Jesus *has* done (his life, death and resurrection) and what he *will* do (return and reign). And while there has been something of a revival in the study of Jesus' ascension,[2] there is a tendency to consider Christ's exalted state simply in relation to the events of his ascension or his parousia. Studies that consider Jesus in his exalted state are relatively rare. However, the Christ that Christians trust in, relate to and love is the Christ who not only lived, died, rose and will come again but also is presently at God's right hand. Christian faith as well as Christian theological reflection must take into consideration this significant aspect of Christ's identity.

This book, then, is a study on the exalted Christ. For our purposes, we will consider his 'exaltation' to be the process by which, as John puts it, Jesus departed 'out of the world' (John 13:1). Generally NT authors focus on the resurrection and the ascension as the events that bring Jesus into his exalted state, though John actually sees the crucifixion as the essence of Jesus' exaltation (e.g. John 3:14). The exalted Christ, then, is Jesus as he is following his exaltation and before his return.

This book and biblical theology

Considering the exalted Christ – his identity, his location and his activity – may seem to be a subject more obviously suited to

---

[1] All Scripture quotations are from the ESVUK unless otherwise noted.
[2] E.g. Farrow 1999, 2011.

systematic theology rather than biblical theology. However, apart from the ongoing need to show the interconnectedness of these two disciplines, considering the temporal structure of the Bible's revelation helps us to see the relevance of this topic in a series devoted to biblical theology.

There are as many proposed 'structures' of the Bible as there are biblical theologians. Graeme Goldsworthy, building on the earlier work of Donald Robinson and Gabriel Hebert, has popularized the schema that is now associated with Moore College.[3] He argues that the organizing principle of the Bible is the 'kingdom of God', and divides the Bible into four main epochs, which each provides development in the revelation of the kingdom of God: the kingdom of God revealed in Israel's prehistory (Gen. 1 – 11);[4] the kingdom of God revealed in Israel's history (Abraham to Solomon); the kingdom of God revealed in prophetic eschatology (Solomon to the end of exile); and the kingdom of God revealed in Jesus Christ (the NT). Goldsworthy further subdivides this final epoch into three aspects:[5]

(1) What Jesus did *for* us in the past, historical gospel event in fulfilment of the promises of the Old Testament.
(2) What the word of Jesus and his Spirit go on doing *in* us as we live in the present our life of faith and in the world as the gospel is proclaimed.
(3) What the end-time consummation *with* us will be when Jesus returns in glory to judge the living and the dead and to bring in the fullness of his kingdom.

Whether or not we accept Goldsworthy's overall structure, this delineation of the New Testament era helpfully distinguishes the different aspects of Christ's work for us. However, in this schema there is a subtle tendency to downplay the *ongoing* significance of Jesus. Whereas in points 1 and 3 Jesus is presented actively ('what Jesus *did* for us' and 'Jesus *returns*'), in point 2 the Spirit and Jesus' '*word*' are presented as the active agents.

Certainly the NT affirms the work of the Spirit (e.g. Rom. 8:14) and the power of Jesus' word (e.g. Acts 6:7); however, it also affirms that Jesus himself *remains* active. For example, he intercedes (Rom. 8:34; Heb. 7:25), he enables Christians to persevere (Rom. 14:4;

[3] See Goldsworthy 2012: 24–27.
[4] Strictly speaking this is not an 'epoch' in Goldsworthy's schema.
[5] The text here is taken verbatim from Goldsworthy 2015: 26; emphasis original.

1 Cor. 1:7–8) and he continues to speak through his apostles (2 Cor. 13:3). Yes, the focus of the NT is on the past (and future) work of Christ but it is by no means silent on his present work.

Further, Goldsworthy's scheme implies that this is a period of Christ's absence. However, the picture across the New Testament is more complicated than simply saying that Jesus leaves and the Spirit comes. For a start, what are we to make of Jesus' famous promise in the great commission, '[B]ehold, I am with you always, to the end of the age' (Matt. 28:20)? This age is fundamentally the age of the *presence* of Jesus. Again, as he concludes his high-priestly prayer in John 17, Jesus expresses the desire that the love the Father has for him may be in the disciples, and that he himself 'may be in them' (17:26). Even though Jesus is leaving and sending the Spirit, he himself will 'be in them'.

However, in the same prayer Jesus affirms that he is 'no longer in the world' even while believers 'are in the world' (17:11). There appears, then, to be something of a tension between the absence and presence of Christ. So, in 2 Corinthians, Paul can state that 'while we are at home in the body we are away from the Lord' (2 Cor. 5:6; cf. 5:8) and he can remind the Corinthians in the same letter that Christ 'is powerful among you' (13:3). One of the questions this book will focus on, then, is how we are to think of this period in redemptive history between Jesus' ascension and his return. In this period what is the relationship between Christ's absence and his presence? If anything, in theological reflection on this question, there is an emphasis on the ongoing *presence* of Christ. So, König is typical when he states that 'Christ has not gone away, and his work on earth has not been interrupted. He continues it without break.'[6] Or Beverly Gaventa who suggests that 'Jesus' ascension does not mean his absence; it simply means that his presence is no longer constrained by place and time'.[7] We will see that these suggestions overlook important strands of NT data which indicate that Christ's absence is more Christologically significant particularly as it relates to his ongoing humanity.

But perhaps the most fundamental question this volume will consider is in what sense, if any, the exaltation of Christ affects his identity. When, for example, Peter affirms that following the resurrection (and ascension), God has 'made him both Lord and Christ,

6 König 1989: 141.
7 Gaventa 2008: 163.

3

this Jesus whom you crucified' (Acts 2:36), what exactly does he mean? Does Christ's exaltation merely reveal his lordship and messianic identity, or does he enter into them in a fuller way following his exaltation?

As such, this book will attend to this somewhat neglected sub-epoch of biblical theology in considering what we can say about Jesus in the present, as the exalted Christ, and so what it means to 'set our minds' on Christ as he is seated at God's right hand.

The plan of this book

This book will examine the exalted Christ through the lenses of his identity (chapters 2–4), his location (chapters 5–8) and his activity (chapters 9–10). In terms of his identity, chapter 2 considers the relationship between the 'earthly Jesus' and the 'exalted Christ' across the NT, and will particularly consider the question of how the resurrection and ascension affect (if at all) his identity. Chapters 3 and 4 will treat the exalted Christ's relationship to the Spirit and to the church and will consider arguments that have effectively collapsed Christ into either the Spirit or the church. In considering his location, chapter 5 looks at the relationship between Christ's exaltation and his absence. Chapters 6 and 7 attend more closely to the relationship between Christ's absence and his continuing possession of a discrete, individual, localizable human body. For Paul, in particular, Christ's absence is a bodily absence. In chapter 8 we examine the presence of Christ by examining one of the most important sections in the NT to deal with Christ's ongoing presence: 2 Corinthians 2 – 4. Here we will see that Christ's presence is both mediated and *epiphanic*; that is, Christ is essentially *made* present. Although this is an essentially passive mode of presence, we will see that this is by no means weak or ineffectual. The final section on the activity of Christ (chapters 9 and 10) is related to chapter 8 in that it portrays Christ's active presence; that is, where he is presented as an agent. In chapter 9 we look at Christ's mediated activity on earth, while in chapter 10 we examine his activity in heaven as he responds to prayer and intercedes for believers. In the final chapter I offer a brief summary and some theological and pastoral reflections.

Chapter Two

The identity of the exalted Christ: the exalted Christ and the earthly Jesus

Introduction: defining identity

Defining the identity of the exalted Christ, on the surface at least, appears to be straightforward. NT writers uniformly consider the Christ who is exalted to be the same person as the Jesus who died. So, for example, in 1 Corinthians 15:3–4 Paul maintains that the Christ who died is the Christ who was raised. In Hebrews 1:3 the one who 'made purification for our sins' is the one who then 'sat down at the right hand of the Majesty on high'. In Revelation 1:7 the one who is returning is the one who was 'pierced'.

However, the question of identity is more complex than it appears at first and attempts to define it fully have put bread on the table for generations of philosophers. For our purposes, it is enough to touch on two aspects of identity that have been highlighted in these discussions.[1] First, identity as 'singularity';[2] that is, 'the specific uniqueness of a person, what really counts about him'.[3] What is it that makes a person unique? Second, identity in terms of relationship. That is, personal 'identity is never merely an individual matter, as though we are what we think'. Rather, it 'is always a social product, the upshot of multiple perceptions'.[4] Our identities are never formed in isolation but are always shaped in relationship with others.[5] And so, to 'tell the story of Jesus is to tell the story of his relationships'.[6]

[1] For a recent survey of theories of identity and their application to biblical studies see Pascut 2017: 10–15.
[2] Grieb 2008: 206.
[3] Frei 1997: 95, cited in Grieb (2008: 206).
[4] Allison 2008: 93.
[5] Ricoeur (1992: 3) is helpful here in his discussion of the 'other'; i.e. the 'otherness of a kind that can be constitutive of self-hood'.
[6] Meier 2001: 2, cited in Tilling (2012: 261).

These two aspects of identity are helpful for organizing our reading of the NT and what it says about the exalted Christ. In this chapter we will consider Christ's identity in terms of his singularity. We will examine the continuity of the exalted Christ and the 'earthly' or 'historical' Jesus (a relationship which has been the subject of considerable debate in NT scholarship). I will show that his personal identity remains the same – the Christ who is exalted *is* the Jesus who was crucified. Nevertheless, we will also see that, in a number of places, Christ's identity seems to be reconfigured by the resurrection. Following the resurrection, the NT can use the language of Jesus' being 'made' Lord and Christ (Acts 2:36) or being 'begotten' as Son (Acts 13:33; cf. Rom. 1:4). It can also use the language of Jesus' receiving a new name (Phil. 2:9; cf. Heb. 1:4; Rev. 3:12). In what sense does Jesus' identity develop or expand following his exaltation?

We will consider Christ's identity in terms of his relationship with others in the following chapters as we consider his relationship to the Spirit and to the church. In chapter 3 we will see that in a number of Pauline passages (including Rom. 8:9–10; 2 Cor. 3:17) and in John's farewell discourse the risen Christ seems to be identified with the Holy Spirit. The language leads some scholars to conclude that following the resurrection 'Jesus himself *becomes* the life-giving Spirit'.[7] We also need to consider the relationship of the risen Christ to the church across the NT. Again, the closeness of this relationship leads some scholars to identify the risen Christ and the church, arguing that the 'line of distinction between Christ and his people has become blurred *if not erased altogether*'.[8]

Continuity in identity: the exalted Christ is the earthly Jesus

The debate

One of the key debates in twentieth-century NT scholarship was between Rudolph Bultmann and his pupil Ernst Käsemann concerning the continuity or otherwise between the 'earthly' (or 'historical') Jesus and the exalted Christ. For Bultmann, the 'historical' Jesus (even if we could access him) is of no relevance whatsoever. To try to reconstruct the historical Jesus would be merely to try to pursue 'Christ

---

[7] Buch-Hansen 2010: 352, emphasis added.
[8] Hays 2008: 195–196, emphasis added.

according to the flesh', which the apostle Paul rules out (2 Cor. 5:16).[9]
For Bultmann what counts is the *proclaimed* Christ. Christ has risen
into the proclamation of the gospel and is encountered there (and only
there). We encounter Christ only in the *kerygma*, the proclamation.
Following the resurrection, the 'proclaimer became the proclaimed'.[10]

Käsemann, for his part, is sympathetic to his former teacher, and
even grants the validity of Bultmann's statement that 'Christ rises
again into the kerygma' (though he does label it 'hyperbole'). However,
his great concern is that the earthly Jesus (and his teaching) is
necessary 'to keep the preached Christ from dissolving into the mere
projection of an eschatological self-consciousness and becoming
the object of a religious ideology'.[11] For Käsemann, seeing how the
church in Germany supported the Nazi regime in the Second World
War convinced him that the preaching of the church needed to be
controlled by the preaching of the earthly Jesus.

On this debate, Sarah Coakley is very perceptive in observing
that the two were actually arguing at cross-purposes because their
understandings of terms were radically different. That is, for Bultmann
continuity meant 'full and complete identity, identity in *all* characteristics, between the prior and the latter states', emphasis original –
which he denied. For Käsemann, it meant 'merely a contentful
enduring of certain *key* characteristics between the two', emphasis
original – which he insisted on.[12] They differ, too, on what is meant
by the 'historical Jesus'. For Bultmann it means the 'historians' Jesus',
while for Käsemann it means the 'earthly [or pre-Easter] Jesus' and
so 'there had to be some substantial continuity if the "risen Christ"
was not to evaporate into a docetic or ghostly variant'.[13] As such,
Coakley suggests, it is necessary to distinguish between epistemology
and ontology, 'between *ontological* states of Jesus' identity (whether
earthly or risen) and *epistemological* forms of response to him
(whether through historical research or decisions of faith)'.[14]

There is no need to enter into this debate more fully except to
observe that there is *both* continuity and discontinuity between the
earthly Jesus and exalted Christ. That is, there are NT texts which
both Bultmann and Käsemann could appeal to. A more careful

---

[9] Bultmann 1969: 220–246.
[10] Bultmann 2007: 33.
[11] Käsemann 1969: 60.
[12] Coakley 2008: 302.
[13] Ibid. 304.
[14] Ibid. 305, emphasis original.

understanding of identity prevents this reductionistic approach; that is, either absolute continuity or absolute discontinuity. There is continuity but also development in Christ's identity.

These two aspects are well illustrated in Luke's two-volume work. In her chapter on the identity of Jesus in Luke–Acts Beverly Gaventa notes Luke's pattern of what she calls 'identity changing'. A character in the Gospel may be first identified but then have his or her identity redefined or qualified in some way. So, for example, the woman introduced as 'bent over' (Luke 13:11), and so defined by her illness, is reidentified as a 'daughter of Abraham' (13:16). Zacchaeus is introduced as a 'chief tax collector' (19:2) and so is a person implicitly who needs to repent (3:12). Jesus then reidentifies him as a 'son of Abraham' (19:9).[15] This reidentification continues into Acts, where Saul is described by Ananias as a notorious man who has done much evil (9:13), but this description is corrected by the risen Lord Jesus. Saul is actually his 'chosen instrument' for carrying Jesus' name 'before the Gentiles and kings and the children of Israel' (9:15).[16] Crucially for Gaventa this process of reidentification is also applied to Jesus: 'As the narrator introduces other characters, only to have them reidentified by Jesus, the narrator also introduces Jesus to readers and hearers in ways that are later amplified or corrected or redirected.'[17] So, for example, Jesus is introduced as a king even before his birth (1:32–33), but throughout his Gospel, Luke redefines and clarifies his readers' idea of what sort of king Jesus is. This reidentification culminates with the sign above the cross identifying him as 'King of the Jews' (23:38). In other words, he is not a king 'in the usual sense of that word'.[18] The redefinition continues into Acts, where Jesus is proclaimed as 'Lord of all' (10:36) and so a king 'in a sense that lies beyond human comprehension'.[19] Gaventa's treatment of Jesus' identity in Luke–Acts is a helpful illustration of how attending to both continuity and development helps us understand his identity more carefully.

Continuity

The very notion of *resurrection* presupposes continuity of identity since the 'posit of an unidentified risen person is oxymoronic'.[20]

---

[15] Gaventa 2008: 153–154.
[16] Ibid. 154.
[17] Ibid. 155.
[18] Ibid. 156.
[19] Ibid.
[20] Jenson 1997: 199.

Throughout the NT it is repeatedly affirmed and demonstrated that the Jesus who lived and died is the same Jesus who was raised and is reigning. The Gospels recount how Jesus predicted his own resurrection, and each Gospel affirms that it is *Jesus* himself who has indeed been raised (e.g. Matt. 28:9; Mark 16:6; Luke 24:36; John 20:14). Similarly, Acts in both its narrative (1:3) and its discourse (e.g. 2:32, where Peter is emphatic: '*This* Jesus God raised up, and of that we all are witnesses') affirms this continuity in identity. This is illustrated in the three accounts of the conversion of Saul. In each one, Saul is confronted with the risen Lord Jesus and in response he asks the question 'Who are you, Lord?' (9:5; 22:8; 26:15). In each case the risen Christ identifies himself as 'Jesus' (9:5; 26:15), or by the more specific 'Jesus of Nazareth' (22:8).

For Paul, it is *Jesus* who was raised (e.g. Rom. 4:24; Gal. 1:1). In Philippians 2:6–11 he cites what many believe to be a pre-existing hymn,[21] which traces the 'story' of Jesus from his pre-earthly life through to his incarnation, death on the cross and, finally, his exaltation by God. It is worth noting with Hays that this passage shows us that

> the distinction between 'the Jesus of history' and 'the Christ of faith' is misleading . . . For Paul, Jesus Christ is a single person whose identity is disclosed in a seamless narrative running from creation to the cross to the resurrection to the eschaton. The historical details of his earthly life, such as his death by crucifixion, are no more and no less part of his identity than his role in creation and his present lordship in the community of those who call on his name.[22]

Development in identity: revelation, name and status

I imagine that most readers of this book do not need to be convinced that the NT affirms a basic continuity in identity between the earthly Jesus and the risen and exalted Christ. In this section we will consider in what sense Jesus' identity undergoes change in his exaltation (his resurrection and ascension). We will examine a number of texts that suggest that he did undergo such change, and we will see that though

---

[21] Whether or not it was does not affect the point I am making here.
[22] Hays 2008: 182.

there are ways that these texts have been misunderstood, nevertheless they help us to see that the resurrection did not leave Jesus unchanged – even at the level of his personal identity.

The need for revelation

Though the Gospels affirm that the risen Christ is *Jesus*, they also affirm that the resurrection has not left him unchanged. This is highlighted particularly in Luke and John, where, following the resurrection, even Jesus' closest followers struggle to recognize him.

Luke describes the two disciples walking on the road to Emmaus and that 'their eyes were kept from recognizing him' (24:16). Even following an extensive discussion with Jesus they do not recognize him. They do so only when 'their eyes were opened' (*diēnoichthēsan* – a passive verb; 24:31). Later the disciples recount that Jesus 'was made known to them' (HCSB; *egnōsthē* – also passive) 'in the breaking of the bread' (24:35).

Similarly, in John's Gospel Mary fails to recognize the risen Jesus. Having gone to his tomb, when she encounters Jesus they have a brief conversation, but Mary recognizes Jesus only when he addresses her by name (John 20:16). Likewise, the seven disciples who have been fishing all night do not recognize Jesus standing at the shore (21:4). When his advice leads to the miraculous catch, the beloved disciple realizes that '[i]t is the Lord' (21:7). The disciples then make their way to the shore to have breakfast with Jesus. Even in this intimate environment there is still uncertainty regarding Jesus' identity. Though John tells us that '[t]hey knew it was the Lord,' he precedes this by stating that 'none of the disciples dared ask him, "Who are you?"' (21:12). Their grasp of Jesus' identity, then, remains somewhat tenuous. It is not obvious or straightforwardly discernible to them that he is the risen Jesus.

Does this lack of recognition on the part of the disciples indicate that Jesus' body was so different that they simply could not have known that it was him? Certainly, his body is clearly a human body. Jesus can be seen with the eye, he can be touched (Luke 24:39; John 20:27); he can eat (Luke 24:43). Even though they fail to recognize him, they still relate to him as another (normal) human being. In fact, it seems that it is his very ordinariness that contributes to their failure to recognize him (the disciples think Jesus is simply another traveller on the road to Emmaus; Mary mistakes him for a gardener).

However, perhaps the disciples' lack of recognition implies more that the ability to grasp that Jesus is risen is not a simple matter of natural observation but of revelation. For Luke, as we have seen, it is only when their eyes are 'opened' and Jesus is 'made known to them' that the disciples grasp who he is. For John, Jesus does not only appear to the disciples but is 'manifested' or 'revealed' (*ephanerōthē* – again passive) to the disciples (21:14). Their way of relating to him has changed following the resurrection. His identity has changed, not in the sense that he is no longer the same individual, but in the sense that he is not apprehended simply with the naked eye. To understand Jesus as the risen Jesus is to have his identity revealed. Of course, this was true during his earthly ministry – a *true* grasp of his identity was only ever a result of revelation (Matt. 16:17; John 3:2–3). And so to grasp fully that Jesus is risen, to identify him as the risen Lord, is not *simply* a matter of observing a natural phenomenon but of revelation. A full apprehension of his identity as risen Lord comes only through revelation.

A new name

The exalted Christ is the risen Jesus. He remains the same person, his identity (considered in terms of his distinct, unique *singularity*) remains constant. However, in a number of places the NT seems to teach that following his resurrection (and/or ascension), Jesus is given a new name. In Philippians 2:9 Paul tells us that following Jesus' death of the cross, God 'has highly exalted him and bestowed on him *the name that is above every name*'. The elevated nature of Christ's name is also apparent in Ephesians 1:20–21, where Paul tells his readers that following the resurrection, God 'seated him at his right hand in the heavenly places, far above all rule and authority and power and dominion, *and above every name that is named*'. In Hebrews 1 the author begins by extolling the supremacy of Christ. At verse 4, he begins to compare Jesus to angels and maintains his superiority over them. Following Jesus' death and his being seated at God's right hand, the author tells us that Jesus became 'as much superior to angels as *the name he has inherited* is more excellent than theirs'. Both Philippians 2:9 and Hebrews 1:4, then, speak of Jesus' receiving a new name following his exaltation. This same idea is expressed in Revelation 3:12, where the risen Lord Jesus tells the church at Philadelphia that for the 'one who conquers', he will make him a 'pillar in the temple of my God' and 'will write on him the name of my God, and the name of the city of my God, the new Jerusalem, which comes down from my God out of heaven, and *my own new name*'. Before returning to these verses, it is worth looking at how names are used in the OT.

11

Names in the Old Testament

Though we do not have space to offer a full survey of the concept of 'name' in the Bible, a few comments may be helpful. Naming someone is a sign of authority, as shown by Adam's naming the animals in the garden: 'whatever the man called every living creature, that was its name' (Gen. 2:19). Further, a person's name is related to his or her reputation or character. The builders of the tower of Babel want to 'make a name' for themselves (Gen. 11:4). For God to make someone's name great is an expression of God's blessing (Gen. 12:2).

The concept of God's name is a rich one in the Bible. In Exodus 3 he tells Moses that his name is YHWH[23] and that this is 'my name for ever, and thus I am to be remembered throughout all generations' (Exod. 3:14–15). And yet a few chapters later the Israelites are reminded to worship only the Lord 'whose name is Jealous' (Exod. 34:14). At the very least this shows that the biblical concept of a 'name' can be more fluid than a Western idea that it is the 'tag' that uniquely identifies a person. In Exodus it can be closely tied to character.

We see this most clearly in Exodus 34:5, where we are told that the Lord proclaims 'the name of the LORD' to Moses. In the very next verse we read that '[t]he LORD passed before him and proclaimed, "The LORD, the LORD, a God merciful and gracious, slow to anger, and abounding in steadfast love and faithfulness."' In other words, proclaiming his name and proclaiming his character seem to be two sides of the same coin. The Lord guards his name and his reputation, speaking through Isaiah:

> I am the LORD; that is my name;
> my glory I give to no other,
> nor my praise to carved idols.
>
> (Isa. 42:8)

And so to profane God's name is to profane his character, and to take the Lord's name in vain is a serious thing and he 'will not hold him guiltless who takes his name in vain' (Exod. 20:7; cf. the execution of the man who 'blasphemed the Name', Lev. 24:11). Conversely, to fear God's *name* is to fear *him* (Deut. 28:58).

There is a strong association throughout the OT between the temple and the Lord's name. The temple is the place where his name dwells

---

[23] In this section and following sections we will switch from 'YHWH' to the more conventional (for English Bibles) 'the LORD'.

(cf. Deut. 14:23; 14:24; 16:2, 6, 11; 26:2; 1 Kgs 3:2; 5:5; 8:29; etc.). Nevertheless, given the ubiquity of God's glory, his name is seen 'in all the earth' (Ps. 8:1, 9). There is also an association between angels and God's name. The Israelites are warned to pay attention to and obey the angel who will guard and lead them because 'my name is in him' (Exod. 23:21). In Judges 13 Manoah is told that he cannot know an angel's name since 'it is wonderful [*thaumaston*, LXX]' (Judg. 13:17–18).[24]

Names are also connected to covenantal blessings in the Bible. God promises to make Abraham's name great (Gen. 12:2); he does the same for David, promising 'I will make for you a great name, like the name of the great ones of the earth' (2 Sam. 7:9). Further, being named by the Lord is connected with redemption and relationship with him. Through Isaiah he tells Israel:

> Fear not, for I have redeemed you;
> I have called you by name, you are mine.
> (Isa. 43:1; cf. 45:4)

Even more wonderfully a few chapters later he promises his people:

> I will give in my house and within my walls
> a monument and a name
> better than sons and daughters;
> I will give them an everlasting name
> that shall not be cut off.
> (Isa. 56:5)

This 'everlasting name' is developed later when Isaiah tells the people that

> nations shall see your righteousness,
> and all the kings your glory,
> and you shall be called by a new name
> that the mouth of the LORD will give.
> (Isa. 62:2)

---

[24] On the intriguing reference to the name of God's son in Prov. 30:4 see Keefer 2016: 38–40. Although Calvin argued for a trinitarian reading of this passage, he conceded that 'with the contentious this passage will not have sufficient weight; nor do I found much upon it' (cited by Keefer [2016: 38]).

One implication of this brief study of names, which anticipates some of the discussion below, is that while a rigid distinction between 'name' and 'title' may be relevant in Western culture it does not quite reflect the more fluid use of the concept of 'name' in the Bible.

The name that is above every name (Phil. 2:9)

Philippians 2:6–11 is one of the most Christologically significant passages in the NT. It moves from Jesus' pre-existence (v. 6) to his incarnation (v. 7) to his death (v. 8) to his exaltation (vv. 9–11). As we saw above, Paul assumes a basic continuity between the 'earthly' Jesus and the exalted Christ. The first half of the passage, or 'hymn' (as many suggest it is), is full of complex exegetical issues, while the second half is, thankfully, less debated.[25] Nevertheless, in verse 9 two are important for our purposes: the meanings of 'highly exalted' (*hyperypsōsen*) and the referent of the 'name that is above every name'.

Following Jesus' death,[26] Paul tells us that God has 'highly exalted' him.[27] Some debate centres on whether this is a restoration to his position of former glory[28] or if the exalted Christ is exalted 'to a place which he had not reached previously'.[29] This is difficult to answer, and may, in fact, be the wrong question to ask.[30] What seems to be clear is that the pattern of Jesus' humiliation and exaltation closely parallels that of the suffering and exaltation of the Suffering Servant in Isaiah 52:13 – 53:12.[31] A strong case can be made that in his exaltation the servant was sharing in the unique divine identity.[32]

These two clauses 'highly exalted him' and 'bestowed upon him the name' are connected by the Greek word *kai*. It may be that Paul understands two successive events: exaltation and *then* bestowal of the name. However, if the *kai* is epexegetic (explanatory), the bestowal of the name *is* the exaltation.[33] That seems to fit this context where

---

[25] Silva 2005: 108.
[26] Here Paul moves straight from Jesus' death to exaltation. In Rom. 8:34 the pattern is death–resurrection–exaltation at the right hand.
[27] The addition of the prefix *hyper* does seem to indicate an intensification of the more frequent *hypsoō*.
[28] Cf. Jesus' prayer in John 17:5: 'And now, Father, glorify me in your own presence with the glory that I had with you before the world existed'.
[29] Martin 1997: 239.
[30] Fee (2007: 396) is probably correct to see the language here as indicating that Christ has been exalted 'to the highest possible degree'.
[31] On these parallels see Bauckham 2008: 43.
[32] Ibid. 44–45.
[33] Silva 2005: 110.

the emphasis is not on the *position* of Christ (at God's right hand) but the *response* of worship to his new name.

So, what is the 'name that is above every name'? Paul immediately continues that because he has this supreme name, 'at the *name of Jesus* every knee should bow, in heaven and on earth and under the earth' (2:10), suggesting that this name is simply *Jesus*. However, the Greek genitive construction 'name of Jesus' (*onoma Iēsou*) could equally indicate 'the name which Jesus possesses or bears'.[34] And so by far the most common suggestion is that the name that Jesus is given is 'Lord' (*kyrios*). That would certainly fit with Acts 2:36 (see below), and also with what Paul goes on to say in verses 10–11: 'so that at the name of Jesus every knee should bow, in heaven and on earth and under the earth, and every tongue confess that Jesus Christ is Lord, to the glory of God the Father'. Here Paul seems to be borrowing from Isaiah 45:23, where the Lord says of himself:

> By myself I have sworn;
>   from my mouth has gone out in righteousness
>   a word that shall not return:
> 'To me every knee shall bow,
>   every tongue shall swear allegiance.'

Behaviour that the Lord (through Isaiah) says will be directed to him, Paul says is directed to *Jesus*. In other words, what we have is the 'recurring, and consistent, phenomenon of [Paul's] transferring the Septuagint's [*kyrios*] (Lord) = Yahweh to the exalted Christ'.[35] As Fee suggests, the 'name that is above every name' can 'hardly be anything other than a reference to the Divine Name in the OT'.[36]

Nevertheless, Silva urges some caution in too quickly assuming that the name bestowed on Jesus is 'Lord'.[37] He suggests that if this identification holds, it would be only 'an inference, not an explicit statement of the text'. Second, he suggests that 'Lord' is really a title, not a name. Third, to understand the genitive construction 'name of Jesus' to indicate a name which Jesus possesses goes against common usage. Silva does not wholly reject the dominant interpretation since the connection between 'Jesus' and 'Lord' is 'close and basic'.[38] Rather,

---

[34] Bauckham 2008: 199.
[35] Fee 2007: 396.
[36] Ibid. 397.
[37] Silva 2005: 110.
[38] Ibid.

he suggests that while the name is 'Jesus', this name has been invested with a new dimension: that of Lord.

Silva is helpful in cautioning against too concrete a separation between Lord and Jesus – particularly given that Paul continues to state that what 'every tongue' confesses is 'that "*Jesus* Christ is Lord"'. Nevertheless, it does seem that what is *new* here is that Jesus is formally given the name *Lord*. We have seen above in the brief survey of names in the OT that there is not a rigid distinction between name and 'title'. Further, if, as seems likely, verses 10 and 11 are a reference to Isaiah 45:23, it is worth noting the verses that precede in Isaiah:

> Declare and present your case;
>   let them take counsel together!
> Who told this long ago?
>   Who declared it of old?
> Was it not I, the LORD?
>   And there is no other god besides me,
> a righteous God and a Saviour;
>   there is none besides me.
>
> Turn to me and be saved,
>   all the ends of the earth!
> For I am God, and there is no other.
> By myself I have sworn;
>   from my mouth has gone out in righteousness
>   a word that shall not return:
> 'To me every knee shall bow,
>   every tongue shall swear allegiance.'
>   (Isa. 45:21–23)

Isaiah here stresses the uniqueness of Yahweh's identity. He is the *only* God. Paul's application of this passage to Jesus, then, implies that he is sharing in 'the unique divine identity'.[39] Nevertheless, though confessing Jesus as Lord in this way assumes his divine identity, this confession is 'to the glory of God the Father' (Phil. 2:11) and so Paul's 'monotheism is kept intact by the final phrase'.[40]

The exaltation of Jesus *does* bring a change in his identity. Not his identity considered in terms of his singularity, what he is in and of

---

[39] Bauckham 2008: 200.
[40] Fee 2007: 400.

himself (he was equal with God from eternity, 2:6), but in terms of his relationships. Nevertheless, this equality with God was something that *in some way* he laid aside in his descent to the cross. After his death, Jesus was exalted as God himself publicly gave him the name *Lord* and by revealing his true identity that he had with him from eternity.

In other words we are not so much dealing with questions of ontology (do the incarnation or resurrection affect the divine nature of Christ?) or even primarily of function (do they affect his *role*) as much as his identity understood in terms of relation. People now relate to[41] – they call on the name of – the exalted Christ in the same way that Jews called on the name of the Lord. However, this means that ideas of *function* cannot be entirely ruled out. To put it somewhat simplistically, part of the function of 'Lord' in the OT is to have people call on your name. As Jesus is publicly given that name he is enabled to fulfil the function in a *fuller* way than he was able to fulfil it in his earthly life.[42] Paul in Romans 10:13 cites Joel 2:32, 'everyone who calls on the name of the Lord will be saved'. In its original context Joel was referring to Yahweh, whereas Paul is referring to Jesus. Would this have been true before Jesus' resurrection/exaltation? Unquestionably yes. But following his public exaltation by God and the public bestowing of the name Jesus, his lordship (and the saving benefits of calling on his name) are announced to the world. His identity 'expands', then, not in the sense of taking on something wholly new (that it did not have before), but by being more widely and clearly known.

Far above every name that is named (Eph. 1:21)
Unlike Philippians 2, in Ephesians 1 Paul clearly distinguishes between the resurrection and ascension of Christ. In praying that the Ephesians would know the power of God, he describes it in verse 20 as the power by which 'he raised him from the dead and seated him at his right hand in the heavenly places'. He continues:

far above all rule and authority and power and dominion, and above every name that is named, not only in this age but also in the one to come. And he put all things under his feet and gave him

---

[41] See Tilling 2012 on how the category of 'relationship' can be used to demonstrate Paul's divine Christology.
[42] Jesus is frequently identified as 'Lord' in his earthly ministry.

as head over all things to the church, which is his body, the fullness of him who fills all in all. (Eph. 1:20–23)

The mention of God's right hand is a clear reference to Psalm 110:1.[43] The exalted Christ is at God's right hand – thus having the power and authority associated with being seated next to God the Father. Paul further qualifies Christ's location as 'in the heavenly places' and 'far above' the rulers, authorities, powers and dominions. The issue of spiritual forces seems to have been a significant one at Ephesus and so Paul gives an extensive list of these before adding 'and above every name that is named' – to reassure readers who might have been worried about a particular evil 'power' that each one imaginable was included.[44]

Locating Christ 'in the heavenlies' seems on the surface to contradict Ephesians 4:10, where Christ is said to have ascended '*far above* [*hyperanō*] all the heavens'. It seems best to see heaven being used in two slightly different ways. In 1:20 it does seem to have a locational, spatial sense rather than being an expression of authority. However, in 4:10 the reference to heaven seems to be used to show Christ's equality with God – who is 'over all' (4:6). In other words, Christ 'can be viewed both locally as in *heaven* (cf. 1:20; 6:9) and at the same time as above the *heavens*, beyond that which can be conceived in terms of created reality'.[45]

In the next verse Paul describes God as having put 'all things under [Christ's] feet' (1:22). Again, there appears to be a contradiction, this time with 1 Corinthians 15:25, where Paul says that Christ 'must reign *until* he has put all his enemies under his feet'. What lies in the future in 1 Corinthians 15 seems to have already been accomplished in Ephesians 1. However, again, the tension is more apparent than real. Part of the issue is that in each passage Paul is drawing on both Psalm 8:6 and Psalm 110:1 and each of these psalms gives a different perspective on God's rule through his agent.[46] Psalm 8 states humanity's superiority over all things ('you have put all things under his feet',

---

[43] Despite the fact that the psalm has *ek dexiōn mou* rather than *en dexia*. This latter form is used by Paul (Rom. 8:34; Eph. 1:20; Col. 1:20) and 1 Peter (3:22), while the more literal *ek dexiōn* is used by the Gospels and Acts. Presumably this is a stylistic variation (as argued by Ellingworth [1993: 102]).

[44] Best 1988: 173.

[45] Lincoln 1990: 248, emphasis added.

[46] In Ps. 8 the agent is humanity in general (though see the reference to the son of man in v. 4). In Ps. 110 the agent is the 'Lord'.

8:6), while Psalm 110 speaks of the need for this superiority actually to be realized:

> Sit at my right hand,
> *until* I make your enemies your footstool.
>   (110:1)

In Ephesians 1 Paul alludes to both Psalm 110:1 ('at his right hand', 1:20) and Psalm 8:6 (he has put 'all things under his feet', 1:22) to underline Christ's exaltation. In contrast, in 1 Corinthians 15:25 when Paul alludes to Psalm 110:1 it is to the *second* half of the verse: 'until I make your enemies your footstool'; that is, the need for Christ's ongoing reign to secure the ultimate subjection of his enemies. However, this *ultimate* subjection is still grounded in Christ's *current* status as having all things in subjection to him, which Paul establishes by alluding to Psalm 8:6 in 1 Corinthians 15:27.

The emphasis then in 1 Corinthians 15:25 is for the need for Christ to continue to reign to bring all his enemies under his feet, and thus *fulfil* God's plan for humanity (Ps. 8:6, cited in 15:27). The emphasis in Ephesians 1:20–23 is that in his resurrection and ascension Christ has already *inaugurated* that plan for humanity. Although on the surface Ephesians 1:20–23 may appear to suggest that evil has already been decisively defeated, later in the letter Paul recognizes the ongoing presence and activity of evil (6:12).[47]

Christ being raised above every name that can be named then is an expression of his exalted status. Christ is exalted from the dead (1:20) to God's right hand, and as such is higher than anyone else in the universe (1:21). There *is* therefore a change in his identity – not in terms of his *singularity* but in terms of his *relationships* to others (in fact to *everyone* else). Although Paul does not here explicitly articulate the same movement as in Philippians 2:6–11, nevertheless it is still present as Christ moves from death to the highest exaltation possible. Christ's exalted name is a reflection of that identity – as reflected in Paul's seamlessly connecting prayer to God the Father to prayer 'in the *name* of our Lord Jesus Christ' (5:20).

The inherited name (Heb. 1:4)
The beginning of Hebrews displays some of the highest Christology in the NT. The author affirms Christ as the mode of final revelation

---

[47] A point made by Best 1988: 181.

and the one through whom God 'created the world' (1:2). He is the 'radiance of the glory of God' and the 'exact imprint of his nature' and 'upholds the universe by the word of his power' (1:3). Although some try to deny or downplay a divine Christology here,[48] the author is making remarkably strong statements concerning the status of the Son in his equality with God. This is not to deny his genuine humanity ('he had to be made like his brothers in every respect', 2:17), which is not held in tension with his deity as if Hebrews is operating with two 'independent Christological traditions that have been loosely combined'.[49] No, Christ as the divine Son of God who is made human is thereby uniquely qualified to act as a mediator.[50] As Bauckham puts it, Hebrews

> attributes to Jesus Christ three main categories of identity – Son, Lord, High Priest – and . . . each of these categories requires Jesus both to share the unique identity of God and to share human identity with his fellow humans. In each category, Hebrews portrays Jesus as both truly God and truly human, like his Father in every respect and like humans in every respect.[51]

The stress, however, in the first paragraph of the book is on Christ in his exalted state, with an emphasis on 'the full and eternal deity of the Son'[52] (the writer will go on to discuss Jesus in the period when he 'for a little while was made lower than the angels', 2:9). The second half of 1:3 presents the narrative of Christ from his death ('[a]fter making purification for sins') to his exaltation ('he sat down at the right hand[53] of the Majesty on high'). He then provides a comment on the implication of this exaltation: 'having become as much superior to angels as the name he has inherited is more excellent than theirs' (1:4).

In what sense did Christ 'become' (*genomenos*) superior to the angels? Hebrews gives significant space (1:4 – 2:9) to establishing the superiority of Christ over angels. There does not seem to be evidence of any kind of angel cult among the readers (as there seems to be in Colossians),[54] which raises the question of the nature of the

---

[48] Dunn 1989: 208.
[49] Lincoln (2006: 85), who rejects this idea.
[50] Ibid.
[51] Bauckham 2008: 236.
[52] Ibid. 237.
[53] Ellingworth 1993: 102: 'a clear though free allusion' to Ps. 110:1.
[54] As noted by Ellingworth (1993: 104).

author's concern. The key seems to be his statement in 2:2 that the law was delivered through angels. Whatever the origin of this belief,[55] the author establishes Christ's superiority over angels as the first stage in his central argument regarding the superiority of the new covenant that Christ established over the old covenant (cf. the contrast between Christ and Moses in 3:5–6).

Although the focus is on Christ's superiority over the angels following his exaltation ('having become as much superior'), the author also maintains the exalted status of Christ before creation (1:2; 1:10). The author seems to be using angels as a 'midpoint' between humanity and God. As such,

> [t]hey mark out the cosmic territory. They function, so to speak, as measures of ontological status. To be above the angels is to be God, to be below the angels is to be human. Above the angels, Jesus transcends all creation, sharing the divine identity as Creator and Ruler even of the angels. Below the angels, Jesus shares the common identity of earthly humans in birth, suffering and death.[56]

The Son, who was with God from the beginning of creation (1:2; 1:10), is in his incarnation made lower than the angels (2:9). Following his purification of sins, he is exalted and so made higher than them again. In that sense he *becomes* again – as a human being – higher than the angels.

But what is the 'more excellent name' that he has inherited? Various suggestions are offered in the literature.

Ellingworth suggests that the name is deliberately left unspecified, because the NT 'including Hebrews suggests that there may have converged around Christ a number of titles, no one of which (not even *theos*, 1:8) was considered supreme'.[57] As such, in this context 'name' is left indefinite enough 'to leave room for the later argument that the one who was eternally God's Son has now through his self-sacrifice been exalted as high priest'.[58]

The most obvious candidate, though, is 'Son' especially given the explanatory 'for' (*gar*) that commences verse 5, where the author goes on to identify Jesus as 'Son'. That is, the first name that is actually mentioned is 'Son'. The problem with seeing the name as 'Son' is that

---

[55] See Lane 1991: 37 for the argument that Deut. 33:2 lies behind this belief.
[56] Bauckham 2008: 241.
[57] Ellingworth 1993: 105.
[58] Ibid.

'elsewhere in Hebrews, sonship is spoken of as a permanent attribute of Christ, not as a title which is given or acquired at the time of his exaltation'.[59] So, for example, the author has already identified Jesus as the Son through whom God created the world (1:2). Moreover, in the rest of Hebrews, 'name' most clearly refers to the name Yahweh (2:12; 6:10; 13:15). The word 'name', as we have seen, has strong biblical background as referring to God himself (Exod. 3:13–15). As such, '[t]he superiority of Jesus' name in a context where his exaltation and divine identity are communicated points to his deity'.[60] However, in reply to these arguments, Schreiner notes that Jesus is referred to as 'Son' four times in this chapter, including in the following verse, which, as we have noted, is introduced by 'for' (*gar*). Moreover, 'in using the word *Son*, the author would be referring to Jesus' exaltation and rule as God *and* man, and such a rule commenced only at his resurrection'.[61] We might add that the distinction between name and title is (as we have argued above) not as rigid in the Bible as in a Western context.

However, Guthrie argues that the name is an expression of Christ's Davidic status. He points out that often interpretations of the 'name' in 1:4 overlook the following context, namely that the author is citing 2 Samuel 7:14.[62] Nathan's oracle in 2 Samuel 7 in the Greek starts with a reference to the Lord's having given David an 'inheritance' (cf. Heb. 1:4, 'the name he has inherited'). The Lord promises to David that he will make him a 'great name, like the name of the great ones of the earth' (7:9). He then promises that David's *Son* will 'build a house for my name, and I will establish the throne of his kingdom for ever' (7:13). In response, David praises God for how in redeeming Israel he made 'himself a name' (7:23) and how in fulfilling his promises to David, his 'name will be magnified for ever' (7:26).

The language of 'greatness' also permeates the 2 Samuel passage (*megas*, 7:9; *megalōsynē*, 7:22–23; *megalynō*, 7:22, 26), anticipating Hebrews' language of Christ's sitting at the right hand of the 'Majesty' (*megalōsynēs*) in heaven (1:3). As such, Guthrie concludes:

> Thus, the use of *onoma* in 1:4, in association with God's right hand as *tēs megalōsynēs*, could be understood as an anticipatory echo of that broader messianic context of 2 Sam. 7 to which our author

---

[59] Ibid.
[60] Schreiner 2015: 60.
[61] Ibid. 61, emphasis original.
[62] Guthrie 2007: 924.

will immediately point in 1:5. The inherited 'name,' then, mentioned in 1:4, is, on this reading, not to be understood as an allusion to the title 'Son,' but rather as an honor conferred by God on the Messiah as the Davidic heir at the establishment of his throne and in association with God himself.[63]

In the end both Schreiner and Guthrie put forward convincing arguments, which are not contradictory. The most obvious candidate for the new name is 'Son'. Yet this should be understood not in a pre-incarnate sense (as it is in 1:2, where the Son is said to have been the one through whom God created the world). Rather, Christ is *identified* and recognized as the Davidic Son – God's king – following his resurrection from the dead. Again, Christ's identity *expands* following the resurrection as God bestows on him the name of 'Son'.

A new name (Rev. 3:12)

In Revelation 3:12 the risen Lord Jesus promises the recipients of the letter to the church at Philadelphia that 'I will write on [the one who conquers] the name of my God, and the name of the city of my God, the new Jerusalem, which comes down from my God out of heaven, and *my own new name*'.

References to specific 'names' are prevalent in Revelation (2:3, 13; 3:1, 5, 8, 12; 6:8; 8:11; 9:11; 11:18; 13:6, 8, 17; 14:1; 15:4; 16:9; 17:5, 8; 19:13, 16; 22:4). Two other verses are particularly relevant to help us understand the referent of Christ's 'own new name' here. Later, John gives a description of the exalted Christ and describes how his 'eyes are like a flame of fire, and on his head are many diadems' and 'he has a name written that no one knows but himself' (19:12). Christ then has a name that is unique to him and which seems knowable only by revelation. Earlier in the book, in the letter to the church at Pergamum, Jesus promises to the 'one who conquers' 'some of the hidden manna' and 'a white stone, with a new name written on the stone that no one knows except the one who receives it' (2:17).

Combining these ideas, it would seem that the Christian believer who remains faithful to Christ, and 'conquers', will be given a new name (2:17). This will actually be Jesus' own 'new name' (3:12), a name that can only be 'known' by revelation (2:17; 19:12), that is known by Jesus and those to whom he chooses to give it.

---

[63] Ibid. 925.

The bestowal of a new name was promised to Israel by God through the prophet Isaiah (62:2; 65:15).[64] Here having a new name is not so much a matter of a new identifying 'label' but rather a change of status, as when a wife changes her name upon marriage. When God's people are called by a new name,

> the nations shall see [their] righteousness,
> and all the kings [their] glory . . .
>
> (Isa. 62:2)

In fact, a new name, according to Isaiah, involves a new creation (65:15–18), even though Jerusalem will actually retain the personal name 'Jerusalem' (65:18).[65] This seems to be the idea behind Revelation's use of the 'new name' motif. It is not a personal name as such, but an expression of a new status. And so, faithful believers will be identified with the name of God and of the new Jerusalem (3:12) as his faithful people. Christ's new name, similarly, relates to his new exalted status – seated with God on his throne (3:21). The fact that this name cannot be known except to the one to whom Jesus chooses to make it known is, again, to be understood against an OT backdrop, where to know someone's name suggests some degree of control over that person.[66] Jesus' new name then points to his identification with both his exalted status with God and his identification with his people (3:12).

Conclusion

In considering these verses which speak of Jesus' new names we have seen (as we saw in the OT) that names are associated with status and titles, and that we cannot force a rigid distinction between names and status. Jesus' new 'names', then, speak of his new status. A name is also the way that someone is identified and these new names speak of an expansion of Jesus' identity not in terms of his own personal singularity so much as in terms of how others relate to him.

A new status

The question for our purposes is what the resurrection and/or ascension do for the identity of Jesus in terms of his status, or his title. We examine three verses – one dealing with Jesus in terms of his

---

[64] Beale 1999: 255.
[65] Ibid.
[66] Ibid. 955.

being 'Lord and Christ' (Acts 2:36) and two dealing with his being God's 'Son' (Acts 13:33; Rom. 1:4).

Lord and Christ (Acts 2:36)

In his speech at Pentecost Peter interprets the phenomena that the crowd have just witnessed as evidence of the end-time giving of the Spirit to God's people as promised in Joel 2. Peter then goes on to speak of Jesus' death and resurrection, and Peter uses two psalms to interpret these events.[67] First, in verses 25–28 he cites Psalm 16 to establish that David predicted Jesus' resurrection. David confidently stated that the Lord would not 'abandon my soul to Hades' nor 'let your Holy One see corruption' (2:27, citing Ps. 16:10). Given that David, in fact, died ('his tomb is with us to this day', 2:29), and knowing that God promised to give his throne to one of his descendants (2:30, referring to the promise of 2 Sam. 7:12–15), Peter reasons that David must have been prophesying about the resurrection of Christ (2:31). Peter then affirms that 'this Jesus God raised up, and of that we all are witnesses' (2:32). Then, in verses 33–36, Peter connects the resurrection to the outpouring of the Holy Spirit, which the crowd has just witnessed, through Psalm 110:1. Receiving the Spirit, whom he then pours out, is a sign of Jesus' exaltation (2:33) and this exaltation was prophesied by David in Psalm 110:1, where he speaks of the Lord's (God's) saying to David's own Lord:

> Sit at my right hand,
> until I make your enemies your footstool.

Having cited the psalm to explain Jesus' exalted status, Peter concludes his reflection on Jesus by stating in verse 36, 'Let all the house of Israel therefore know for certain that God has made him both Lord and Christ, this Jesus whom you crucified.'

What exactly does Peter mean by saying that God 'has made' (*epoiēsen*) Jesus both Lord and Christ? Did Jesus *become* Lord and Christ by virtue of his resurrection, implying that he was not so before?

A number of twentieth-century commentators drew some quite significant Christological implications from this verse. Wrede suggested that it proved that there was 'in primitive Christianity a view in accordance with which Jesus was not the messiah in his earthly

---

[67] Eskola 2001: 162.

life'.[68] Similarly, Bultmann suggested that the verse proves that 'Jesus' messiahship was dated from the resurrection'.[69] Barrett saw it as out of step with the rest of Luke's Christology, suggesting that the verse is 'clear proof that Luke is at this point using a source' since 'he would not have chosen to express himself in this way'.[70]

Kavin Rowe is a recent scholar who has strongly argued that Peter's speech (via Luke) is not suggesting that Jesus *became* Lord and Messiah at this point.[71] After all, Luke identifies Jesus as Lord even when he is in his mother's womb (Luke 1:43) and recounts the angel's announcing to the shepherds the birth of 'Christ the Lord' (Luke 2:11). Unless we believe Luke to be hopelessly incoherent (and/or a terrible editor of sources), it cannot be that Jesus *became* Lord and Christ at the resurrection in an unqualified sense. How then do we understand the statement that God *made* (*epoiēsen*) him Lord and Christ?

Rowe notes that Jesus is consistently and repeatedly referred to as Lord (*kyrios*) throughout Luke's Gospel *except* for the period where he recounts the 'mocking, trial, execution, and burial of Jesus'.[72] The last reference is made during Peter's denial in 22:61–62 when 'the Lord' turns to look at Peter, and he remembers what 'the Lord' had said and then weeps bitterly. As Rowe comments:

> It is just here, at the moment that Jesus is rejected by his last disciple and begins to be mocked and beaten, that the word [*kyrios*] disappears from the story. This silence is striking; it is in fact the silence of death, that which the human verdict upon the identity of Jesus brings upon the Lord. Not until the other side of the resurrection does [*kyrios*] reappear (24.3, 34).[73]

As such, Rowe argues that the resurrection brings *recognition* of Jesus' *prior* lordship. The language of 'making' in Acts 2:36 does not indicate an 'ontological transformation in the identity of Jesus or his status (from not [*kyrios*] to [*kyrios*]) but an epistemological shift in the perception of the human community'.[74] The verb

---

[68] Wrede 1971: 216, cited in Rowe 2007: 42.
[69] Bultmann 2007, 1: 27, cited in Rowe 2007: 42.
[70] Barrett 1994: 151.
[71] This paragraph is a summary of Rowe's article.
[72] Rowe 2007: 52.
[73] Ibid.
[74] Ibid. 55.

poieō, then, according to Rowe, essentially here means 'to make known'.[75]

Rowe's reading has been critiqued by others. So, Zwiep agrees with his observation that Jesus' 'lordship' is found across Luke's writings. However, he argues that as an aspect of Jesus' identity, his 'lordship' should not be regarded as a static concept but as something fluid and dynamic that develops across the corpus.[76] Using Ricoeur's concept of 'retroactive realignment of the past',[77] Zwiep argues that pre-resurrection references to Jesus' lordship are primarily *anticipatory*. We see a parallel in the description of Jesus as 'Saviour' in 2:11. Given that his saving death lies in the future, this title anticipates his future work.[78] Nevertheless, Zwiep pulls back from suggesting that 'Jesus' pre-Easter career was considered to be non-messianic'.[79] Rather, to say Jesus was 'made . . . both Lord and Christ' is, for Luke, 'materially identical with saying that Jesus was "exalted" by God in/at his resurrection'.[80] As such, the meaning of the term *kyrios* 'gets its shape and contours' from the completed narrative of Jesus' life.[81]

J. Daniel Kirk similarly objects to Rowe's suggestion that what Peter is talking about is merely the recognition of Jesus' identity as Lord and Messiah. Quite simply, he argues, 'to make' [*poieō*] does not mean 'to make known' [*gnōrizō*]. God has actually *done* something.[82] However, this is not to say that Peter is speaking of a change of ontology or Jesus' 'inherent identity'. No, these titles represent a 'function [Jesus] performs within the story of Israel'.[83] However, Kirk does recognize that Jesus is referred to as Lord and Christ throughout Luke's writings. He builds on Rowe's observation that lordship

[75] On the validity of this rendering, ibid. n. 65 notes: (1) as one of the most common Greek verbs, *poieō* has a 'remarkably' large range of meaning and so context is particularly important for the meaning in a particular instance; (2) in his discussions of the verse, Athanasius seems to have viewed it as essentially meaning the equivalent of 'to make known'; (3) in Luke 1:51 Luke seems to use the verb with a similar meaning (cf. NRSV, AV).

[76] Zwiep 2010: 147.

[77] Ibid. 151. He gives the following example: 'To say that "in 1717 the author of *Le Neveu de Rameau* was born" is anachronistic. What we mean is "the person who would later write *Le Neveu de Rameau* was born in 1717."'

[78] Ibid. 153.

[79] Ibid. 155.

[80] Ibid.

[81] Ibid.; cf. Strauss (1995: 144), who states that only at 'his exaltation-enthronement, however, is Jesus installed in the full authority as reigning Christ and Lord'.

[82] Kirk 2016: 409.

[83] Ibid.

language is missing in the lead up to the cross, and so suggests that the point Luke is making (through Peter) is that 'what Jesus was on earth prior to his suffering and death he becomes once again, but to a *fuller and more real degree*, in heaven'.[84]

Kirk and Zwiep, then, do not fully contradict Rowe's view. They both hold that God's 'making' Jesus to be 'Lord and Christ' in the resurrection should not be understood in an unqualified sense, as if he was not Lord and Christ before. Nevertheless, whereas Rowe sees Jesus being revealed to be what he really was, Kirk and Zwiep, I think, more fully take into account the *laying aside* of Jesus' lordship that happens at the cross. And so the resurrection *does* affect Jesus' identity inasmuch as an enthronement does affect the identity of a king.

Rowe, Zwiep and Kirk actually lie on a spectrum in terms of how they understand the resurrection to impact Jesus' identity in Acts 2:36. Rowe understands the resurrection to be only revelatory: Jesus was fully Lord, then laid aside his lordship at the cross and was then shown to be Lord again at the resurrection. Zwiep lies at the other end of the spectrum. For him, references to Jesus as Lord before Easter are primarily (though not entirely) anticipatory – it is the resurrection that enthrones him as Lord. Kirk lies in between. Jesus *is* Lord before the resurrection, but enters into his lordship in a fuller and more real sense at and following the resurrection. Kirk both captures the strength of Peter's language of 'making' *and* maintains the reality of Jesus' identity as Lord and Christ throughout Luke's writing up to this point. Jesus' resurrection, then, is his 'enthronement' so that 'the one who was born Christ and Lord, but whose lordship is silenced through crucifixion, is made Lord and Christ through his literal enthroning at God's right hand'.[85]

The parallel with Jesus as 'Saviour' in Luke is instructive.[86] Jesus is identified as 'Saviour' as early as his birth (2:11). However, this is not *only* in anticipation of his later work. Rather, he does acts of 'salvation' throughout the Gospel (e.g. 7:50; 23:35). In a very real sense he is the Saviour *throughout* the Gospel. However, it is fundamentally his work on the cross that defines, completes even, his identity as Saviour. Jesus is Lord throughout his earthly ministry. His resurrection does not merely demonstrate this but *defines* and *completes* his lordship.

---

[84] Ibid. 410, emphasis added.
[85] Ibid. 408.
[86] Noted, as we observed above, by Zwiep.

Son of God (Acts 13:33; Rom. 1:4)
In this section we will examine two verses that seem to speak of Jesus' becoming Son of God following his resurrection.

Acts 13:33
In Acts 13:16–41 Luke gives us an account of Paul's first speech, delivered at Pisidian Antioch. He begins by recounting Israel's history up to the failure of Saul as king (vv. 17–21). Having removed Saul, God 'raised up' (*ēgeiren*) David as a king 'after [his own] heart' (v. 22). Paul then jumps from David to Jesus: 'Of this man's offspring God has brought to Israel a Saviour, Jesus, as he promised' (v. 23). Paul surveys Jesus' ministry, moving quickly from John the Baptist's announcement of Jesus (v. 24) to an explanation for the people's rejection of Jesus (vv. 27–28) to the execution of Jesus (v. 29). He then turns to the resurrection of Jesus, stating that God was the one who raised (*ēgeiren*) him from the dead (v. 30) and that Jesus 'appeared' to many who were now witnesses of his resurrection (v. 31). Paul then begins to draw the theological implications of Jesus' resurrection. He starts by affirming that 'by raising Jesus' God has 'fulfilled' what he promised to the fathers (v. 32), as 'it is written in the second Psalm'. He then quotes Psalm 2:7:

> You are my Son,
> today I have begotten you.
> (v. 33)

In the rest of the sermon he continues (in a similar vein to Peter in Acts 2) to establish from the OT that God's holy one would not 'see corruption' (vv. 34–37), proclaims forgiveness of sins and justification available in Jesus (vv. 38–39) and concludes (v. 41) by warning his hearers not to be the fulfilment of what the prophets say about 'scoffers'.

There are many complexities in how Paul's argument proceeds,[87] but it is his use of Psalm 2:7 that is most relevant for our study. The first question to be addressed is what Paul means when he says, 'what God promised to the fathers, this he has fulfilled to us their children by *raising [anastēsas]* Jesus' (vv. 32–33). Is Paul referring to Jesus'

---

[87] Novakovic 2012: 213: 'Paul's speech in Acts 13 provides the most sophisticated argument in the New Testament of the way the resurrection of Jesus fulfils God's promise to David.'

resurrection[88] or does he mean something like 'bringing [Jesus] on to the stage of history'?[89] If we understand the reference to Jesus' being born, then the meaning of the psalm quotation may be 'the raising up of Jesus as Messiah at his birth, where the coming of the Spirit on Mary is tantamount to a divine begetting'.[90]

The main reasons for understanding 'raising' as 'being raised onto the plane of human history' are (1) the absence of the qualifier 'from the dead', which is present in verses 30 and 34, where the resurrection is clearly in view; and (2) the parallel with verses 22–23, where David is 'raised up' (*ēgeiren*) to be king, and this is fulfilled by bringing Jesus to Israel.[91] That is, in verses 22–23 Jesus' fulfilment of the Davidic role relates to Jesus' whole life and ministry, suggesting the same is true in verse 33.

However, there are also very strong arguments in favour of seeing verses 32–33 as referring to Jesus' resurrection from the dead:[92] the verb *anistēmi* can be used to refer to the resurrection even when the qualifier 'from the dead' is not present (2:24, 32); the immediate context (vv. 30, 34) refers to the resurrection; when *anistēmi* (or *egeirō*) is used to refer to someone coming 'onto the scene', a title is used (e.g. 3:22, 'a prophet') rather than simply a proper name as here.

On balance, these latter reasons, particularly the fact that the context refers to Jesus' resurrection (and the same verb is used in v. 34), suggest that Jesus' resurrection from the dead is in view. As Jipp suggests, 'A reference to his earthly ministry would entirely interrupt the flow and logic of Paul's sermon.'[93] If that is the case, how does Jesus' resurrection from the dead relate to his being 'begotten' as God's Son?

As we saw with 'Lord and Christ' in 2:36, Luke has already referred to Jesus as the 'Son of God'. His identity of Son is clearly established from birth (Luke 1:35) and from the beginning of his ministry (Luke 4:3).[94] He does not deny the title 'Son of God' when asked if he

---

[88] So most commentators; e.g. Peterson 2009: 392.
[89] Barrett 1994: 645.
[90] Marshall 2007: 585.
[91] Summarizing Strauss 1995: 162–163.
[92] Again summarizing ibid.
[93] Jipp 2016: 52.
[94] In fact, the main purpose of the temptation narrative in 4:1–13 is to establish that Jesus is the *true* Son of God. Zwiep does not discuss this passage in depth but it would seem harder to see an instance of Ricoeur's 'retroactive realignment of the past' with this title given the key part it plays in Luke's narrative.

identifies with it at his trial before the Sanhedrin (Luke 22:70). Clearly then, Luke does not expect Acts 13:34 to be understood as teaching that the resurrection *makes* Jesus God's Son in an absolute, unqualified sense. Nevertheless, as with 2:36, the language is strong and more is in view than *simply* a disclosure of what was already true. Whether we see Christ's being 'installed'[95] or being 'enthroned',[96] it seems that Paul understands that Jesus' 'resurrection–ascension brings him to the *full experience* of his messianic destiny in a heavenly enthronement and rule'.[97]

Paul is not making a point about Jesus' pre-existent relationship with his Father, but how the resurrection allows him to enter into the full reality of his Davidic role. As Novakovic puts it, in recounting Paul's sermon here in Acts 13:

> Luke shows that Jesus fulfils all three components of Nathan's oracle in 2 Sam. 7:12–16: he is David's seed (v.23), who was enthroned and declared God's son by virtue of his resurrection from the dead (vv.32–33), and whose dominion is everlasting because he will no more return to corruption (vv.34–37). In this way, Luke closes the circle he opened in Luke 1:32–33, when the angel announced that all three of the elements would be fulfilled in Jesus: 'He will be great and will be called the Son of the Most High, and the Lord God will give him the throne of his father David, and he will reign over the house of Jacob forever, and of his kingdom there will be no end.'[98]

Romans 1:4

Having read Luke's account of Paul's sermon in Acts, we turn to a similar Christological affirmation at the beginning of Romans. Here Paul connects Christ's identity as Son to his resurrection. At the beginning of the letter Paul describes himself as an apostle 'set apart for the gospel of God' (1:1), and then proceeds to define the gospel as being promised beforehand 'through his prophets' in the 'holy Scriptures' (1:2). He then discusses the content of the gospel and starts with the simple statement that it concerns God's 'Son'. What follows in the next couple of verses is a description of God's Son. Most commentators agree that Paul is quoting a fragment of a hymn

---

[95] Kirk 2016: 410.
[96] Novakovic 2012: 213.
[97] Peterson 2009: 392, emphasis added.
[98] Novakovic 2012: 213.

or creed,[99] but they disagree concerning how much he has edited or adapted it.[100] Although there may be some value in reconstructing the redactional process Paul applied to the text he inherited, far more important is the final form he included in his letter, as this reflects what he thinks about Christ.[101]

Paul gives us two parallel statements regarding Christ: he was 'descended from David according to the flesh' (1:3) and he was 'declared to be the Son of God in power according to the Spirit of holiness by his resurrection from the dead' (1:4).[102] Not only is nearly every word and phrase in these two verses disputed but so is the relationship between the two parallel statements: does the second follow the first *temporally* or is the first the *cause* of the second?

We will return below to the relationship between the two statements, but first we will consider the meaning of the individual phrases. Paul first describes God's Son as '*tou genomenou ek spermatos Dauid kata sarka*'. The first issue is the meaning of the verb *ginomai*. Paul uses it to refer to Christ in Galatians 4:4 ('God sent forth his Son, born of woman, born under the law') and Philippians 2:7 ('[Christ Jesus] made himself nothing, taking the form of a servant, being born in the likeness of men'). In both cases, although a birth is presupposed, the emphasis 'appears to be on change of status from a heavenly mode of existence to an earthly one rather than on ordinary human birth'.[103]

Jesus then comes into human existence *ek spermatos Dauid*. It is common to understand this as a reference to the source of Jesus' earthly lineage: 'from the seed of David'. Recently, however, Bates has suggested that the prepositional phrase be understood instrumentally: Jesus came into (earthly) existence *by* the seed of David. It is, Bates argues, a reference (albeit oblique) to 'Mary's contribution to Jesus' human production and family lineage'.[104] Bates makes this argument by noting the thematic parallel with Galatians 4:4 ('having come into being by means of a woman'[105]); observing that some early Christian writers connected the expression to Mary (see Irenaeus, *Against Heresies* 2.16.3; Ignatius, *Ephesians* 18.2); and arguing that by construing *ek spermatos Dauid* instrumentally this 'precisely

---

[99] See the discussion in Bates 2015: 109 and Novenson 2012: 170.
[100] See Bates 2015: 112–114, assessing Jewett 2007: 105–108.
[101] Bates (2015: 112) rightly critiques the common suggestion that the creed that Paul inherited (and adapted) was adoptionist.
[102] I have quoted the ESVUK here but I depart from it below.
[103] Bates 2015: 115.
[104] Ibid. 117.
[105] This is Bates's translation.

preserves the parallelism' with the phrase *ex anastaseōs nekrōn* in verse 4.

Bates's last reason is the weakest aspect of his argument and represents a misunderstanding of the nature of parallelism; that is, the assumption that the preposition has to 'be grammatically identical because it occurs at the same point [as another occurrence of the same preposition] in a parallel structure'.[106] Moreover, if Paul had wanted to refer to Mary, this seems a rather oblique way to do it. It seems best to understand this in line with the traditional interpretation: Jesus was in the line of David.

Paul further qualifies this 'birth' with 'according to the flesh' (*kata sarka*). While Pauline references to 'flesh' are frequently negative (e.g. Rom. 8:3; 1 Cor. 3:1; Gal. 3:3), they are not necessarily so and the context here suggests that Paul does not mean the phrase negatively. Frequently a negative meaning is argued on the basis of the parallel with *kata pneuma* in the following verse.[107] That is, since *kata pneuma* (according to the Spirit) is clearly positive, *kata sarka* must stand in contrast and be negative. However, as Johnson shows, again this misunderstands the nature of this parallelism.[108] It also fails to take into account the strong thematic parallel with Romans 9:5, where Christ's human origins are described as *kata sarka* and these are clearly meant positively, or at least neutrally. Use of 'flesh' here does however connect Christ's humanity with the notion of 'weakness' (rather than sinfulness).

In Romans 1:3 Paul is underlining that Christ 'truly and fully entered into the sphere of human existence'.[109] However, the use of the word 'flesh' here, though it is not 'pejorative', does suggest 'that we have not arrived at a full understanding of Jesus if we only look at him from the standpoint of "the flesh"'.[110]

The next verse gives us this fuller perspective and it is equally debated. Paul starts with another participle *horisthentos* (paralleling *genomenou*). The verb *horizō* is frequently translated 'to declare' (e.g. ESVUK, HCSB) but most commentators recognize that the meaning is closer to 'designate' or 'appoint' (NIV).[111] So, for Paul, Jesus is 'appointed' Son of God. The tendency to translate the verb as 'declare' may derive

---

[106] Johnson 2017: 479.
[107] Dunn 1973: 49, cited in Johnson 2017: 484.
[108] Johnson 2017: 484.
[109] Bates 2015: 121.
[110] Moo 1996: 47.
[111] See particularly Acts 17:26, 31; Heb. 4:7.

from a reticence to suggest a form of adoptionism whereby Jesus is 'made' or 'appointed' Son of God; that is, he was not the Son of God until the resurrection. However, as Moo points out, Paul has already affirmed Jesus' divine sonship: the gospel is 'God's gospel' concerning 'his Son' (v. 3), and so it is 'the *Son* who is "appointed" Son'.[112]

The next qualifying phrase is 'in power' (*en dynamei*). This could be understood to qualify *horisthentos* ('decisively established'[113]) or *huiou theou* ('son-of-God-in-power; that is, 'the powerful Son of God' (HCSB). Most commentators settle for the second reading and they do so on the basis of the 'need to demarcate the second occurrence of "Son of God" from the first'.[114] Cranfield offers three parallel uses of 'in power' (Mark 9:1; 1 Cor. 15:43; 1 Thess. 1:5), which he argues suggests that the phrase in Romans 1:4 qualifies 'Son of God'.[115] However, Fitzmyer offers the same three passages as possible reasons for understanding the phrase to qualify the verb![116]

Overwhelmingly the NT usage of 'in power' is adverbial.[117] Further, it is more likely that Paul is qualifying the one verb with three adverbial phrases. Christ was 'appointed' Son of God – and this was done 'in power', 'according to the Holy Spirit' and 'by his resurrection from the dead'. As such, it would seem that the first two phrases further qualify the last one: his resurrection was 'powerful' and 'according to the Spirit of holiness'. This reference to the Spirit is most likely a reference to the new sphere of existence into which the risen Christ entered upon his resurrection (cf. 8:5).[118]

We have a very similar thought, then, to Acts 13:33: the resurrection does *change* the identity of the risen Christ. He is not simply *shown* or *declared* to be the Son of God; his resurrection means that he is powerfully appointed Son of God *in the realm of the Spirit*. While he was son of David in the realm of the flesh, the resurrection brings him into a new realization and experience of the divine Sonship that was his from before his birth and which he possessed in his earthly life but which is now fully realized.

---

[112] Moo 1996: 48, emphasis original.

[113] Fitzmyer 1993: 235.

[114] Moo 1996: 48.

[115] Cranfield 1975, 1: 62.

[116] Fitzmyer 1993: 235. He actually settles for it qualifying 'Son of God'.

[117] E.g. Mark 9:1, 'the kingdom of God comes with power'; Rom. 15:13: believers 'abound in hope by the power of the Holy Spirit'. See also Rom. 15:19; 1 Cor. 15:43; 2 Cor. 6:7; Col. 1:29; 1 Thess. 1:5; 2 Thess. 1:11; 1 Pet. 1:5. 1 Cor. 2:5 and 4:20 are possible exceptions (although in the latter 'in power' may qualify an implied verb 'to be').

[118] Moo 1996: 50.

We see something of a parallel later in the letter where Paul describes believers as 'sons of God' (8:14). However, he also writes that we will only enter into the full experience of our sonship when we are raised from the dead (8:23) – when our bodies are redeemed. Our experience, then, mirrors Christ's – who was fully God's son before this resurrection but entered into the full experience of his sonship following his resurrection from the dead.

Conclusion

Does the resurrection and ascension change the identity of Jesus? We have seen that the NT resists a simplistic answer to this question. Twentieth-century debates concerning the relationship of the Jesus of history and the exalted Christ tended to operate with reductionistic assumptions of the nature of continuity; that is, either absolute continuity or absolute discontinuity. However, we have seen that there is both continuity and development.

There is continuity in that the Jesus who died is the same person who rose and who ascended to God's right hand. 'The historical details of his earthly life, such as his death by crucifixion, are no more and no less part of his identity than his role in creation and his present lordship in the community of those who call on his name.'[119]

However, the resurrection does not leave the identity of Jesus unchanged. We saw this as we considered the need for revelation following his resurrection. Even his closest followers could not innately and naturally recognize him. For Luke, we saw that only when their eyes are 'opened' (24:31) do they grasp who he is. For John, Jesus does not only appear to the disciples but is 'manifested' or 'revealed' to them (21:14). Their way of relating to him has changed following the resurrection. His identity has changed, not in the sense that he is a different individual, but that he cannot be apprehended simply with the naked eye.

We also saw that Jesus' identity undergoes development when we consider his name. In each case we saw that the aspect of his name was connected to his identity in terms of its *revelation*; that is, his name reflected what was true of him. In Philippians 2:9, following his exaltation, Jesus receives 'the name that is above every name'. We saw that his identity as the divine Lord 'expands', then, not in the sense of taking on something wholly new (that it did not have before), but

[119] Hays 2008: 182.

35

by being more widely and clearly known. In Ephesians 1:21 the concept of the name is connected to his exaltation – his exalted name reflecting the move he makes from death to being seated at God's right hand. Hebrews 1:4 speaks of Jesus' inheriting a 'more excellent' name – that of the Davidic Son: a name by which Jesus is identified and recognized following his resurrection from the dead. Finally, in Revelation 3:12 we saw that Jesus' new name points to his identification with both his exalted status with God and with his people.

Finally, we turned to consider verses in the NT where, following his resurrection, Jesus is described as being made 'Lord and Christ' (Acts 2:36) and 'Son of God' (Acts 13:33; Rom. 1:4). In both cases we saw that Jesus was not becoming someone entirely new (i.e. as if prior to the resurrection he was not Lord, Christ or Son). However, nor is the resurrection a *mere* demonstration of what was true of Christ already. No, we argued that the resurrection actually does change Jesus in bringing him into the *full* expression of his identity as Son, Lord and Christ. We saw that there was a parallel with Jesus' identity as Saviour which he had before the cross, but that he fulfilled or realized by his death on the cross. Similarly, for Paul in Romans 8 believers are 'sons' of God already, but they enter into the fullness of their sonship following the redemption of their bodies (Rom. 8:23). I argued that for Jesus his resurrection brings about the full experience and expression of his identity.

Chapter Three

The identity of the exalted Christ: the exalted Christ and the Spirit

Introduction

In this chapter we examine a number of interpreters who understand Paul to be collapsing the identity of Christ and the Spirit. So, in Romans 8:9–10 Paul switches between the Spirit's dwelling in believers to Christ's dwelling in them. This suggests to some that, at least at the level of experience, Christ and the Spirit cannot be distinguished. In 1 Corinthians 15:45 Paul describes Christ as a 'life-giving' spirit, suggesting that the risen Christ has become 'a' if not 'the' Spirit. Perhaps even more starkly, in 2 Corinthians 3:17 Paul states that 'the Lord is the Spirit', suggesting, again at the very least at the level of experience, that Christ and the Spirit are indistinguishable. Finally, in Ephesians 4:10 the one who 'descended' is seemingly equated with the one who 'ascended' suggesting to some that the descending Spirit is one and the same as the 'ascending' Christ.

For John's Gospel we explore a more narrow range of interpretation associated with the University of Copenhagen. Two scholars, Gitte Buch-Hansen and Troels Engberg-Pedersen, have offered readings of John's Gospel against the background of first-century Stoic metaphysics. This leads them to conceive of the Spirit in material terms and so, they argue, reduce the seeming tension in John's identification of Christ and the Spirit.

We will see that these diverse interpretations fall on a number of points. They all have in common a resistance to understanding the Spirit in personal terms. However, once his personality is established and we understand the *relationship* between Christ and the Spirit, it prevents us from collapsing their identity. Neither Paul nor John articulates a full-blown doctrine of the Trinity, but we will see that the elements of this doctrine are not far from the surface of their writings.

The exalted Christ and the Spirit in Paul

The Spirit of God dwells in you . . . Christ is in you (Rom. 8:9–10)

In Romans 8:9 Paul states that the Spirit of God dwells in believers. In the very next verse he comments that *Christ* is in them. Paul's language here has led to certain interpretative tendencies whereby Christ and the Spirit are effectively collapsed into one another. We will briefly outline one such interpretation before turning to examine Romans 8:9–10 in more detail.

Christ experienced by the believer as the Spirit?

For some interpreters the indwelling of Christ and the indwelling of the Spirit are simply 'identical' since the 'spirit is none other than Jesus Christ'.[1] As such Christ is not mediated *through* the Spirit but *as* the Spirit. For others, while the Spirit and Christ can be distinguished in that they are not to be identified without remainder, at the level of *experience* they are indistinguishable. So, for example Dunn, commenting on Romans 8:9–10 (and other similar passages), suggests that such passages

> make it abundantly clear that for Paul *no distinction can be detected in the believer's experience between exalted Christ and Spirit of God* . . . If the Spirit of God is now to be recognized only by the Jesus-character of the spiritual experience he engenders, then it is also true that for Paul Christ can be experienced now only in and through the Spirit, *indeed only as the Spirit* . . . The exalted Christ and the Spirit of God are one and the same so far as the believer's experience is concerned . . . That is to say, in Paul's understanding the exalted Christ is not merely synonymous with the Spirit, has not been wholly absorbed as it were by the Spirit . . . the equivalence between Spirit and Christ is only a function of the believer's limited perception . . . Christ [is] experienced as Spirit and 'limited' to Spirit in his relationship with men.[2]

Similarly, Ziesler suggests that

> If the Spirit and Christ are not to be confused, neither in practice from the believer's point of view can they be distinguished. Because

[1] Betz 2000: 333.
[2] Dunn 1989: 146–147, emphases added.

the Spirit communicates Christ, his earthly work and his present authority, Paul can pass from one to another almost without noticing. Christ is in us and the Spirit is in us (Rom. 8:9f); we are in Christ and in the Spirit (Rom. 8:1, 9) . . . It is because the Spirit now conveys Christ and conversely since *Christ now encounters mankind as the Spirit*, that such sets of statements can be drawn up . . . Christ and the Spirit in effect define one another . . . Christ is exalted and in a sense absent, as Christ. He is present and active in lordship, however, because he is now understood and experienced as the Spirit.[3]

For Dunn and Ziesler, while Christ and the Spirit are not synonymous, they are indistinguishable at the level of experience. In terms of Christ's identity he is now experienced *as* the Spirit. Christ's identity, then, effectively collapses into the identity of the Spirit.

Christ present to the believer by the mediation of the Spirit (Rom. 8:9–10)

However, if Romans 8 is read as a whole we see that Paul does maintain a distinction between Christ's and the Spirit's identities, even on the level of experience. We will see this as we understand both Paul's dominant personal (or 'hypostatic') concept of the Spirit and the fact of Christ's *absence* (cf. 8:34). All too often Romans 8:9–11 is simply read in isolation and this, I will argue, distorts the relationship between Christ and Spirit such that they are effectively collapsed into one another. While there is, as we shall see, a degree of synonymity in 8:9–11 between Christ's and the Spirit's dwelling in the believer, neither is this an absolute identity nor should this passage be read in isolation from the rest of the chapter. If the Spirit is understood as a personal entity as the rest of the chapter suggests, then his mediation of the absent Christ is a *personal* mediation. While it is an extremely 'effective' mediation, nevertheless it must not be understood in such a way that the absence of Christ is overridden. As such, the idea of Christ being present *as* the Spirit is ruled out.

The extent to which Paul presents the Spirit in personal terms in Romans 8 has been disputed. On one end of the spectrum are scholars such as Fee, who argues that a number of motifs across the Pauline corpus (not just in Rom. 8) 'presuppose the Spirit as person'.[4] Horn

---

[3] Ziesler 1983: 48, emphasis added.
[4] Fee 1994: 831; cf. Bertrams 1913: 144–171.

is more circumspect. In his developmental scheme he suggests that this personal conception of the Spirit is found only in the last stage of Paul's pneumatology – in his letter to the Romans.[5] Rabens is similarly cautious in applying the language of 'personhood' to the Spirit. He suggests that we 'should go no further than to say that . . . Paul understands the Spirit as having personal traits'.[6] Kuss is perhaps even more reticent to apply the term 'person' to the Spirit. He notes a number of instances in Paul where the Spirit is described as 'acting' in a seemingly personal way.[7] However, these are personifications that are similar to others that Paul uses (for example with death, sin or the law) and so cannot be pressed to imply full-blown personhood.[8]

These cautions are to a certain extent valid. The personality or otherwise of the Spirit cannot be established by a simple appeal to the language of personification and there may be deeper philosophical problems with the term 'person' itself. However, one aspect of Romans 8 is consistently underemphasized (even if it is acknowledged), namely the intercession of the Spirit. This is usually treated as merely one of the 'personifications' of the Spirit that Paul employs in this chapter, like 'leading' (v. 14) or 'bearing witness' (v. 16). However, when Paul describes the Spirit himself as 'interceding'[9] for the 'saints' with 'wordless groaning' according to the will of God (v. 26), we are moving beyond the realm of personification and into the realm of personal relationship. Here is the Spirit's *relating* in prayer to God.

Paul opens his treatment of the Spirit's intercession by describing it in terms of helping us in our weakness (v. 26). Importantly, this is introduced by the adverb 'likewise' – Paul is comparing the Spirit to something he has already said. Although the antecedent of this adverb is widely disputed,[10] perhaps the best view is to see the 'likewise' picking up on the repeated reference to 'groaning' that he has already made.[11] So, in verses 19–22 the creation groans (v. 22), waiting for the liberation 'from its bondage to decay' (v. 21). In verses 23–25 'we Christians' groan (v. 23), waiting for the redemption of our bodies

[5] Horn 1992: 60.
[6] Rabens 1999: 177.
[7] Kuss 1963–78: 580.
[8] Ibid. 581.
[9] The compound verb *hyperentynchanō* is not used anywhere else in the Greek Bible, perhaps coined by Paul in anticipation of 'the expression "for [*hyper*] the saints" of the following verse' – so O'Brien 1987: 73, n. 8.
[10] See the discussions in Holdsworth 2004: 341 and Smith 1998: 36.
[11] Balz 1971: 93. The following summary is based on O'Brien 1987: 68.

(v. 23). In verse 26 the Spirit himself intercedes 'with groanings too deep for words'. This groaning becomes more and more specific from creation to Christians to the Spirit himself. The 'likewise' in verse 26, then, is a reference to the fact that the Spirit *too* groans.

Paul unpacks believers' weakness specifically as lack of knowledge of *what* to pray ('we do not know what to pray for as we ought', v. 26). The parallel between the two phrases 'as we ought' (*katho dei*, v. 26) and 'according to the will of God' (*kata theon*, v. 27) suggests that Paul means that we do not know what to pray because we do not know the will of God. Our prayers, like everything in creation, have been subject to 'futility' (v. 20). This ignorance on our part is overcome by the intercession of the Spirit himself. Our inability to pray, then, is matched by the Spirit's own intercession. Paul sees the Spirit's helping believers by *praying* for them according to the will of God.

The content of the Spirit's prayer is described by Paul as 'inaudible groanings' (v. 26). This phrase has led some interpreters to suggest that the Spirit's distinct praying is not in view. Rather, the Spirit somehow 'inhabits' believers' own prayers. Key to this idea is the contention that these inaudible groanings actually refer to glossolalia (tongues) uttered by believers. This suggestion goes back at least as far as Origen and Chrysostom,[12] but was revived in the twentieth century by Ernst Käsemann, particularly in his Romans commentary.[13] One of the more recent articulations has been by Fee, who argues on the basis that what is in view here is the believer's 'prayer in the Spirit'.[14] However, Paul seems to go out of his way to insist that it is the *Spirit* who intercedes for us. He uses 'but' (*alla*) as a strong contrast to the 'actions' of believers, who *do not know* what to pray; he uses the pronoun to emphasize that it is the Spirit *himself*[15] who intercedes; and this intercession is not *by* the saints but *for* the saints (v. 27) with inaudible groanings.

This description of intense prayer, then, goes beyond mere personification. In describing the Spirit as interceding, Paul is showing the Spirit's relating as a person. As such, this suggests that in this context the *other* personifications (e.g. putting evil deeds to death by the Spirit, 8:13; being led by the Spirit, 8:14; the Spirit of sonship by whom we cry 'Abba Father', 8:15; the Spirit witnesses with our Spirit,

---

[12] For references see Gieniusz 1999: 222, n. 730.
[13] Käsemann 1980: 241.
[14] Fee 1994: 579–586; cf. Engberg-Pedersen 2010: 67.
[15] Gieniusz 1999: 223.

8:16) are more than that – in turn they are evidence of Paul's operating with a personal conception of the Spirit here.

Before returning to 8:9–10, one other aspect needs to be noted: the *heavenly location* of Christ and his intercession there. The presentation of Christ in 8:34 as being 'at the right hand of God', where he 'is interceding for us', is important in connection with the intercession of the Spirit for two reasons. First, it underlines the fact that Christ is absent. However we understand his indwelling in 8:10, it cannot be absolutized or conceived as a presence without remainder. Any *embodiment* of Christ in the believer must be understood in the light of his location at God's right hand, and the mediation of the Spirit understood accordingly. Second, and related to this, is the fact that while Christ is present as interceding in heaven at God's right hand, the Spirit is present as interceding 'in the midst of' or 'with' believers. True, the Spirit is not localized per se in 8:26–27, but the context suggests that his intercession is occurring in the midst of the earthly life that the believer experiences in weakness (8:26). This is significant because the Spirit is presented as operating *in parallel* with Christ. It is not simply that Christ's intercession is mediated to us through the Spirit. No, the Spirit is operating as a discrete (though not independent) agent. He serves – albeit in a highly qualified sense (see below) – as a *substitute* for an absent Christ. While the absent Christ intercedes in heaven, the Spirit is the one who intercedes for believers in their very midst. The two intercessions are related but cannot be collapsed into one another.

Attending to the significance of the *absence* of Christ and the parallel activity of the Spirit who *acts* as a *discrete* agent in Christ's absence helps us to consider the nature or mode of Christ's embodiment *by the Spirit* in 8:9–11.

Paul begins Romans 8:9 by stating that believers are in the Spirit and not in the flesh 'since' (*eiper*)[16] the Spirit of God dwells (*oikei*) 'in you'.[17] If someone does not have the Spirit of Christ, this person does not belong to Christ. In contrast, if *Christ* is in the Christian then while the body may be 'dead', the Spirit is 'life' through

---

[16] On the translation 'since' see Cranfield 1975, 1: 388.

[17] Paul could, however, mean that the Spirit dwells 'among them', in their midst. Jewett (2007: 409) argues for this on the basis of the strong parallels found in Judaism (Exod. 29:45–46; *T. Levi* 5.2). He suggests that the individual language of verse 9c ('someone') stands *in contrast* to the collective language of verse 9a–b. This is correct, but the contrast is not on the individual–collective axis, but on possession or non-possession (*ouk echei*) of the Spirit. As such, it seems better to understand 'you' distributively as referring to the individual.

righteousness. Paul expands on this by stating that if 'the Spirit of him who raised Jesus from the dead' dwells (*oikei*) in them, then 'he who raised Christ Jesus from the dead' will also give life to their 'mortal bodies'. He will do this through the Spirit who already indwells them (8:11).

Two aspects of this passage especially demand attention. First, Paul seems happy to switch without comment from 'Spirit of God' to 'Spirit of Christ'. The former phrase in Judaism seems to speak of God's own presence.[18] As such, the analogous phrase 'Spirit of Christ' suggests the experience and presence of Christ.[19] The Spirit within the Christian is nothing less than the Spirit of *Christ*. Paul's intention, then, is 'to connect the work of the Spirit to the Roman Christians' belonging to Christ and his dwelling within them *as Christians*'.[20] The Spirit mediates the presence of Christ in the same way that he mediates the presence of God.

Second, as we have seen, Paul is also happy to switch between Christ's being in the believer and the Spirit's being in the believer. It is this perceived synonymity between Christ's indwelling the believer and the Spirit's indwelling the believer that has prompted the understanding of the Spirit as being in some sense equivalent to Christ. For example, for Jewett 'it raises problems for later trinitarian thought' but 'there seems little doubt "that Christ and the Spirit are perceived in experience as one"'.[21] However, this is incorrect. We have already seen from the context of the rest of the chapter that the presence of the Spirit does not nullify the absence of Christ. Christ *is* at the right hand of God and is interceding there (8:34) while the Spirit is interceding in the midst of believers. There *is* distinction at the level of experience.

Further, while Paul does indeed describe Christ as 'in you' (8:10), the language of the presence of the Spirit is *more* concrete. It is the Spirit who *dwells* within (*oikei*, 8:9, 11; *enoikountos*, 8:11) believers; it is the Spirit whom believers *possess* (*echei*, 8:9). There is *not* an *absolute* synonymity or reciprocity between the Spirit and Christ in this immediate passage or indeed the chapter as a whole.[22]

How are we, then, to understand the embodiment of Christ in the believer (8:10)? The location of Christ as absent from believers at

[18] Fatehi 2000: 163.
[19] Hermann 1961: 65.
[20] Fatehi 2000: 207, emphasis original.
[21] Jewett 2007: 491, citing Dunn 1988a, 431.
[22] See Fatehi 2000: 269.

God's right hand (8:34) combined with Paul's *emphasis* on the indwelling of the Spirit suggests that it is reasonable to understand Paul to mean that Christ is in believers *by his Spirit*.[23] However, the emphasis on the *personality* of the Spirit in this chapter clarifies the nature of this mediation as a *personal* mediation. That is, the Spirit does not make Christ present *materially* or (purely) *experientially*. Rather, he is *in some senses* a *substitute*. Not a substitute who can ever fully be disconnected from his sender (as the very expression 'Spirit of Christ' suggests). However, neither can he be fully *collapsed* even at the level of experience with his sender. The bodily presence of Christ in the individual believer is qualified by the mediation of the Spirit.[24]

Christ, then, is not 'embodied' in the believer in a *spatial* or *material* sense *as* the Spirit but is present in a *personal* sense *by* the presence of the Spirit himself in the believer. The relationship between Christ and Spirit is such that if the Spirit is present to the believer, then Christ is. The depth of the relationship between Christ and the Spirit (inherent in the very phrase 'Spirit of Christ' with its parallels to 'Spirit of God') means that the 'density' of mediation that the Spirit provides is such that if the Spirit is 'in' a person, in a *real* sense Christ is too. However, this 'real' presence of Christ is a qualified presence. The presence of Christ by the Spirit must be understood in the context of the absence of Christ. These two aspects of the Christian's experience are held together most clearly in Romans 8, a chapter which helps us to see both the personal dimension of the Spirit's mediation and the Spirit's acting as a 'substitute' for the absent Christ. The *absence* of Christ is too often overlooked when scholars examine the relationship between Christ and the Spirit. By ensuring that we do not neglect the *heavenly location* of Christ (Rom. 8:34), the nature of his 'embodiment' by the Spirit comes into clearer focus. It is neither a material embodiment nor an experiential identification *without remainder*. To have the Spirit is to have Christ because the Spirit is the Spirit *of* Christ, not because the Spirit *is* Christ nor even because the Spirit is experienced *as* Christ.

Christ as life-giving spirit (1 Cor. 15:45)

In Romans 8 we have seen that although Paul appears to collapse the identity of the exalted Christ into the Spirit, this is not the case, and

[23] Cf. Eichholz 1983: 274.

[24] On the parallel text Gal. 2:20 see Carson (2002: 165–166), who suggests that *en emoi* here may have the meaning 'in relation to me' or 'on my behalf'; i.e. 'Christ lives on my behalf'.

that even at the level of experience he maintains a clear distinction between them. However, in 1 Corinthians 15 Paul seems to take a step further to define the risen Christ as 'a' (or even 'the') Spirit. In 15:45 he begins his comparison between the first and last Adams. As he begins this comparison, he cites Genesis 2:7: 'The first man Adam became a living being'. He then states a contrast that the 'last Adam [became] a life-giving spirit [*pneuma zōopoioun*]' (15:45 NIV). Here the resurrected Christ seems to be equated with the Spirit.

We will more fully explore 1 Corinthians 15, and what it says concerning the body of the exalted Christ, in chapter 6 below. But at this point I make a few remarks concerning this verse and its seeming equating of Christ and the Spirit.

First, it is important to note that the Holy Spirit is not explicitly mentioned in 1 Corinthians 15. In fact, the description of Christ as 'life-giving spirit' may not actually be a reference to the Holy Spirit at all. Rather, as is frequently pointed out, Paul's terminology is significantly conditioned by his citation of Genesis 2:7. That is, he primarily uses the description as an antithesis to the statement that the first Adam was a 'living being'[25] or even a living 'soul'. Just as Adam's nature is characterized by but *without being reduced to* 'soul' or *psychē*, so Christ's nature is characterized by but *without being reduced* to 'spirit'. That is, he is *spiritual.*

So, not only is it unlikely that this verse contains a reference to the Holy Spirit; more fundamentally, to identify Christ and the Spirit would essentially negate the ongoing humanity of the exalted Christ. Affirming the humanity of the exalted Christ is a crucial aspect of Paul's aim in this chapter. In his summary of the gospel at the start of the chapter, Paul narrates Christ's history from his death to his resurrection to his appearances to the Twelve, five hundred other brothers and last of all to Paul himself. At each point in the narrative, as we have seen, there is a continuity in the identity of Christ. The one who died is the one who rose and is the one who appeared to the early church. Further, this ability to appear presupposes that in his resurrected state Christ maintains an identifiable body that can appear and be observed (15:6–8). In 1 Corinthians 15 Paul wants to establish the truth of the resurrection of Christ (15:12–34) and his ongoing bodily nature (15:35–57). As such, the descriptions of Christ's appearances serve his argument.[26] They thus establish that

[25] So Fee 1987: 790.
[26] Schmisek (2011: 82) interprets the 'seeing language' in both 9:1 and 15:8 as referring to an interior experience. However, he then asserts that the visions therefore

45

Christ possesses an *identifiable* body, which, in turn, proves the resurrection *of the body*. This chain of argument would not hold if these appearances were simply equivalent to OT theophanies. As such, Christ must be distinguishable from the Holy Spirit, who, for Paul, could never be thought of as 'appearing' in bodily form.

As Paul continues, we have further evidence of the ongoing humanity of Christ. In 15:18 'in Christ' language is applied to those who have died. Paul maintains that those who have died 'in Christ' *will* be raised. To say otherwise is to deny the fact of Christ's resurrection. Christ has been raised as the 'firstfruits' of those who have died (15:20) and there is an organic connection between Christ and those who are his (15:23), so that what happens to the former happens to the latter. At Christ's coming (15:23), those who belong to Christ will be raised. Further, Christ is compared to Adam: Just as all who are in Adam die, so all who are in Christ will be made alive (15:22). Importantly, though both Christ and Adam are being conceived as more than mere individuals, the comparison turns on the fact that both Adam and Christ are human beings: just as 'by a man came death, by a man has come also the resurrection of the dead' (15:21). The future resurrection will come through a human being – one who is currently absent. Even in his transformed bodily state, the risen Christ retains his humanity and can be distinguished from other human beings. To consider Christ merely in transcorporeal, supraindividual purely *spiritual* terms would be to deny the fact of his ongoing humanity. Even as Paul assumes the first *Adam* to have had a representative and corporate function, he was still an individual human being (15:21).

Further evidence concerning the ongoing humanity of Christ is seen in 15:23–28. Here Paul details what will happen at Christ's coming (15:23). Paul outlines the eschatological climax to the Son's reign when he will hand his kingdom over to God the Father. This will happen only when he has destroyed every 'rule, authority and power' (15:24). Paul explains this in the next verse with an allusion to Psalm 110:1 (LXX 109:1) combined with Psalm 8:6 (LXX 8:7), where he states that Christ must reign until 'he has put all his enemies under his feet' (15:25). He then states that the last enemy to be defeated is death (15:26) and establishes this point by citing Psalm 8:6, stating

(note 26 *cont.*) do not necessitate 'a physical object of the vision'. If this were Paul's meaning, his appeal to a vision would contribute nothing to his overall argument in chapter 15, where it is precisely the claim of a bodily, tangible resurrection that Paul is seeking to maintain.

that God has placed everything under Christ's feet (15:27). In appealing to this Scripture, Paul is showing that Christ fulfils the commission that was given to *human beings* (Ps. 8:5). Christ, then, in his eschatological victory over death, is fulfilling God's charge to *humanity* and is showing himself to be the true Adam. The risen Christ, then, *must* remain a human being. Paul continues in 15:47–48 to describe Adam ('the first man was from the earth') in contrast to Christ ('the second man is from heaven'). The risen Christ in heaven remains a human being. Finally, Christ's humanity has an important eschatological transformative function in that believers will be transformed to bear his image (*eikōn*), just as they have borne the image (*eikōn*) of Adam (15:49). This Adam–Christ parallel would break down if Christ were to lose his distinct, human bodily form.

That Christ remains a human being, then, is of fundamental importance to this chapter and, as such, must take hermeneutical priority over Paul's antithetical use of Genesis 2:7 – which can, *in any case*, be read in a way that does not equate Christ and the Holy Spirit.

The Spirit of the Lord (2 Cor. 3:4–17)

In 2 Corinthians 3:6 Paul describes himself and his apostolic colleagues as 'ministers of a new covenant, not of the letter but of the Spirit. For the letter kills, but the Spirit gives life'. This long-debated differentiation is worked out in the following argument, which climaxes in 3:17 with Paul's stating that 'the Lord is the Spirit'. If we understand 'Lord' (*kyrios*) to refer (as it most frequently does in Paul) to Christ, then here Paul seems explicitly to *identify* Christ and the Spirit: Christ *is* the Spirit.

Margaret Thrall provides a clear, recent summary of the main positions on 3:17. The three main groups differ on the meaning of the *kyrios*, who is identified with the Spirit: (1) simply 'God' (considered abstractly); (2) Christ or (3) 'the Lord' of 3:16. The first option is unlikely,[27] and we will return to the third option when we consider the passage in more detail. For our purposes, though, the second option is the most interesting – is Paul making an identification between Christ and the Spirit, and if so what is the nature of this identity? If 'Lord' does refer to 'Christ' in 3:17, then, Thrall argues, there are four main ways of understanding the relationship between Christ and the Spirit. The first two are fairly unlikely, namely that

---

[27] Thrall 1994, 1: 279. The presence of the article before *pneuma* weighs against understanding Paul to be saying 'God is spirit'.

'Christ is the inward spiritual meaning of the Old Testament',[28] or 'Christ is spirit'.[29] That leaves the idea that Paul is somehow identifying Christ with the Holy Spirit either in an absolute sense or in a functional sense (a 'dynamic' identity). We will consider both these positions in turn.

An absolute identity between Christ and Spirit

Commenting on 2 Corinthians 3:17 and verses where Paul switches between 'in Christ' and 'in [the] Spirit' (e.g. Rom. 8:9–11), Hendrikus Berkhof argues that for Paul 'Christ and the Spirit are identical and that the Spirit *is* Christ in action' and as such 'we go far beyond the traditional connection between Christ and the Spirit'.[30] He notes that 'traditional theology' avoids the word 'identity' to express the relationship between the Spirit and the exalted Lord and speaks instead of 'an identity in functions'. Berkhof, however, argues that this position is 'untenable'.[31]

However, another proponent of Spirit-Christology, Lampe, actually argues that Paul was inconsistent precisely because he pulls back and does *not* identify Christ and Spirit. He argues that Paul was inhibited 'from completing [his] partial identification of Christ with Spirit by [his] concept of the pre-existence . . . of the actual person Jesus Christ'.[32] He argues that, in contrast, Christian *experience* does not correspond with the idea of the Spirit's simply mediating Christ's presence. Rather, 'when we speak of the "presence of Christ" and the "indwelling of the Spirit" we are speaking of one and the same experience of God'.[33] As soon as one regards the Spirit as distinct from Christ (as Lampe argues that Paul does), the Spirit 'then has to be regarded as a second and subsidiary manifestation of God's outreach towards man'.[34] Lampe argues that 'this reduction of the Spirit to a second, and very ill-defined, place in God's outreach towards the world could have been avoided if the term "Spirit" had been allowed to express the totality of God in his creativity'.[35] Lampe argues, however, that Paul did not make this absolute identification because

[28] Ibid.
[29] As with the interpretation 'God is spirit', the definite article before *pneuma* rules this out.
[30] Berkhof 1977: 25, emphasis added.
[31] Ibid. 28.
[32] Lampe 1977: 117.
[33] Ibid. 118.
[34] Ibid.
[35] Ibid.

he wanted to affirm 'the personal pre-existence of Jesus Christ as Son of God, the continuing personal "post-existence" of Jesus Christ, resurrected and ascended and also experienced by present believers, and the future return of the ascended Christ in glory'.[36]

So, both Lampe and Berkhof reject the idea of the Spirit's simply mediating Christ's presence. Berkhof argues that the Spirit *is* Christ in action. Hence, to experience the Spirit is to experience Christ. Lampe wishes that Paul had been less restrained and, in fact, been more consistent in his understanding of Christian experience.

A dynamic identity between Christ and Spirit

Hamilton is typical of those who argue for a dynamic or functional identity between Christ and the Spirit. He argues that in 2 Corinthians 3:17 Paul 'equate[s] the source of the benefits with the agent of their distribution'.[37] That is, 'the Spirit so effectively performs His office of communicating to men the benefits of the risen Christ that for all intents and purposes of faith the Lord Himself is present bestowing grace on His own'.[38] The Spirit actually 'brings the ascended Lord to earth again' and 'bridges the gap between transcendence and immanence'.[39] Hamilton uses the analogy of an actor playing a role so well that he seems to become the person he is portraying. It is '*in just this sense* that the Lord is the Spirit'.[40] The Spirit 'portrays the Lord so well that we lose sight of the Spirit and are conscious of the Lord only'.[41]

For Hermann, this dynamic understanding flows from his understanding of the Spirit, namely that the expression *pneuma* 'is not a self-clarifying concept, but is a dynamic expression of the presence and reality of the exalted Lord in his Church'.[42] It is the question of the *experience* of the Spirit that is key.

What we have, then, is a similar spectrum to what we saw with Romans 8:9–10, ranging from Christ *identified* as the Spirit or *experienced* as the Spirit.

Again, the identity of Christ is effectively collapsed into that of the Spirit. In both cases the notion of mediation is to a greater or lesser extent missing. Even with a dynamic understanding of the relationship

[36] Ibid. 119.
[37] Hamilton 1957: 6.
[38] Ibid.
[39] Ibid.
[40] Ibid., emphasis added.
[41] Ibid.
[42] Hermann 1961: 51, my tr.

between Christ and the Spirit, the question of the *distinction* between Christ and Spirit and hence any 'eschatological reserve' in the believers' experience is effectively eroded.

Identifying the Lord of 2 Corinthians 3:17

We will examine Paul's wider argument to determine the identity of the Lord in verse 17 who is equated with the Spirit.

Part of Paul's aim in chapter 3 is to establish the effectiveness of his ministry – an effectiveness that rests not on the 'letter' (3:6) but on the work of the Spirit. In contrast to Moses, who would keep himself veiled to prevent the Israelites seeing that the glory of his face was fading,[43] Paul and the apostles are 'very bold' (3:12). Paul then plays on the motif of the veil by using it as a reference both to the physical object that covered Moses' face and to the spiritual covering that remains over hearts when the old covenant is read (3:14–15). Only in Christ is this spiritual veil taken away (3:14). Verses 14b–16 contain two thematically parallel pairs that follow this basic pattern:

A   Statement about covering by veil remaining to this day (v. 14b);

B   Statement about veil being removed 'in Christ' (v. 14c);

A'   Statement about covering by veil remaining to this day (v. 15);

B'   Statement about veil being removed upon 'turning to the Lord' (v. 16).[44]

It would seem on first glance that 'turning to the Lord' (B': v. 16) parallels 'in Christ' (B: v. 14c), thus implying that Christ is the Lord who is then identified as the Spirit in verse 17. However, the picture is more complicated when we examine verse 16 in more detail. It has been argued that in this verse Paul is specifically drawing on the Greek of Exodus 34:34. If we observe the two texts (woodenly translated) next to each other we can see both the similarities and the differences:

Exodus 34:34	2 Corinthians 3:16
Whenever (*hēnika d'an*)	Whenever (*hēnika d'an*)
was entering (*eiseporeueto*)	one turns (*epistrepsē*)

---

[43] Watson 2004: 293.
[44] For more detail on the parallelism see van Unnik 1963: 163.

Moses

before the Lord (*enanti kyriou*)	to the Lord (*pros kyrion*)
to speak to him (*lalein autō*)	
he was removing the veil	the veil is removed
(*periēreito to kalymma*)	(*periaireitai to kalymma*)

Three differences are especially notable:[45] the change in verb (and tense) from 'was entering' (*eiseporeueto* – imperfect) to 'turning' (*epistrepsē* – aorist);[46] the omission of Moses as the subject; and the change from the imperfect middle (*periēreito*) to the present middle (*periaireitai*).[47] However, as Belleville notes, the similarities must not be overlooked: the particular form of 'whenever' (*hēnika d'an*) is found only here in the NT; the verb *periaireō* is found only here in Paul; the reference to a veil being removed is unique to 2 Corinthians 3:16 and Exodus 34:34; and the syntax of the two verses is identical.[48]

On the basis of these differences and similarities commentators have argued for a range of relationships between the two texts: from Wong who argues that 3:16 is simply 'a Pauline creation'[49] to Horn who, while he admits that it is not a citation, argues that it is 'a specific application of the OT text'[50] to Hafemann who argues that it is 'the most explicit reference to Exod. 32–34 in our passage'.[51] The similarities surely do point to *some* kind of relationship, but how do we account for the differences? Has Paul changed the specific description of Moses' entering the tabernacle and removing the veil to a more general statement to the effect that 'anyone who turns to the Lord has the veil removed'?[52] Paul may simply be providing his own translation of Exodus 34:34 and referring directly to Moses' entry into the presence of Yahweh.[53] However, most commentators argue that Paul has deliberately changed a verb that basically refers to physical movement (*eisporeuomai*) to one that refers to turning, often with reference to conversion (*epistrephō*).[54]

---

[45] Belleville (1991: 251) argues that the other differences are minimal.

[46] An aorist subjunctive used to express a future condition.

[47] Or possibly passive.

[48] Thrall 1994, 1: 268, n. 547.

[49] Wong 1985: 67.

[50] Horn 2000: 67.

[51] Hafemann 1995: 387, cited in Watson 2004: 297, n. 47. Watson himself argues that the syntax and the scriptural background 'make the reference to Moses unambiguously clear'.

[52] Furnish 1984: 202.

[53] See Wong 1985: 56, n. 27, for a list of commentators who take this position.

[54] Ibid. 58. The change in tense also most likely suggests that Paul is broadening the reference, with the aorist subjunctive *epistrepsē* functioning in a future sense.

Perhaps more significant, though, is the omission of the subject. The loss of Moses from the text suggests to some that Paul is 'cutting the sentence loose from its immediate narrative moorings'.[55] However, equally it is worth noting that Paul does not simply add a generic 'whoever'. The text simply reads, 'whenever *he* turns to the Lord, he removes the veil', suggesting a clear if not explicit reference to Moses.[56] As such the changes Paul has introduced, while admittedly pointing to a broader application of the text, do not, in fact, cut it loose from the original Exodus text altogether. As such the statement 'the Lord is the Spirit' is an *interpretative* and hence *pneumatological* statement rather than a *Christological* one. Paul is identifying the Lord in the text as the Spirit, not making an assertion about Christ.

It is often pointed out that when citing the LXX Paul's use of 'Lord' nearly always refers to Christ.[57] However, Paul is not *simply* bringing the OT text into the present. The actors in the original scene as Paul alludes to it remain Moses and Yahweh.[58] Hays has aptly summarized the difficulty that interpreters have with this passage, namely that

> its central figure, Moses, bears within himself metaphorical tensions that resist reduction into a one-for-one allegorical scheme . . . Moses pre-figures Christian experience, but he is not a Christian. He is both the paradigm for the Christian's direct experience of the Spirit and the symbol for the old covenant to which that experience is set in antithesis.[59]

Paul is emphasizing that the Spirit is the divine agent whom *we* experience in the present just as Moses encountered Yahweh in the past.[60] Paul is essentially arguing that 'within the sanctuary, which is the dwelling place of the Lord who is the Spirit, the unveiled Moses signifies the reality of Christian worship'.[61] Thus the text resists a simplistic Lord = Christ identification. Paul's use of 'Lord' already

[55] Hays 1993: 147.
[56] Watson 2004: 297.
[57] Fee 2007: 631.
[58] The idea that Paul is alluding to the Lord as the pre-existent Christ (e.g. Thrall 1994, 1: 272) seems unlikely – otherwise Paul would surely have specifically identified the Lord as Christ in v. 17 rather than the Spirit.
[59] Hays 1993: 144.
[60] Thrall 1994, 1: 281.
[61] Watson 2004: 297.

has a degree of flexibility in that as much as he applies it to Christ in the present, he also knows that it refers to Yahweh in the Old Testament. Here he brings the Spirit into that same relationship. The Spirit too is 'Lord'. When someone turns to 'the Lord', whether Moses' turning to Yahweh, or a Gentile's turning to Christ, it is the *Spirit* who is the Lord at work.[62]

Paul, then, does not *identify* (either dynamically or ontologically) Christ and the Spirit. What this passage does highlight, though, is the *agency* of the Spirit. The Spirit is key to the removal of the veil (v. 16) and *where* the Spirit operates, there is freedom (v. 17). As such, while there is no *direct* identity made between Christ and the Spirit, in their impact on the believer they are inextricably linked. The Spirit who brings freedom is the Spirit *of the Lord* (v. 17). This complex switching in the referent of the term 'the Lord' points to an underlying complexity in the relationship between Christ and the Spirit. The qualification 'Lord' here is used in differentiation from the Spirit. Presumably as we move away from the Exodus text, it seems reasonable to understand 'Lord' to refer, as it usually does in Paul, to Christ. Thus while the Spirit and Christ *share* the divine status of 'Lord', they can be distinguished at the personal[63] level so that the Spirit can be identified as the 'Spirit of the Lord'. Though this relationship is complex it does point to the Spirit's suitability in mediating Christ. The depth of their relationship – *approaching* identity without their being collapsed into one another – means that as the Spirit is encountered, so too is Christ.

The one who descended is the one who ascended (Eph. 4:10)

In Ephesians 4, in his discussion of the gifts Christ gives to the church, Paul cites Psalm 68:18 in verse 8 to establish the point that just as God received gifts from his captives when he triumphed over his enemies, the risen Christ distributes gifts following his own triumphant ascension. The issues regarding Paul's use of the psalm are numerous and complex.[64] For our purposes, though, we focus on Paul's subsequent exposition of the psalm in verses 9–10 when he states:

---

[62] This is the position essentially argued by Fee (1994: 311–312). However, later (2007: 179) he changes his view and argues that 'Lord' should be understood to refer here to Christ.

[63] See the discussion of this term in the section on Rom. 8 above.

[64] For a helpful, recent discussion see Arnold 2010: 246–252.

In saying, 'He ascended,' what does it mean but that he had also descended into the lower regions, the earth? He who descended is the one who also ascended far above all the heavens, that he might fill all things.

A number of scholars see the language of descent here as referring to the descent of the Spirit at Pentecost.[65] Here the suggestion is made, for example by Harris, that the descent referred to in verses 9 and 10 occurred *after* the exaltation of verse 8 and so refers 'to the descent of Christ *as* the Spirit who distributes gifts (gifted leaders) to his church'.[66] Fowl, for example, takes it this way and so suggests that verse 10 represents 'an extraordinary assertion of the identity of the Son and the Spirit'.[67] Harris, however, pulls back from expressing an absolute identity between Christ and the Spirit but suggests that there is 'a functional relationship amounting to experiential identity'.[68]

However, this collapsing of the Son and the Spirit goes against other parts of Ephesians, where we see the Son and the Spirit though clearly connected also to be carefully distinguished. So, in 1:17 Paul prays 'that the God of our Lord Jesus Christ, the Father of glory, *may give you the Spirit* of wisdom and of revelation in the knowledge of him'. Here the Spirit is given by Christ. As such, it seems better to see the descent and ascent as both referring to one and the same person, either the Spirit or Christ.

Not only does the context suggest Christ rather than the Spirit is in view (4:7); Paul's wording underlines that the sequence is descent and then ascent. Again, this makes it unlikely that the *descent* is referring to the coming of the Spirit.[69] Paul's point is that that Christ who was powerful enough to conquer his enemies is powerful enough to equip his people to maintain their unity and continue their growth in him (4:11–16).[70]

The exalted Christ and the Spirit in John's Gospel

The parallels in activity between Jesus and the Holy Spirit in John's Gospel have been frequently observed. As Thompson summarizes:

---

[65] See ibid. 253, n. 27, for a partial list of recent commentators.
[66] Harris 1996: 193, emphasis added.
[67] Fowl 2012: 138.
[68] Harris 1996: 192.
[69] Hoehner 2002: 536.
[70] See Thielman 2010: 273.

Jesus teaches (7:14–15; 8:20; 18:19), as does the Spirit (14:26).
Jesus gives testimony (5:31–32; 8:13–14; 7:7), as does the Spirit (15:26).
Both Jesus (7:17; 8:26; 14:10) and the Spirit (14:26; 16:13–14) speak of what they have heard.
Both Jesus (1:18; 4:25) and the Spirit (16:13) disclose and reveal.[71]

This overlap of function and the closeness with which John associates Jesus and the Spirit can make delineating their relationship tricky. On one side is the danger of so differentiating Jesus and the Spirit that the latter is simply seen as an unqualified 'replacement' for Jesus.[72] This idea is often not expressed carefully and does not adequately capture the dynamic nature of the relationship between Jesus and the Spirit.

However, perhaps more problematic is the tendency to collapse the identity of the Spirit into Jesus. This can be seen in strands of both German and Anglo-American scholarship. Woll provides a helpful summary of earlier German scholarship,[73] and essentially agrees with Hans Windisch's observation that the text of the farewell discourse (John 14 – 16) in its final form suggests that the return of Jesus is to be identified with the coming of the Spirit.[74] Marianne Meye Thompson highlights the ease with which a scholar like Raymond Brown can slip from describing Jesus as coming back 'in and through the Paraclete' (and thus maintaining some sort of distinction between Jesus and the Paraclete) to describing Jesus' presence to believers 'as the Paraclete' which confuses their identities.[75] Thompson rightly notes that both these formulations 'in and through the Paraclete' and 'as the Paraclete' are found 'widely and indiscriminately without much attention to the differences between them', thus merely underscoring 'how difficult it is to interpret the Gospel precisely at this point'.[76]

As an example of the difficulty of pinning down the exact nature of the relationship, Smalley describes the Paraclete as 'the alter ego of Jesus' who 'acts in the church and in the world for the risen Jesus, and *as* Jesus'.[77] It is hard to pin down what exactly he means by

---

[71] Thompson 2015: 320.
[72] Brown 1970: 143, cited in Thompson 2015: 320.
[73] Woll 1981: 70–79.
[74] Ibid. 78; Windisch 1968: 3.
[75] Brown 1970: 1143, cited in Thompson 2001: 180.
[76] Thompson 2001: 180.
[77] Smalley 1998: 261, emphasis added.

'as Jesus'. Similarly, Burge suggests that '[i]n a very real way, in the Spirit Jesus has come back'.[78]

Others have more directly equated the coming of the Spirit with the actual return of Christ in the fullest sense. Bultmann famously understood John to be collapsing not just Jesus' resurrection and parousia but Pentecost too so that the experience of the Spirit's coming is not external to the disciple but an internal experience of faith.[79] Or more recently, Martyn, who, commenting on 14:23, suggests that '[j]ust as the Word did not remain in heaven, but rather came and dwelt among us, so the Risen Lord *does not remain in heaven*, but rather comes to dwell with his own'.[80]

However, in this section I want to examine briefly a more recent strand of scholarship that posits an absolute identity between Jesus and the Paraclete before considering the text of John itself. Two recent works by scholars associated with the University of Copenhagen have applied a Stoic understanding of *pneuma* to their reading of John to the effect that they understand that Jesus and the Spirit should be absolutely identified.

Gitte Buch-Hansen: Jesus himself becomes the life-giving Spirit

Buch-Hansen situates her 2010 study in conversation with, among others, Wayne Meeks. Meeks had suggested that the Gospel of John deliberately employs confusing, even 'irrational, disorganized and incomplete metaphors'[81] on the lips of Jesus for the purpose of community formation. That is, by using confusing language (observe how even an initially sympathetic Nicodemus fails to grasp what Jesus is talking about in John 3), John is able to emphasize Jesus' strangeness to the world and so strengthen the distinctiveness of the Johannine community. Hence, on this understanding, language in John which seems to evade logic has a specific purpose.

Into this category comes Jesus' discourse about his departure and the coming of the Spirit with the tensions between 'his identity/not-identity with the coming spirit and about his simultaneous leaving and coming (14:28)'. These tensions are understood to 'generate a collapse of the syntactic logic of language'.[82]

---

[78] Burge 1987: 148.
[79] Bultmann 2007, 2: 57.
[80] Martyn 2003: 142, emphasis added.
[81] Meeks 1972: 68.
[82] Buch-Hansen 2010: 394.

Gitte Buch-Hansen, however, suggests that a Stoic understanding of *pneuma* enables us to read John and his portrayal of Jesus' teaching without the need to view it as 'incomprehensible'.[83] Her argument is complex and comprehensive and I do not have space to do anything other than sketch the main lines.

Buch-Hansen suggests that John's teaching about Jesus' future, namely 'the *synchronicity* of Jesus' leaving and coming, the *fusion* of spaces, the *blurring* of established identities', is only contradictory if one assumes 'the (modern) understanding of the subject's body-bound integrity and a dualistic world view'.[84] If one reads it through the lens of a first-century Stoic world view, the tensions disappear. Essentially she sees a parallel between John and Paul in 1 Corinthians 15:45, where Jesus is described as transforming into a 'life-giving spirit'. The turning point of John's Gospel is 13:1, when John describes Jesus' *metabasis* from the world. Typically understood as his 'depart-ure' (so ESVUK, NIV, etc.), Buch-Hansen rather understands it as Jesus' 'transition'. This transition is at the heart of the Gospel, namely Jesus' transition 'as the Son of God to the next generation of divinely-begotten children (1:2–3)'.[85] That is, Jesus' transition takes place in two stages. He first becomes 'spirit' and then that life-giving spirit is infused into believers to transform them.

Drawing parallels with Philo's application of Stoic cosmology to explain the transition of devout men to heaven, Buch-Hansen understands John's Gospel to be drawing on the Stoic understand-ing that *pneuma* is actually a form of matter and teaching a form of what the Stoics conceived as *anastoicheiōsis* ('interchangeability of elements'[86]). Thus she is not suggesting that Jesus leaves his body behind (John 20 rules this out); rather, he undergoes a transformation 'in which the elements of soul and body – "blood and flesh" – are transformed into the highest, lightest, swiftest, and most dynamic element of the divine continuum, the divine [*pneuma*]'.[87]

Thus Jesus goes *and* returns, and can be identified with *and* dis-tinguished from the *pneuma* (since this does not exhaust what can be said about him). Nevertheless, according to Buch-Hansen, we can conclude that for John, 'Jesus himself becomes the life-giving Spirit'.[88]

---

[83] Meeks 1972: 54.
[84] Buch-Hansen 2010: 352, emphasis original.
[85] Ibid. 1.
[86] Ibid. 306, n. 395.
[87] Ibid. 402.
[88] Ibid. 352.

Troels Engberg-Pedersen: the Paraclete is Jesus himself

In a similar manner to Buch-Hansen, Troels Engberg-Pedersen draws on Stoic metaphysics to explain John's Gospel. He also views John as sharing a Stoic view of *pneuma* as matter and, as such, stresses that many Johannine expressions do not need to be read metaphorically. For example, the language of indwelling can be understood to describe the concrete possession of the material *pneuma*. The disciples will literally and substantively receive the *pneuma* within their bodies (thereby becoming able literally to remain *in* the 'Jesus-vine' just as he remains *in* them, 15:4), and this is what explains that they will henceforth 'bear much fruit' and act on the love command. Not only will they now know; they will also act on their knowledge. When the *pneuma* has been infused into and taken over their bodies, they *cannot but* act on their knowledge.[89]

Engberg-Pedersen applies this understanding of *pneuma* to explain the relationship of Jesus to the Paraclete in John's Gospel. The promises in 14:15–24 are that the reception of the Paraclete by the disciples will lead to their *fully* being in Jesus and God and they will *fully* (and finally) understand that 'I am in my Father, and you in me, and I in you' (14:20). And so their reception of the Paraclete means a '*fully* adequate relationship – with *Jesus*'.[90] Because the Paraclete brings knowledge of *Jesus*, Engberg-Pedersen concludes that 'the two figures of (the risen and returning) Jesus and the "Paraclete" are not in the end to be distinguished'.[91] That is, 'it seems virtually impossible not to see Jesus here as talking of himself *as* the "Paraclete"'.[92]

But how do we explain the distinction between Jesus and the Paraclete that is made when, for example, Jesus refers to the Spirit as *another* Paraclete? Engberg-Pedersen argues that Jesus be understood in terms of a Stoically conceived amalgam or 'mixture' (*krasis*) of 'two entities: Jesus of Nazareth (in his body and flesh) and the *pneuma* he received in the baptism scene'.[93] When Jesus returns, he does so in a 'disamalgamated' form *as pneuma*. That *pneuma* is the 'Paraclete'. Though Jesus departs in one form, he also immediately returns in what is either the same or else a slightly different form, namely as

---

[89] Engberg-Pedersen 2017: 274.
[90] Ibid. 279, emphasis original.
[91] Ibid.
[92] Ibid, emphasis original.
[93] Ibid. 277.

nothing but *pneuma*, which is nevertheless also the form that makes him be what he both was and is: Jesus *Christ*.[94]

And so, the best way to relate Jesus' identity with, but also his difference from, the Paraclete is to understand the *pneuma* 'as both present *in* that "amalgam" and also independently present in the form of the 'Paraclete'.[95] Nevertheless, it is still correct, according to Engberg-Pedersen, to conclude that 'the "Paraclete" *is* Jesus himself'.[96]

Christ and the Spirit distinguished

Engberg-Pedersen and Buch-Hansen have proposed very bold interpretations of John. Both rely on the assumption that John's readers would have understood and been familiar with a Stoic conception of *pneuma*. However, fundamentally, as a number of reviewers have pointed out,[97] their assumptions regarding a Stoic background to John's understanding of *pneuma* are problematic. Engberg-Pedersen, building on the work of Martin Hengel, has done much to break the Jewish–Hellenistic division, as if the two 'worlds' were hermetically sealed. However, it remains that there are serious and considerable differences between Stoic and OT concepts of *pneuma*. Neither Buch-Hansen nor Engberg-Pedersen draws heavily on the OT as a source of John's understanding of the Spirit – except as mediated through Philo.

This leads them to neglect and downplay the dynamic relationship between Jesus and the Spirit. Engberg-Pedersen seeks to maintain a distinction between the Spirit and Christ so that the *pneuma* is 'both present *in* that "amalgam" and also independently present in the form of the "Paraclete"'.[98] However, by conceiving the Spirit in material terms, any sense of personal relationship between him and Christ is effectively overlooked. And yet John, as we have seen with Paul, while not articulating a full-blown doctrine of the Trinity, lays the groundwork for that later doctrine, a crucial component of which is the personality of the Spirit. John describes him doing, as we have seen, the very things that Jesus has done (see above). And yet, he remains distinct from Jesus: 'whatever he hears he will speak, and he will declare to you the things that are to come. He will glorify me, for he will take what is mine and declare it to you' (John 16:13–14). Further, it is not simply the case that what Jesus did the Paraclete now

---

[94] Ibid.
[95] Ibid. 280, emphasis original.
[96] Ibid.
[97] E.g. Jobes 2011 and Levison 2012.
[98] Engberg-Pedersen 2017: 280.

does. If that were so, it would be possible to see the Spirit as simply a 'replacement' for the absent Jesus or even Jesus himself in another form. But critically, the Spirit's primary role is of testifying *to* Jesus (16:14–15).[99]

Part of the difficulty involved in discerning how John understands Jesus and the Spirit to be related turns on the potentially different referents to the language of 'coming' in the farewell discourse. This seems to operate on three levels. So, in 14:3 Jesus says that he will 'come again', presumably here referring to his parousia since he immediately adds that the purpose of this coming is to take believers to himself. However, in 14:18, having just pledged that he will give the Spirit to be in them and with them for ever, Jesus promises, 'I will not leave you as orphans; I will come to you'. Does this refer to the return of Jesus to his disciples following the resurrection? Or a spiritual coming to the disciples?

In 14:23 Jesus further promises that if anyone loves him and keeps his word, 'my Father will love him, and we will come to him and make our home with him'. Here the promise of a spiritual dwelling is widened to all post-resurrection believers. This is a similar promise to 14:21 that 'whoever has my commandments and keeps them, he it is who loves me. And he who loves me will be loved by my Father, and I will love him and manifest myself to him.'

It can be hard to untangle the referents to these different comings, but it seems that Jesus does speak about his coming to them following the resurrection (16:16); his coming to them *through* the Spirit (14:18); and his final coming, following which he will take them to be with him (14:3; 17:24).

Attending to each of these allows us, again, to see that Jesus does not promise an unqualified presence with believers before he comes again to take them to himself that they may be 'where' he is (14:3; 17:24). Christ, in other words, is absent from believers in the meantime (cf. 'I am no longer in the world, but they are in the world', 17:11). And while, to anticipate our later discussion, the Spirit does mediate Christ's presence, he does not override his absence.

No, in John as in Paul, even at the level of experience Christ and the Spirit remain distinct. As Thompson puts it (on 14:23):

Jesus speaks of his presence, his Father's presence, and the Spirit's presence with the disciples. In some fashion, Jesus, the Father, and

---

[99] Thompson 2001: 181.

the Paraclete will all be 'with' believers. Just as Jesus does not 'replace' the Father but rather makes the Father known, testifies to him, and discloses him, so the Spirit does not 'replace' Jesus but makes Jesus known, testifies to him, and discloses him to the disciples. In this manner, the Spirit does not *replace* Jesus, or even become the real presence of Jesus; the Spirit makes the presence of Jesus real.[100]

Conclusion

In our last chapter we considered the identity of the exalted Christ in 'singular' terms; that is, we explored how his identity develops following the resurrection and ascension. In this chapter in considering his relationship with the Spirit, we have seen how John and Paul can *almost* speak of the Spirit and Christ interchangeably. To have the Spirit is, in some real sense, to have Christ (Rom. 8:9–10); it means that as believers we are not bereft of Christ's presence (John 14:23). However, neither Paul nor John takes the further step of fully identifying, *even at the level of experience*, Christ and the Spirit. The Spirit's presence does not negate or override Christ's absence, because the two while intimately related nevertheless remain distinct. And so to have the Spirit is not to have Christ in an unqualified sense, because the Spirit is not Christ. Along the way we have noted that neither Paul nor John offers a full-blown doctrine of the Trinity. However, the relationship they presuppose to exist between the Spirit and Christ patently lays the groundwork for this later doctrine. This is seen in the way both writers can move between the Spirit and Christ in a way that expresses their most intimate connection and relationship, without nevertheless overriding the distinction between them. Their relationship is such that to have the *Spirit* dwelling in you is to have *Christ* dwelling in you *by the Spirit*.

---

[100] Ibid., emphasis original.

Chapter Four

The identity of the exalted Christ: the exalted Christ and the church

Introduction

In this chapter we are going to consider the question of how the church as *Christ's body* has an impact on our understanding of his identity. That the exalted Christ is affected by what happens to his church seems undeniable. In the repeated account of Saul/Paul's conversion in Acts, each time Luke recounts that the risen Lord Jesus asks Saul not 'Why are you persecuting the church?' but 'Why are you persecuting *me*?' (9:4; 22:7; 26:14). That the church in some sense reveals or discloses the identity of Christ seems reasonable. Not only does Jesus tell his disciples that people will know that they are his disciples if they love one another (John 13:35), but Paul states that the 'manifold wisdom of God' is made known 'to the rulers and authorities in the heavenly places' *through* the church and that is according 'to the eternal purpose that he has realized in Christ Jesus our Lord' (Eph. 3:10–11). Jesus taught that acceptance or rejection on judgment day turns on the fact that how people treat his followers ('the least of these my brothers') is how they treated him (Matt. 25:40, 45).

However, in a similar way to what we saw in the last chapter with the Spirit, some commentators posit a relationship between Christ and church which blurs their distinction – at least on a bodily level. That is, the church is understood to be the *exclusive* body of the exalted Christ. This view was made popular in the English-speaking world by J. A. T. Robinson in his 1952 monograph *The Body.* Here he suggests that the church is the body of Christ in an absolute sense since it is 'in literal fact the risen organism of Christ's person *in all its concrete reality*'.[1] The church 'is in fact no other than the glorified

---

[1] Robinson 1952: 51, emphasis added.

body of the risen and ascended Christ'.[2] Robinson's idea has found expression in contemporary systematic theology. So, Robert Jenson in his *Systematic Theology* notes that 'in a Copernican universe [there] is no plausible accommodation for the risen Christ's body'.[3] However, if 'there is no *place* for Jesus' risen body, how is it a body at all'?[4] Jenson concludes that although

> Paul clearly thinks of the Lord as in some sense visibly located in a heaven spatially related to the rest of creation, the only body of Christ to which Paul ever actually refers is not an entity in this heaven but the Eucharist's loaf and cup and the church assembled around them.[5]

Similarly, Graham Ward in an essay on the body of Christ in *Radical Orthodoxy* contends that

> [t]he body of Jesus Christ is not lost, nor does it reside now in heaven as a discrete object . . . The body of Jesus Christ, the body of God, is permeable, transcorporeal, transpositional . . . We have no access to the body of the gendered Jew . . . because the Church is now the body of Christ, so to understand the body of Jesus we can only examine what the Church is and what it has to say concerning the nature of that body . . . God in Christ dies and the Church is born. One gives way to the other, *without remainder*.[6]

In the first section of this chapter we will examine 1 Corinthians 12, the passage where Paul seems to identify Christ and the church (especially v. 12) most explicitly and where the arguments of Jenson et al. above seem to have the most purchase. However, we will see that Paul pulls back from positing a strict identity between Christ and the church. This anticipates what we will see in chapter 6, where we will see that the NT unambiguously maintains that the exalted Christ *does* continue to possess a discrete, localizable and physical body. In the second half of the chapter, however, we will consider how Christ's relationship with the church, particularly the church described as his body, affects our understanding of his identity. While the church

---

[2] Ibid.
[3] Jenson 1997: 202.
[4] Ibid., emphasis original.
[5] Ibid. 204.
[6] Ward 1999: 176–177, emphasis added.

cannot exhaust the identity of the exalted Christ, nevertheless his relationship with the church does have significant implications for how we understand the identity of the exalted Christ.

The church as the exclusive bodily expression of the exalted Christ?

Paul describes the church as the body of Christ in a number of places (e.g. Eph. 1:23; 4:12; Col. 1:18), but his most sustained discussion is found in 1 Corinthians 12. In verse 12 Paul turns from the 'oneness' of the Spirit (12:1–11) to the oneness of the body – which though it is made up of many members remains one body. This does not apply simply to any generic human body but also to Christ. However, Paul does not simply compare the *church* to a many-member body but compares *Christ* himself. So he begins the comparison, 'For just as the body is one and has many members, and all the members of the body, though many, are one body'. If he completed the comparison by saying, '*so it is with the church*', it would be unremarkable. However, he actually says, '*so it is with Christ*'. That is, *Christ* himself has many members. Similarly, in 6:15, Paul does not say, 'Do you not know that your bodies are members of *the church*?' but ' Do you not know that your bodies are *members of Christ*?' Is Christ, then, being conceived as a corporate entity made up of many members? We will see that, in one sense, the answer is yes! Christ *is* a corporate entity, however he is not *exclusively* so, and even these verses cannot be used to absolutize the relationship between Christ and the church. As we have seen, some exegetes posit an *identity* between Christ and the church, which has, in turn, led to emphasis on the church as an 'expansion' of the incarnation[7] and the resurrection body of Christ being revealed 'not as an individual, but as the Christian community'.[8]

Jerome Murphy-O'Connor argues that it is not surprising that Paul makes a direct link between the church and Christ in 1 Corinthians 12:12 since for Paul 'the community is Christ'.[9] He argues that the community and Christ are *functionally* identical. That is, 'the community mediates the salvation won by Christ', and as such, is 'the incarnational prolongation of the mission of the saving Christ'.[10] In terms of 'the reality of salvation the community is the physical

---

[7] E.g. Kelly 2014: 62–91.
[8] Robinson 1952: 58.
[9] Murphy-O'Connor 1977: 375.
[10] Ibid.

presence of Christ'.[11] In a more recent article, Murphy-O'Connor clarifies and rearticulates his position:

> It would be absurd to imagine that Paul confused the individual Jesus Christ and the local church. Time and time again his letters make it clear that one was not the other. The identity of predication, therefore, cannot be explained in terms of being. The only remaining possibility is function. The local church prolongs the ministry of Jesus. The words he spoke are not heard in our contemporary world unless they are proclaimed by the community. The power that flowed forth from him to enable conversion is no longer effective today unless mediated by the community. What Jesus was in his physical presence to his world, the church is in its physical presence in our world. It is this identity of function that justifies the double predication of 'Christ'. The local church is Christ in the world.[12]

Murphy-O'Connor is right in his distinction between the individual Jesus Christ and the local church. However, at the same time, a number of problems remain with his understanding of the body of Christ.

First, Murphy-O'Connor's argument that Paul's comparison in 12:12 'For just as the body . . . so it is with Christ' means that he is *equating* (not merely comparing) Christ and the body is making Paul's language bear too much weight. In his opinion, the only other option, which he rejects in passing, is that Paul 'made an accidental slip'.[13] However, it may simply be that Paul is elliptically referring to the body of Christ. In other words, Paul's thought is that what is true of any body is true of Christ's body, namely that though it is made up of diverse members it is a unity. And in fact, that is precisely what Paul goes on to argue in the following verses (13–27), starting with the work of the Spirit in baptizing the Corinthians into one body (*not* 'into Christ', v. 13) and culminating with the description of the Corinthians as 'the body of Christ' (v. 27).[14] To read verse 12 as positing an unqualified identity between Christ and the church is not the only way to read the verse, and in the context, I would argue, not the best reading.

[11] Ibid. 376.
[12] Murphy-O'Connor 1999: 191.
[13] Murphy-O'Connor 1977: 375.
[14] So Ziesler 1983: 62.

Second, the structure of the chapter counts against equating Christ and the church. As a section, 1 Corinthians 12:12–26 breaks into three subsections – 12:12–14, where Paul establishes that the church like any other body is a unit made up of many parts; 12:15–20, where he establishes the necessity of a body possessing many parts; and 12:21–26, where he describes the dependence of the different parts on each other. In 12:27–31 Paul sums up the argument he began in 12:4 by tying the two parts (12:4–11 and 12:12–26) together.[15] So, in 12:27 the imagery of the body is explicitly applied to the church. Paul's point is not to equate Christ and the church but to underline the fact that the body to which the Corinthians are joined by the Spirit is not just *any* body but is the body *of Christ*. This is the point he makes in anticipation in verse 12. The two verses are essentially saying the same thing and so verse 12 cannot be pressed to yield a metaphysical understanding of the church in relation to Christ.

Third, and more fundamentally, it seems that Murphy-O'Connor is conflating related but distinct Pauline ideas. Paul's concern in 1 Corinthians 12:12 is the relationship between Christ and the church, not the relationship of Christ to the world through the church. Any 'identity' of Christ and church in 1 Corinthians 12:12 is *not* made in terms of 'function' or 'mission' to the world but in the context of the *spiritual relationship* between Christ and the church. That is, their unity is grounded on the work of the Spirit, who baptizes believers into the one body (v. 13). Murphy-O'Connor argues that Paul also predicates 'Christ' of the community in 1 Corinthians 6:15, where Paul asks the Corinthians if they do not know that 'your bodies are members of Christ'.[16] However, this is not a predication of the church and Christ but part of the argument at the end of which Paul concludes by stating that whereas sexual union relates to the physical body (6:16), union with the Lord is a *spiritual* union (6:17). Murphy-O'Connor does not explicitly *deny* this aspect,[17] but in seeing the relationship between Christ and the church primarily in terms of a *functional identity*, he underplays this important dimension that unlocks the nature of the relationship between Christ and the church. This spiritual union is of such an order (as significant as the marriage union) that Christ and the church are *one* with one another.

---

[15] Fee 1987: 617.

[16] Murphy-O'Connor 1999: 191. I discuss this passage more fully below.

[17] Murphy-O'Connor 1991: 126: 'The community is "Christ" insofar as it is the sphere where the saving power of the Spirit is at work,' cited in Fitzmyer 2008: 477.

Perhaps the most important error is that Murphy-O'Connor effect-ively makes Christ *dependent* on the church to extend his ministry when he states that the 'power that flowed forth from [Christ] to enable conversion is no longer effective today unless mediated by the community'.[18] However, Christ is Lord over the church and may choose to operate through it but not in such a way as to make himself dependent on it.

Certainly Murphy-O'Connor is not atypical in his positing of a functional identification between Christ and the church. On 1 Corinthians 12:12, Luke Timothy Johnson suggests that Paul 'requires us to think in terms other than of simple comparison', but that

> 'Christ' in this context cannot be the empirical Jesus who ministered in Palestine some twenty years earlier and then was crucified. It can refer only to the present social body that is the assembly, which Paul daringly terms 'the Christ'. Paul means, I think, that the Corinthian assembly *is*, in a very real (that is, in an ontological and not merely moral) sense, a bodily expression of the risen Jesus who has become life-giving spirit (1 Cor. 15:45) . . . If Paul were asked, 'Where is the body of the resurrected Jesus now?' he has given his response in 1 Cor. 12: 'The body of the resurrected Christ is this assembly (12:27) – together with all those who call on the name of the Lord in every place, theirs and ours' (1:2).[19]

Johnson also appeals to 1 Corinthians 8:12, where Paul rebukes the Corinthians for wounding the weak conscience of a fellow believer. To do so is to 'sin against Christ'. This phrase 'assumes the strongest sort of connection between each member of the community (or the community as a whole) and the resurrected Lord'.[20] As with Acts 9:5 (etc.), Johnson suggests that something more than a 'moral' idea of identifying with the weak is in view.

However, as with Murphy-O'Connor, Johnson goes too far in his (incorrect) understanding that the body of the exalted Christ is *exclusively* located in the church. We will see in chapter 6 that the risen Jesus maintains a distinct, individual body. Having said that, Johnson is helpful in emphasizing the corporate nature of Christ's identity. In other words, the church *does* have an impact on Christ's identity.

---

[18] Murphy-O'Connor 1999: 191.
[19] Johnson 2012: 233–234, emphasis original.
[20] Ibid. 235.

Richard Hays is more circumspect in his study of 1 Corinthians 12:12–27 when he suggests that in this passage the term 'Christ' actually refers to a 'multimembered corporate entity' so that 'Jesus is personally united with his people in such a way that they become his "body"'.[21] As such, after his resurrection, 'Jesus' identity is not *confined* to a single localized physical body'. No, because 'he embraces and receives into himself all those whom he calls' this means that 'he manifests his identity to the world through this complex corporate reality'.[22] This is a helpful insight that I will develop below. However, Hays extends too far when he suggests that the 'line of distinction between Christ and his people has become blurred if not erased altogether'.[23]

The corporate identity of Christ

In the first section of this chapter we have seen that it is not correct to posit a relationship between Christ and the church to the extent that the latter exhausts the bodily identity of the former. However, this does not mean that the church is unconnected from the identity of Christ. As we have seen, the church is the 'body' of Christ; Christ is the 'head' of the church. To persecute the church is to persecute Christ (Acts 9:5); how people treat his followers ('the least of these my brothers') is how they treated him (Matt. 25:40, 45).

Of course these could be of a piece with the typical concept of a messenger representing the one who sends him or her, so that what you do to the messenger you do to the sender. Jesus articulates this in John 13:20: 'Truly, truly, I say to you, whoever receives the one I send receives me.' In this sense as the representatives of Christ in the world, Christians reveal Christ's identity, just as Israel were meant to reveal Yahweh's identity in the OT. However, John and Paul in particular with their concept of union with Christ suggest a more organic relationship. Both writers see the church connected to Christ with a spiritual relationship that goes beyond mere representation.

This is not the place to track out a full concept of the doctrine of 'union with Christ', and we will return to explore how the church mediates the presence of Christ in the world when we consider 2 Corinthians 3:3 ('the letter of Christ'). However, in this section we do want to explore union with Christ from the Christological angle.

---

[21] Hays 2008: 195.
[22] Ibid., emphasis added.
[23] Ibid. 195–196.

Often it is examined in terms of soteriology – examining how union with Christ relates to justification, what impact it has on believers' salvation, and so on. We want to consider what the union does for our understanding of the identity of the exalted Christ.

Christians spiritually united to Christ (1 Cor. 6:17)

In 1 Corinthians 6:15 Paul states that the bodies of believers are 'members' of Christ. Thus the union between Christ and believer is expressed corporeally. However, in 1 Corinthians 6:17 Paul states that the one who is 'joined' to the Lord is 'one spirit' with him. This would appear to be something substantially different from the 'bodily' union with a prostitute that Paul has just warned against in 6:16. Bodily and spiritual union thus appear to be distinct modes not to be conflated with one another. Though members of Christ, believers then are united with Christ spiritually, not physically. However, May has argued that in making the comparison between the two unions, Paul is stressing their similarity rather than emphasizing the difference between *body* and *spirit*.[24] This can be seen when (wooden) translations of the two clauses are compared:

v. 16a	he who is joined	to the prostitute	is one body
v. 17	he who is joined	to the Lord	is one spirit

May admits that the difference between *body* and *spirit* is 'not without significance' but suggests that the grammatical similarities are more striking and point to a comparison rather than contrast. As such, he argues that the latter 'pneumatic union must *include* some notion of somatic union'.[25] He does this on the basis that 6:16–17 is best understood as a development and explanation of 6:15, where Paul reminds the Corinthians that their *bodies* are members of Christ, before strongly rejecting the suggestion that a person should take 'the members of Christ' and make them 'members of a prostitute'. If Paul then goes on to *contrast* somatic and pneumatic union, it would be difficult, May contends, to see how it would *develop* his contention in verse 15. May goes on to explore the nature of this corporeal union and argues that these verses primarily indicate that the spiritual nature of this union does not preclude an *impact* on their bodies. Paul wants to underline that what they do with their bodies matters because their bodies belong to Christ.

[24] May 2004: 115.
[25] Ibid. 116, emphasis added.

Paul has reminded the Corinthians that 'God's Spirit dwells in you' (3:16) and is about to tell them that their 'bodies are temples of the Holy Spirit' (6:19). It is the Spirit of God who produces and secures union with Christ.[26] As such, this passage speaks of the relationship between the bodies of believers and Christ in terms of ownership and lordship rather than any materiality or physicality. Nevertheless, it does stress that Christ can be potentially (negatively) affected (as we saw in Acts 9:5) by his union with believers. Believers are one spirit with Christ. If they become sexually united to a prostitute they become 'one body' with her (6:16). By implication then they are uniting the 'members of Christ' with a prostitute.

We need to be careful that we do not understand this in a crudely materialistic way. Nevertheless, the exalted Christ it seems is bound to believers in a way that their actions do affect him. The exalted Christ is conceived as a corporate person but not only do his actions affect believers (e.g. Rom. 5:10); their actions affect him.

The church as the body and fullness of Christ (Eph. 1:23)

Equally significant is Ephesians 1:23, where Paul states that Christ is head of the church (1:22) 'which is his body, the fullness of him who fills all in all'. The basic phrase 'the church is the fullness of Christ' can be understood two ways. We could understand 'fullness' passively; that is, 'that which is full of something [BDAG 2]'. So, the church is full of Christ. Or we could understand 'fullness' actively; that is, 'that which fills [BDAG 1]'. So, the church is that which fills (or completes) Christ.

Although the second view does have a strong pedigree,[27] on balance understanding 'fullness' passively seems to fit with the theology of Paul's letter. When he uses *plērōma* and related words in the rest of the letter in connection with believers, believers are always passive and are the ones who are filled, whether with God's fullness (3:19) or with the Spirit (5:18).[28]

The church, then, is being filled. We next need to consider *who* is filling it by examining the rest of the verse: *tou ta panta en pasin plēroumenou*. We will leave the phrase *ta panta en pasin* and concentrate on the participle *tou plēroumenou*. This participle is either middle or passive in form. If the participle is a middle, then Christ is the one who fills the church but with the nuance of his acting 'on his own

---

[26] Ciampa and Rosner 2010: 261.
[27] See Thielman 2010: 114.
[28] Ibid. On the possible exception of 4:13 see Arnold 2010: 266.

behalf' or 'for his own benefit'. Understanding a true middle is certainly possible and *ta panta* is then understood as the direct object of the verb and *en pasin* as an adverbial phrase. Understood this way, Christ fills all things (for himself) in 'every way'.[29] However, as Thielman points out, this does not seem to fit the context, which 'emphasizes how God's action through Christ benefits the church, not how Christ's action benefits himself'.[30]

If there is anything approaching a consensus, it is with those who take the participle as a passive and understand Paul to be saying, 'The church is being filled by the one who (in turn) is being filled.'[31] Paul does not identify who or what is filling Christ but it seems reasonable to assume that he understands God to be the one who fills Christ (cf. Col. 2:9).[32] The problem with understanding the participle to be passive is the difficulty in rendering *ta panta en pasin*. If the participle is passive then *ta panta* cannot be the direct object and so *ta panta en pasin* is frequently taken as adverbially modifying *plēroumenou*. On this reading it is understood as something like 'completely'. This renders the entire phrase 'the church is filled by Christ, the one who is being filled completely [by God]'.[33] Thielman acknowledges that this 'use of the phrase [*ta panta en pasin*] would be unusual' but suggests that we have to understand it this way 'in light of the difficulties involved in taking [*plēroumenou*] as anything but passive'.[34] However, it is also possible to take *ta panta* as a retained accusative of respect[35] – Christ is being filled *with* all things. This certainly fits 1:10, where Paul expresses God's plan 'to unite' all things in Christ.[36]

However, we can examine one final possibility. That is, to understand the participle as a middle with an active sense (i.e. without the normal 'personal interest' dimension of the middle). With this we can take *ta panta* as the direct object of *plēroumenou* and understand *en pasin* as an adverbial modifier, 'in every way'. The frequent objection to this interpretation is that Paul uses the verb *plēroō* in the active voice in 4:10 and 5:18. In other words, if Paul had meant the verb to have a purely active meaning, he would have used the active form, as he does in these other two verses. However, Paul can use the same

---

29. To take *en pasin* in one possible way.
30. Thielman 2010: 115.
31. So Hoehner 2002: 299; Thielman 2010: 115.
32. Hoehner 2002: 299; Thielman 2010: 115.
33. So Hoehner 2002: 285; Thielman 2010: 107.
34. Thielman 2010: 115.
35. See Wallace 1996: 439.
36. Best 1988: 104.

verb in both active and middle forms with little change in meaning. So, in Colossians 1 the verb *karpophoreō* appears in the middle (v. 6) and the active (v. 10) with little or no discernible difference in meaning.[37] Further, an active sense accords with 4:10, where Paul describes Christ as the one 'who ascended far above all the heavens, that he might fill[38] all things'.

Granted this is a very complex sentence and so our conclusions must be suitably cautious, it seems reasonable to understand that Paul is describing the church as Christ's body: 'the fullness, i.e. that which is being filled by him who is filling all things in every way'. As Lincoln states:

> Here, as in 1:22b, ecclesiological and cosmic perspectives are juxtaposed in a way that underlines the Church's special status, for although Christ is in the process of filling the cosmos, at present it is only the Church which can actually be called his fullness.[39]

Paul does not indicate, at this stage at least, that the church is the means by which Christ fills the cosmos. However, when he returns to the thought in 4:10, the logic of the argument seems to be that he ascended to fill all things by giving gifts (of apostles, prophets, etc.) to the saints for the work of ministry so that the body of Christ might be built (4:11–12).[40] As this happens, the body (which is the fullness of Christ) realizes this fullness as it grows into unity and attains to 'mature manhood, to the measure of the stature of the fullness of Christ' (4:13). Christ, then, expresses his fullness as Christians speak the word to one another and the church grows.

For our purposes, we can simply conclude that the exalted Christ is being conceived in cosmological terms. In a way not true of the earthly Jesus, the exalted Christ can and does fill the church. Paul does not unpack the nature of this filling or the means by which Christ accomplishes it, but the cosmological description of Christ is a development in his identity following his resurrection and exaltation.

The church as the bride of Christ (Eph. 5:32)

In Ephesians 5:22–33 Paul draws parallels between the relationship of husband and wife and the relationship of the church and Christ.

---

[37] Lincoln 1990: 77.
[38] The verb here is active.
[39] Lincoln 1990: 77.
[40] See Orr 2018.

So, the 'husband is the head of the wife even as Christ is the head of the church' (5:23) and so wives should 'submit in everything to their husbands' just 'as the church submits to Christ' (5:24), while husbands are to love their wives 'just as Christ does the church' (5:29). His argument culminates with Paul's drawing the tightest possible parallel between the marital union of husband and wife and the union between Christ and the church. So, in verse 31 he cites Genesis 2:24: 'Therefore a man shall leave his father and mother and hold fast to his wife, and the two shall become one flesh,' and although this applies to the marriage relationship, Paul's citation of it comes between two statements that speak of the relationship between Christ and the church. We can see this if we lay out the text as follows:

5:30   'we are members of his body';
5:31   Citation of Gen. 2:24: 'Therefore a man shall leave his father and mother and hold fast to his wife, and the two shall become one flesh';
5:32   'This mystery is profound, and I am saying that it refers to Christ and the church'.

Paul's phrase in 5:32 'and I am saying' or perhaps better 'but I say' is used only here and in Matthew (5:22, 28, 32, 34, 39, 44) when Jesus gives his own authoritative interpretation of the Genesis text[41] and points forward to the surprising nature of his interpretation in Ephesians 5.[42] The surprise is that the Genesis 2:24 'one flesh' verse is cited to establish the nature of the union between Christ and the church (rather than between husband and wife in the Ephesian church), so that believers are bodily united with Christ. The description of believers as 'members' of his body is an organic image: the word is 'never used of a member of an organization but always used of a member of an organism'.[43]

Commentators struggle to pin down the exact nature of the connection between Christ and the church that Paul articulates here. So, Son suggests that in 'Paul's mind, the one body unity that believers form together with Christ has something in common with the one flesh unity created between the husband and wife in marriage'.[44] It

[41] Hoehner 2002: 779.
[42] Thielman 2010: 390.
[43] Hoehner 2002: 768.
[44] Son 2009: 23.

seems, though, that we can be stronger. As Arnold points out in 5:30–32 (as opposed to 5:24, 25, 28), Paul has not used any comparative particles. That is, Paul does not say 'we are members of his body *just as* the husband and wife are one flesh in marriage'.[45] Paul is going 'beyond analogy or comparison into an affirmation of reality'.[46] Paul is assuming that there is a typological 'correspondence between creation (Gen. 2:24) and redemption (Christ and the church)'.[47]

The strength of the correspondence between the marriage relationship and that between Christ and the church again is something that only applies to the exalted Christ and suggests a development in his identity. Just as the identity of a husband or wife is fundamentally conditioned by their marriage, the relationship between Christ and the church affects Christ and not simply the church.

Conclusion

In this chapter we have seen that the most common passage used to argue for an exclusive bodily identity between Christ and the church will not bear the weight it is often asked to bear. Paul in 1 Corinthians 12:12 is not making a strict identification between Christ and the church. This anticipates the argument of chapter 6, where we see that the exalted Christ does possess his own distinct, localizable body. However, we have also seen that there is a development in the identity of the exalted Christ and that his relationship with the church is not the same as before the resurrection and ascension. Christ is conceived as a corporate person who is spiritually united with the bodies of believers (1 Cor. 6:15–17), who fills the church in anticipation of the time when he will fill all things (Eph. 1:23) and whose relationship with believers is as strong as the marriage bond between husband and wife (Eph. 5:23).

---

[45] Arnold 2010: 396, emphasis original.
[46] Ibid.
[47] Ibid.

Chapter Five

The location of Christ: ascension, exaltation and absence

Introduction: the location of Christ

Where is Jesus now? It is a deceptively simple question but one that generations of Sunday school teachers have trembled at hearing. The obvious answer is that Jesus is in heaven, as affirmed by a number of NT texts: he is at God's right hand (e.g. Rom. 8:34; Col. 3:1; Heb. 1:3; 1 Pet. 3:22). Luke (24:50–53) and Acts (1:9–11) both describe Jesus' ascent into heaven. Paul, in fact, describes Christ as having 'ascended far above all the heavens' (Eph. 4:10). Jesus in his prayer in John 17 states (in anticipation), 'I am no longer in the world' (17:11). In his sermon in Acts 3 Peter tells the crowd that Jesus is the one 'whom heaven must receive until the time for restoring' (3:21). So, the NT is crystal clear: Jesus is in heaven.

However, there are also a number of NT texts which affirm that Jesus, in some sense, remains with us. The fundamental and frequent Pauline description of the believer as being 'in Christ' (Rom. 12:5; 1 Cor. 1:2; 2 Cor. 1:21; etc.) admittedly does not have to indicate a sense of location,[1] but the description of Christ as dwelling in the believer (e.g. Gal. 2:20; Rom. 8:10) locates Christ with the believer. Paul also prays that Christ might 'dwell in the hearts' of his Ephesian readers (Eph. 3:17). Further, we have Jesus' solemn promise to his disciples at the end of Matthew's Gospel: 'Behold, I am with you always, to the end of the age' (28:20). So, the NT is also crystal clear: Jesus dwells in and with believers.

On the surface, then, we seem to have a tension, even a contradiction between some texts locating Christ in heaven and some locating him in and with the believer. In the context of debates

---

[1] Though, of course, it can. On this see Campbell 2012: 408. Campbell's book is the outstanding treatment of the Pauline motif of union with Christ.

concerning the Lord's Supper and the nature of the body of Christ, Martin Luther came up with an ingenious way to resolve this tension. Noting that Paul locates Christ at God's right hand, he argued that

> since [my opponents] do not prove that the right hand of God is a particular place in heaven, the mode of existence of which I have spoken also stands firm, that Christ's body is everywhere because it is at the right hand of God which is everywhere.[2]

That is, since heaven and the right hand of God are everywhere, then Christ can be located there *and* in the believer without contradiction. It is a neat and appealing solution and not without some basis in the NT. The problem is that it does not account for what we might call the *absence* of Christ. That is, it is not simply that some texts locate Christ in heaven, but that they describe him as *absent* from believers. So, Paul expresses the desire to depart (i.e. die) so that he can 'be with Christ, for that is far better' (Phil. 1:23), the implication being that in the present he is *not* with Christ. Similarly, Paul states that while believers are 'at home in the body, we are away from the Lord' (2 Cor. 5:6) and suggests that 'we would rather be away from the body and at home with the Lord' (2 Cor. 5:8). It is only when we die (Phil. 1:23) or when Jesus returns that we 'will always be with the Lord' (1 Thess. 4:17). In the present he remains *absent* from believers even as he dwells in them.

This chapter and the following two will proceed then by considering the location of Christ through the lens of his absence. To anticipate our conclusion, we will see that his absence is a function of his on-going humanity and possession of a discrete, localizable body that cannot be collapsed into believers. Because he remains localizable, he is *bodily absent*. As such, his presence is always a *mediated* presence. That is not to say that it is an insignificant or *light* presence. We will see that because of his relationship with the Holy Spirit, Christ *is* present to believers in a real way. But it is never an unqualified presence – that remains for the future.

In this chapter we will examine his absence as it relates to his ascension and exaltation.

---

[2] Luther 1961: 213–214.

Absence and the promise of presence (Matthew)

In Matthew's Gospel we see this same tension between the absence and presence of Christ. In a number of places Jesus speaks of his future coming as Son of Man (24:27, 30, 37, 39, 44; 26:64) and Lord (24:42), implying his absence from earth. In the meantime, however, he also reassures his disciples that he will be with them to the very end of the age (28:20).

In fact, a number of scholars argue that the note of presence is actually so dominant in the Gospel that it should effectively override any idea of Christ's absence. Mark Harris notes that the theme of presence forms something of an 'interpretative bracket' for the Gospel, moving as it does from describing Jesus as 'Immanuel' ('God with us') in 1:23 to Jesus' promise to be with the disciples to the end of the age at the conclusion to the Gospel (28:20).[3] Unlike the other Gospels, Matthew has no account of the ascension. Rather, this 'alone of all of the Gospels keeps Jesus on earth throughout the narrative and makes no attempt to remove him at the end. Indeed, to do so would negate his final promise'.[4] In Matthew's narrative world Jesus remains on top of the mountain 'to which Jesus had directed them' (28:16).[5]

How then are we to understand the language of Jesus' *coming* in Matthew's Gospel, implying as it does his absence? Mark Harris has argued that not only should Matthew's language of parousia (24:3, 27, 37, 39) be understood as 'presence' but the language of 'coming' (*erchomai*) should be understood in terms of '*continuous* (i.e. as yet incomplete) motion'.[6] He further notes that 'neither a destination nor a place of departure is given; the "Son of Man" is usually just said to be "coming"'.[7] As such, he concludes that the 'coming Son of Man' theme in Matthew's Gospel is 'consistent with a more *continuous* view of presence than is often supposed'.[8]

As such, Harris rejects a more typical view that understands the coming as referring to a future coming of Christ from heaven.[9] His main grammatical reason for making this argument is that 'the

---

[3] Harris 2014: 52; Hays 2016: 162.
[4] Harris 2014: 56.
[5] Ibid. 57.
[6] Ibid. 64, emphasis original.
[7] Ibid.
[8] Ibid., emphasis original.
[9] Ibid.

verb [*erchomai*] in these kinds of sayings is mostly in the present tense'.[10]

Harris is correct to argue that Matthew emphasizes the ongoing presence of Christ but his handling of Matthew's 'coming' language is not convincing. For a start he overlooks a very significant use of the verb. So, in his article he makes no mention of Matthew 16:27, 'For the Son of Man is going to come [*erchesthai*, present infinitive] with his angels in the glory of his Father, and then he will repay each person according to what he has done.' It is very hard to see how this could refer to anything other than a future coming.[11] This omission alone, I think, calls his thesis into question.

Second, he does not give due consideration to the syntactical structures in which the present-tense verbs are found. For example, in 24:30, while the verb *erchomai* (coming) is a present participle, it is functioning as the object of a *future* verb ('they will see the Son of Man coming'). The construction cannot be read as anything other than a reference to the Son of Man's *future* coming. Or in 24:42 Jesus warns his hearers to stay awake because they 'do not know on what day your Lord is coming'. The reference to a 'day' casts the coming to a point in the future – a fairly common use of the present tense in Greek.[12]

Third, he does not attend to the narrative contexts of a number of the references to the coming. So, again even though the verb *erchomai* is present, the reference to the Son of Man's coming in 24:44 is clearly future: 'the Son of Man is coming at an hour you do not expect'. The reference to an 'hour' speaks against the idea of a continuous coming. Further, this statement is used as a pivot between two parables: 24:42–43, where Jesus speaks about a thief coming to rob a house, and 24:45–51, where he speaks of a master returning suddenly to surprise a wicked servant. In both cases the parallel with Jesus' coming is clearly future. There is also no discussion of chapter 25:1–13, the parable of the foolish and wise virgins and their different fates following the coming of the bridegroom (25:10). Nor is there any discussion of 25:14–30 and the parable of the talents, which turns on the return (*erchetai*) of the master (25:19).

So, Harris has overlooked and misconstrued Matthew's use of coming language applied to Jesus. Overwhelmingly, the language

[10] Ibid. He provides the following data: present tense: 16:28; 21:9; 23:39; 24:30, 42, 44; 26:64; aorist tense: 10:23; 25:31.
[11] Hagner 1998: 485.
[12] Wallace 1996: 536.

of coming refers to Jesus' *future* coming. As such, while there is undoubtedly an emphasis in Matthew's Gospel on the *presence* of Jesus,[13] his future coming presupposes his current absence.[14] And so we are brought back to the questions of how we understand the relationship between his presence and absence, and how we explain the fact that Matthew does not recount Jesus' ascension.

Richard Hays offers an intriguing possibility, namely that Matthew 28:20 may be modelled on Moses' departure and commissioning of Joshua in Deuteronomy, but with differences that are Christologically significant:

> [W]hile both Deuteronomy 31:23 and Matthew 28:20 speak of continuing divine presence, in one case the reference is to God's ongoing presence with Israel in the *absence of Moses*, whereas in the other the manner of God's ongoing presence is precisely through the continuing *presence of Jesus* to the end of the age. This does not mean that there is no figural link between Jesus and Moses; rather it means that readers are called upon to discern the similarities and dissimilarities at the same time. To put the point somewhat crudely, in Matthew's concluding commissioning scene, Jesus assumes the roles *both* of Moses (authoritative teacher departing) *and* of God (continuing divine presence). Both ranges of signification are triggered by the very same narrative typology.[15]

Hays's observations seem sound: Matthew is describing Jesus in terms that evoke connections to Moses at the end of Deuteronomy. This points to Jesus' departure and hence bodily absence. Even though this is not specifically spelt out in the narrative (i.e. there is no ascension scene), Jesus' absence would have been obvious to the early Christian readers of Matthew's Gospel.

Hays is also right to suggest that Christ's ongoing presence is cast in terms of divine presence. However, we must not overlook Christ's mediated presence by the Spirit. It is frequently suggested that

[13] Harris (2014) puts considerable weight on 26:64 '*from now on you will see the Son of Man seated at the right hand of Power and coming on the clouds of heaven*' to suggest that Christ's coming is a *continuous* coming that occurs 'from now on'; i.e. from his resurrection. The reference to 'coming' here is more likely a reference to Dan. 7:13, suggesting that from this point on Jesus will be identified as Lord (Ps. 110:1) and Son of Man (Dan. 7:13).

[14] Cf. 9:15 and 26:11, which Harris (2014: 58) argues refer to the time between Jesus' death and resurrection.

[15] Hays 2016: 145, emphases original.

Matthew has very little to say about the ongoing role of the Holy Spirit,[16] but one significant verse is Matthew 10:20. Here Jesus is assuring his disciples that when they are 'dragged before governors and kings for my sake' (10:18), they are not to worry what to say since 'what you are to say will be given to you in that hour' (10:19); that is, 'it is not you who speak, but the Spirit of your Father speaking through you' (10:20). The Spirit will be God's agent of comfort and equipping for the disciples in the future.[17] Thus the abiding presence of Christ does not do away with the need for the ongoing work of the Spirit.

Matthew's Gospel, then, while it stresses the ongoing presence of Christ, does not negate his absence, and though not emphasizing it is consistent with the idea that the Spirit mediates Christ's presence.

Absence, ascension and glory (Luke–Acts)

Luke ends his Gospel with a description of Jesus' leaving the disciples and being 'carried up into heaven' (24:51).[18] He then begins his second volume with a description of the same event in Acts 1:9–11. This description of Christ's ascension and statements like those of Peter in Acts 3:21, where he describes how heaven 'must receive [Jesus] until the time for restoring all things' (i.e. until Jesus' return),[19] has led a number of scholars to suggest that in Acts, Luke has an 'absentee Christology'.[20] The ascended Lord Jesus is a character of the past, and so readers of Acts 'do not meet Jesus himself as an active and present character within the story of Acts'.[21]

However, others have recognized that while Jesus is clearly absent *in some sense*, he is not a passive character in the narrative. That is, 'Jesus is now present in heaven, at God's right side, but in such a way that he can continue to be active on earth'.[22] On this understanding Christ in Acts is presented as 'absent but not inactive'.[23] Some, though, extend his ongoing activity to imply that 'Jesus' ascension

[16] E.g. Luz 2005: 635.

[17] That this is referring to the future seems clear from the language of bearing witness before governors, kings and Gentiles.

[18] See below on the textual issues.

[19] The way most scholars understand 'the restoration of all things'. See Walton 2016: 123.

[20] Moule 1966: 179–180; though as Sleeman (2009: 13) shows, Moule did nuance this position over time.

[21] Walton 2016: 123, summarizing Conzelmann 1960: 170–206.

[22] Walton 2016: 140.

[23] Zwiep 2016: 18.

does not mean his absence; it simply means that his presence is no longer constrained by place and time.'[24]

That Christ remains active in the book of Acts seems evident, but nevertheless Luke does stress his absence, perhaps more strongly than any of the other Gospel writers. And we see this particularly in Luke's descriptions of the ascension. This event, however, has been the subject of no small amount of scholarly debate. We will begin with two areas that are of particular concern for us: the timing of Jesus' ascension and the question of whether it does relate to Jesus' exaltation or is merely a relocation. We will then turn to consider how Luke's descriptions of the ascension inform our understanding of the absence of Christ.

When did Jesus ascend?

On the surface there seems to be a tension between Luke's account of the ascension in Luke 24 and in Acts 1. In the former, the time references could be read to indicate that the ascension actually occurred on the same day as the resurrection itself. Luke 24:1 ('the first day') and 13 ('that very day') locate verses 1–35 on the day of resurrection. There are then no time markers (e.g. 'a few days later', etc.) for the rest of the chapter, suggesting that, at least on one reading, the ascension and resurrection occur on the same day. This would obviously then present a conflict with the reference to 'forty days' of appearances in Acts 1:3. There have been a range of suggestions.[25] The most common is to argue that Luke has compressed his narrative in his Gospel and given a more chronologically accurate description in Acts 1.[26]

However, recently de Jonge has offered a fresh interpretation to the effect that we should read Luke 24 at face value as indicating that Christ did ascend on the day of his resurrection. There is no contradiction with Acts 1 if we understand verses 1–3 as a summary of Luke's Gospel and verses 4–14 to be a 'repeat or reprise of Luke 24:47–53'.[27] De Jonge lays out the parallels as follows:[28]

1. The supper on the day of the resurrection and Jesus' order to stay in Jerusalem and wait for the Holy Spirit (Acts 1:4–8 // Luke 24:47–49);

---

[24] Gaventa 2008: 163.
[25] For helpful summaries see Zwiep 1997: 90–92, and especially de Jonge 2013: 154–158.
[26] Peterson 2009: 114, n. 47.
[27] De Jonge 2013: 164.
[28] Ibid.

2. The ascension from the Mount of Olives (Acts 1:9–11 // Luke 24:50–51);
3. The return of the eleven to Jerusalem (Acts 1:12–13 // Luke 24:52);
4. The devotion of the disciples in Jerusalem (Acts 1:14 // Luke 24:53).

How then do we explain Acts 1:3 where Luke tells us that Jesus 'presented himself alive to [the disciples] after his suffering by many proofs, appearing to them during forty days and speaking about the kingdom of God'? De Jonge views verses 1–3 as a 'Summary of Luke's "first volume": Jesus' activity until he was taken up to heaven [vv. 1–2] of which his appearances during forty days are conclusive evidence [v. 3]'.[29] As such he concludes:

> In Acts, Luke dates Jesus' ascension to the day of the resurrection, just as he had done in the Gospel. The forty days mentioned in Acts 1:3 are viewed by Luke *as subsequent to the ascension, not as previous to it*. The forty days are not the term fixed for the ascension; they are not linked with the ascension at all. They are linked with the post-Easter, post ascension appearances.[30]

The implication of this interpretation is that the appearances that Christ makes to the disciples during this forty-day period are appearances *from* heaven. In fact, de Jonge goes further and argues that it is the resurrection itself that is the actual moment of Christ's 'assumption' into heaven. So, on the road to Emmaus, Jesus' words to the disciples suggest that he has *already* been glorified (Luke 24:26).[31] And so, the descriptions of Christ's ascension in Luke 24 and Acts 1 are actually both simply functioning as 'closures' to appearance stories.[32] Luke does use 'some traditional "apocalyptic stage props" current in rapture stories', but these are not enough to suggest that the accounts are anything other than simple appearance closure stories.[33]

---

[29] Ibid.
[30] Ibid. 164–165, emphasis added. The appearances over forty days are to give the disciples sufficient credibility as witnesses of the risen Christ; so Dunn 2001: 305–307.
[31] Ibid. 168.
[32] Ibid. 167.
[33] Ibid.

As a result, de Jonge argues that Christ is actually in heaven from the moment of the resurrection and that all his appearances are from there. There is, thus, no need, to speculate that Jesus was in a state of transition between the resurrection and ascension, 'glorified but not yet exalted'.[34] Nor is there need to speculate where Jesus is between the resurrection and the ascension – he is 'in Paradise' (Luke 23:43), and 'at the right hand of God' (Luke 22:69).[35]

Christ then is exalted to heaven at his resurrection. What is described in Luke 24 and Acts 1 'is another event' and is simply the closure of his appearance at the end of the day of his resurrection.[36] This event would be followed by more appearances over the next forty days.

De Jonge's interpretation is both fascinating and attractive. If correct, it would neatly and convincingly resolve the exegetical issue of the relationship between the ascension accounts in Luke 24 and Acts 1 as well as theological issues raised by the traditional understanding of the forty-day gap between the resurrection and ascension (e.g. Jesus' location at that time, etc.). However, there are significant problems with his interpretation that, on balance, mean that it is unlikely to be correct.

First, de Jonge overstates the issue when he claims that the (traditional) reading which posits a forty-day gap between resurrection and the ascension on the basis of Acts 1:3 creates a 'blatant chronological contradiction'.[37] There are four episodes recounted in Luke 24: the women and the eleven finding the tomb empty (1–12); the two disciples encountering Jesus on the road to Emmaus (13–35); Jesus appearing to and instructing the disciples (36–49); the ascension at Bethany (50–52). The temporal connections are strong for the first three: 'on the first day of the week' (1); 'that very day' (13); 'as they were talking about these things' (36).[38] However, the ascension episode is simply introduced by 'and' (*de*), which can but does not *necessarily* indicate contemporaneous time.[39] There is, in other words, no necessary reason for reading Luke 24 as recounting events that all occurred on one day.

---

[34] Lofhink 1971: 274, cited in de Jonge 2013: 168.

[35] De Jonge 2013: 168.

[36] Ibid. 170.

[37] Ibid. 158.

[38] The construction is a genitive absolute. Strictly speaking, the phrase 'while they were speaking about these things' (*tauta de autōn lalountōn*) does not have to refer to the same time as the conversation at the end of v. 35.

[39] Porter 2016: 126.

Second, de Jonge's reconstruction (at least partly) relies on the rendering of the verb *synalizomenos* in Acts 1:4 as 'eating together with [them]' and thus referring to the same event as Luke 24:43, when Jesus eats broiled fish with the disciples. De Jonge lists a number of early commentators who take the word this way, notes the reference to the disciples eating with Jesus after the resurrection in Acts 10:41 and suggests that the grammatical form of the word as a nominative singular renders the meaning 'coming together' (most English versions) impossible since this would require a nominative plural. De Jonge's rendering of the verb is certainly *possible*,[40] and perhaps even more likely than the more common translation.[41] However, this does not necessarily mean that this instance of 'eating' together is the same as the event described in Luke 24:42–43, where Jesus is said to have eaten the fish *before* or *in front of* (*enōpion*) them.[42]

Third, the reference to Bethany in Luke 24 does not quite fit if Luke 24 all takes place on the same day. So, Jesus tells them to stay in Jerusalem until they are 'clothed with power from on high' (24:49) but then *immediately* (on this reading) leads them out of the city to Bethany (about 1.5 miles [2.4 km] from the city).[43]

These first three objections simply raise questions about *the need* and *likelihood* for de Jonge's interpretation. However, more fundamentally his interpretation misses the significance of the ascension event for both Luke and Acts, which I will discuss below.

The ascension: exaltation and/or relocation?

De Jonge does raise an important question: Is the event presented in Luke 24 and Acts 1 an account of Jesus' *exaltation* or of his *relocation* (or 'rapture') to heaven? I will argue below that it is both. However, Arie Zwiep has argued very strongly that the 'form' of the ascension event suggests that it should primarily be understood as a 'rapture' event; that is, a description of Christ's relocation to heaven.

Zwiep provides a very helpful survey of scholarship that has compared the ascension scenes in Luke and Acts to similar post-mortem scenes in Graeco-Roman literature ('disembodied spirits,

---

[40] See the discussion in BDAG 964.1.

[41] Though his argument about the need for a plural verb is perhaps overstated – see BDAG 964.2.

[42] See further Porter 2016: 127.

[43] Ibid. 126.

revenants (people coming back to life), heroes, and translated mortals').[44] Of particular interest is Prince, who argues that although there are particular similarities with 'translation and apotheosis traditions', the portrayal of Jesus in Luke 24 'surpasses all expected modes of post-mortem apparitions by virtue of the fact that it draws upon them all and distinguishes itself from them all'.[45] Although not denying the significance of Graeco-Roman assumption stories, Zwiep suggests that 'the ascension corresponds with the biblical and early Jewish rapture traditions on a more structural level' particularly with respect to what he has called the 'rapture-preservation paradigm',[46] which he defines as follows:

> The rapture is usually announced in advance in some revelatory experience, either as a divine word of instruction or as a remark by the author. In preparation of the event to come, the rapture candidate is commanded to instruct those that stay behind to ensure that his teachings will not perish. This period of final instructions is not infrequently a period of forty days (forty being a quite conventional biblical number of course). The highly standardized description of the rapture is usually conjoined with a remark about the local and temporal *termini ad quem* of the raptured person's preservation in heaven and his envisaged role in the endtime drama, not infrequently with an eschatological return implied.[47]

In his earlier *Ascension of the Messiah* he demonstrates how this model is attested in early Jewish traditions (biblical as well as other early Jewish traditions) about Elijah, Enoch, Ezra, Baruch, Moses and Melchizedek.[48]

What distinguishes the Jewish background from the parallels in Graeco-Roman literature is the issue of divinization. This was routinely assumed in the latter, but because of Israel's strong monotheism was ruled out by the former. This leads Zwiep to distinguish carefully between 'rapture' texts (like in Luke and Acts) and 'exaltation' texts (like the commissioning scene in Matthew's Gospel). The former have to do with geographical relocation, the

---

[44] Zwiep 2016: 14.
[45] Prince 2007: 289, cited in Zwiep 2016: 14.
[46] Zwiep 2016: 14.
[47] Zwiep 2001: 340.
[48] Zwiep 1997: 36–79.

latter with a change in status.[49] As such, Zwiep denies that the ascension of Jesus as described in Acts 1 'marks his exaltation'.[50] For Luke, exaltation of Christ is consistently tied to his resurrection. Zwiep, then, agrees with the implications (if not the precise chronology) of de Jonge's article and suggests:

> Scholars who separate the exaltation from the resurrection and mark the ascension as the occasion of Jesus' heavenly exaltation often interpret the appearances of the risen Lord as appearances 'on the road,' appearances in some quasi-earthbound state in which Jesus was risen but not yet exalted. If, as other scholars hold, the exaltation is to be located at, or is at least closely associated with, the resurrection at Easter Sunday, the appearances are more likely to be understood as appearances of the already exalted Lord from heaven, the ascension simply concluding the last of a series of departures to heaven.[51]

As with de Jonge, Zwiep downplays the significance of the ascension event in Luke 24 and Acts 1 with respect to the status of Jesus. Jesus' exaltation has already taken place with the resurrection; the ascension is simply a 'relocation' event. In the next section we will consider how the ascension of Christ relates to his absence before considering if the ascension is, in fact, related to his glorification.

The ascension in Luke–Acts and the absence and glorification of Christ

There is some debate concerning the text of Luke 24:50–52, given that the 'Western' text of Acts has a shorter reading of this paragraph, omitting the significant phrases 'and he was carried up into heaven' (v. 51) and 'they worshipped him' (v. 52).[52] With these removed, the only reference to Christ's ascension would be that Jesus 'parted from them' (v. 51). If these phrases were not original, it could be argued

[49] So Zwiep disagrees with Wright (2003: 655), who maintains that the ascension accounts should be read against the backdrop of Dan. 7 and Daniel's vision of the exaltation of the Son of Man to the Ancient of Days and *not* against the 'strange story of Elijah'.

[50] Zwiep 2016: 17.

[51] Ibid. 22.

[52] The Western text is generally longer than other text forms; nevertheless, there are a number of passages that contain significant omissions which Westcott and Hort labelled as 'non-Western interpolations': Matt. 27:49; Luke 22:19b–20; 24:3, 6, 12, 36, 40, 51–52. See the discussion in Metzger 1994: 164–165.

that 'the notion of the ascension of the risen Christ as a visible transfer from earth to heaven was only a secondary and later development in early Christian thought'.[53] The textual issues concerning the 'Western' text of Acts are complex but in this instance it seems reasonable to conclude that the omitted phrases are indeed original. Not only are they testified to by the earliest manuscript of Luke (P75);[54] the shorter text is not even uniformly testified to across the Western texts. Zwiep has convincingly shown that the Western reviser consistently 'removes any suggestion that Jesus ascended physically – with a body of flesh and bones – into heaven'.[55]

With the longer text, then, we have a clear description of Jesus not only 'departing' from the disciples, but of being 'carried up into heaven' (24:51). His departure, then, is 'accomplished via a dual movement, away and up'.[56] The description of his movement is not incidental but seems to underline both his absence (departure) and exaltation (elevation to heaven).[57] The latter idea is underlined by the fact that the disciples respond by worshipping Jesus (24:52), the only time they do so in this Gospel. Luke is the only Gospel to narrate Jesus' ascension to heaven, and it is significant that Luke concludes his narrative in this way.[58] Earlier, Luke had recounted Jesus' claim at his trial that 'from now on the Son of Man shall be seated at the right hand of the power of God' (22:69). Though Luke does not specifically locate Christ at God's right hand until Acts 2:33, his ascension to heaven is 'the beginning of his heavenly reign' and, as such, 'a vindication of Jesus' since it 'shows that the claim [at his trial] was true and that his execution was unjust'.[59] The ascension certainly does seem to be associated with Jesus' exaltation to heaven, but we need to turn to Acts to discern more fully how Luke understands their relationship.

In Acts 1 Luke gives a second and fuller description of the ascension. Following his command to the disciples to wait in Jerusalem for the promised Holy Spirit (1:8), Luke tells us that as the disciples looked on, Jesus was 'lifted up' and a 'cloud took him out of their sight' (1:9). As the disciples gaze into heaven, two angels (presumably)

---

[53] Epp 1981: 144–145, cited in Zwiep 2010: 11.

[54] P4 contains only portions of Luke 1 – 6.

[55] Zwiep 2010: 35.

[56] Green 1997: 861.

[57] Ibid.

[58] See Witherington 1998: 112 for a helpful discussion as to how Luke's account still coheres well with the other Gospels.

[59] Bock 1996: 1945.

appear and tell the disciples that '[t]his Jesus, who was taken up from you into heaven, will come in the same way as you saw him go into heaven' (1:11).

Luke is certainly emphasizing the absence of Christ with his description of the ascension. Sleeman lists four factors that underline that at 'its irreducible core, the ascension of Jesus in Luke and Acts is a spatial relocation'.[60] First, the emphasis on seeing with four verbs of sight employed (*blepō*, v. 9; *atenizō*, v. 10; *emblepō, theaomai*, v. 11) 'focus[es] attention on Jesus' physical body'.[61] Second is the statement by the angel that Jesus 'will come in the same way as you saw him go into heaven' (v. 11). Third, the conclusion to the Gospel of Luke with its emphasis on the physical nature of Jesus' risen body is the backdrop against which Luke expects us to read the ascension account in Acts 1. Finally, the Gospel's account of the ascension in 24:50–51 also stresses Jesus' physical nature. As Sleeman concludes, '[f]ramed in these various ways, the mode of Jesus's ascension is physical and embodied, as is his promised return'.[62] As such, 'the ascension is *the* moment of spatial realignment in Acts (cf. 1:1–2a), and Acts as a narrative cannot be understood without ongoing reference to the heavenly Christ'.[63] 'That Jesus is no longer physically present on earth means that [the apostles] become *necessary* witnesses. There is no means by which to access Jesus other than through *their* testimony.'[64]

However, even in the narrative itself there are hints that more than spatial relocation is going on. Zwiep is surely correct to see allusions to OT 'rapture' stories and so the scene may also have parallels to the assumption of Elijah in 2 Kings 2.[65] As such, it concerns 'the passing on of the power and authority of Jesus' witnesses so that they might continue the kingdom work he had begun'.[66] However, the narrative points to an understanding that the ascension is tied to Jesus' glorification.

The reference to the cloud enveloping Jesus may be an allusion to Daniel 7:13, part of Daniel's vision where he sees the Son of Man coming 'with the clouds of heaven . . . to the Ancient of Days' (cf. Luke 21:27). Luke may also have expected readers to have made connections with the 'cloud as the visible token of God's glory

---

[60] Sleeman 2016: 158.
[61] Ibid.
[62] Ibid.
[63] Sleeman 2009: 80, cited in Zwiep 2016: 17, emphasis original.
[64] Sleeman 2009: 77, cited in Zwiep 2016: 18, emphases original.
[65] See Palmer 1987: 431–432, cited in Witherington 1998: 112.
[66] Witherington 1998: 112.

associated with the tabernacle in the wilderness (e.g., Exod. 40:34–35)'.[67] The motif points to Jesus' glory as he ascends. Indeed, Luke has already made a connection between the presence of a cloud and glory in his description of the transfiguration (9:34).[68]

So, while Zwiep may be correct to argue against an overemphasis on Daniel 7, nevertheless it seems that there are indeed allusions to Daniel 7. The words of the angels, that Jesus 'will come' (future of *erchomai*) in the same way that he has gone (i.e. in a cloud), again hint at an allusion to Daniel 7. Jesus has told his disciples that the Son of Man will be seen 'coming in a cloud with power and great glory' (Luke 21:27).

So, was Jesus glorified at his resurrection or at his ascension? To answer this we need to examine Peter's speech in Acts 2, where we see Peter apply exaltation language to *both* the ascension and the resurrection. In verses 22–23 he narrates the crucifixion of Jesus, to which God responds by raising him up (2:24). Peter explains the significance of this by expounding Psalm 16:8–11. He shows that the promise not to let the king be abandoned to the grave or to see corruption (2:27) was not fulfilled in David, since 'his tomb is with us to this day' (2:29), but in the resurrection of Jesus. But Peter continues to describe how Jesus has been 'exalted at the right hand of God, and having received from the Father the promise of the Holy Spirit, he has poured out this that you yourselves are seeing and hearing' (2:33). When does this exaltation to the right hand of God occur? Peter has been speaking only about the resurrection to this point, so we could understand him to be referring only to the resurrection, but he immediately adds, 'for David did not ascend into the heavens' (2:34). It his ascension 'into the heavens' that completes his exaltation to the right hand of God.

It seems that the resurrection and the ascension are inseparably related. They are both associated with the exaltation and glorification of Christ, with the latter completing the former. It is not that the resurrection secures the glorification of Christ and the ascension is simply a relocation event, nor that the ascension is the moment of Christ's glorification and the resurrection is not (implying that the post-resurrected pre-ascended Christ is not fully glorified). They are more organically connected. However, it is important that only with Christ's ascension to heaven is the Spirit poured out (2:33).

---

[67] Peterson 2009: 115.
[68] Ibid.

As Sleeman concludes:

> Acts projects this embodied Jesus as eternally seated on David's throne, at God's right hand, never to see decay or physical corruption (2:30–36). Whatever our understanding of space and place, Acts claims Jesus' ascension as a paradigm-shifting relocation that alters the balance of space.[69]

Absence for a little while (John)

One commentator has argued that the most pressing question of the farewell discourse in John's Gospel (John 13:31 – 16:33) can be formulated as follows: 'How is the Absentee present? How can the one who has returned to the Father establish a relationship with the disciples, who have remained in the world?'[70]

In John 14:18 Jesus reassures the disciples by saying, 'I will not leave you as orphans; I will come to you.' Is he referring to his resurrection or his return at the parousia?[71] Part of the answer lies with the meaning of 'a little while' in what Jesus continues to say: 'Yet a little while and the world will see me no more, but you will see me. Because I live, you also will live' (14:19). Despite the unusual use of 'coming' language (found in the other Gospels in connection with the parousia), the majority of scholars see this as a reference to the resurrection. Apart from anything, the strongly personal language 'I will come to you . . . you will see me' suggests that he is specifically referring to the disciples encountering him after the resurrection.[72] Further, the reference to Jesus' living is most likely a reference to his resurrection.[73]

Later in the farewell discourse Jesus again turns to consider his absence from the disciples, telling them, 'A little while, and you will see me no longer; and again a little while, and you will see me' (16:16). This prompts the understandable response from the disciples, 'what is this that he says to us?' (16:17) and 'what does he mean by "a little while"? We do not know what he is talking about' (16:18). Again, some interpreters have argued that 'the little while' refers to the period between Jesus' death and resurrection, and others for the

---

[69] Sleeman 2016: 158.
[70] Zumstein 2008: 104.
[71] For a comprehensive list of scholars and their views on this issue see ibid. 108.
[72] Carson 1991: 501.
[73] Zumstein 2008: 110.

period of absence before his parousia.[74] The strongest arguments rest with those who believe the death and resurrection are in view. For a start the references to 'a little while' in John's Gospel up to this point have all been referring to his death and resurrection (7:33; 12:35; 13:33; 14:19).[75] Second, Jesus' response to the disciples' confusion is that they will have grief while the world rejoices but their sorrow will turn to joy (16:20), namely when Jesus sees them again their 'hearts will rejoice' and 'no one will take your joy from you' (16:22). This reference to joy fits more with Jesus' 'promise of joy to his disciples *throughout* the Christian era (15:11)' and with 'John's report of the disciples' reactions [of joy] when they saw the resurrected Christ' (20:20).[76]

So, does Jesus in John's Gospel have anything to say about his post-ascension absence and future return? Despite the prevalent scholarly idea that John portrays an exclusively realized eschatology, Jesus does speak about his absence and return. First, he speaks about the work of the Holy Spirit in reminding them of the things that he has said to them (14:25) and warns them of the future threat of death they face, a warning he did not give them before, since, he tells them, 'I was with you' (16:4). Both of these presuppose his absence, as does his simple statement that because he is going to the Father 'you will see me no longer' (16:10).

Jesus is clear that he will continue to make himself present *by* the Spirit (14:21, 23; 17:23) and he calls the disciples to 'abide in me' (15:4). But he also speaks about a future presence, when believers will be *with* Jesus where he is. He consoles the disciples that this is the aim of his going to the cross: 'And if I go and prepare a place for you, I will come again and will take you to myself, that where I am you may be also' (14:3). It is also part of his prayer for those who will believe in him in the future: 'I am no longer in the world' (17:11); 'I desire that they also, whom you have given me, may be with me where I am, to see my glory that you have given me because you loved me before the foundation of the world' (17:24).

We also have the enigmatic encounter between Jesus and Mary in 20:17, when Jesus asks Mary not to touch him 'for I have not yet ascended to the Father'. Instead, she is to go to the disciples ('my brothers') and tell them 'I am ascending to my Father and your

---

[74] Again, for a helpful list for both views see ibid. 116.
[75] Zumstein 2008: 117.
[76] Carson 1991: 543, emphasis original.

Father, to my God and your God' (20:17).[77] In this context Mary is probably embracing or clinging to Jesus since it is hard to imagine Mary's simply prodding Jesus.[78] The reason Jesus gives for Mary not to touch him is that he has 'not yet ascended to the Father'. Are we then to understand the fact that Jesus later allows Thomas to touch him (20:27) to imply that he has ascended in between?

No, the key seems to be in the motive behind the touching. Thomas is told to touch because he does not believe;[79] Mary is told not to touch because she misunderstands the nature of Jesus' resurrection. She misunderstands that though Jesus has risen from the dead, his ongoing presence with them will be mediated by the Spirit. It will not be a bodily presence.[80]

John tends to see the cross, resurrection and ascension as one event. However, in the narrative we are in the middle of this event and so Jesus has not yet ascended but is ascending. While John may stress a realized eschatology and with it emphasize the presence of the Spirit, he still maintains the absence of Jesus following the ascension.

Absence and exaltation (Hebrews)

Perhaps the book in the NT that has most to say about the location of Christ is Hebrews. Here Christ is given a definitively heavenly location. The assumptions behind Hebrews' cosmology have been the subject of extended scholarly debate and particularly the question of whether the author is operating with a Platonic or Philonic cosmology. Despite recent attempts to rehabilitate this view,[81] it does seem that the scholarly consensus is that despite surface similarities, Hebrews operates with a distinctly Jewish apocalyptic and distinctly un-Platonic cosmology (e.g. there is no anti-materialistic perspective regarding the created order).[82]

The author seems to operate with a standard biblical (cf. Gen. 1:1; Ps. 113:6) 'two-story model of the created cosmos';[83] that is, the earth

[77] A number of (weird and wonderful!) proposals have been made as to why Jesus prohibits Mary from touching him – see Keener 2003: 1193. For example, this may be an allusion to Lev. 15:19–23; i.e. a woman having her monthly period making unclean anything she touches. But, as Keener 2003: 1193 rightly notes, 'apart from lacking clues in the text, this position would violate Johannine thought about purity as well as about gender (e.g., 2:6; 4:9)'.

[78] So Keener 2003: 1193.

[79] Carson 1991: 645.

[80] Brown 1970: 1012.

[81] E.g. Svendsen 2009.

[82] Adams 2009: 138.

[83] Ibid. 130.

and the heavens. However, he also seems to distinguish between the visible or created heavens and heaven as God's abode. So, that 'heaven' can refer to 'sky' is seen, for instance, in Hebrews 11:12, where Abraham is said to have as many descendants 'as the stars of heaven'.[84] Heaven meaning 'the dwelling place of God' is in view when the author describes Christ as 'seated at the right hand of the throne of the Majesty in heaven' (8:1).[85]

Hebrews 12:25–26 is an interesting passage in that it contains both the basic heaven–earth distinction and the further heavens–heaven distinction. In verse 25 the author reminds his readers that since rejecting those who spoke to them on *earth* led to punishment, how much more serious it is if they reject him (i.e. God) who speaks from *heaven*. However, in the next verse he quotes Haggai 2:6: 'Yet once more I will shake not only the *earth* but also the *heavens*.'

Hebrews seems to view Jesus as undertaking a journey *through* the heavens *to* heaven, the dwelling place of God.[86] So, the author tells us that following his resurrection Jesus has 'passed through the heavens' (4:14) and is now 'exalted above the heavens' (7:26; cf. Eph. 4:10). This would imply that he is now located *beyond* the heavens. However, the author also describes Christ as the 'one who is seated at the right hand of the throne of the Majesty *in* heaven' (8:1) and as having entered 'into heaven itself, now to appear in the presence of God on our behalf' (9:24). It would seem that he has passed through the visible heavens to enter into heaven – the very dwelling place of God.

Caution is required, though, as Hebrews' 'language about heaven is impossible to fit into a single constant schema'.[87] Further, as the writer's main interest 'in contrast with Philo' is not cosmology, 'conclusions about his cosmology have to be inferred from implied statements in the text'.[88] And so although Hebrews seems to locate Christ in heaven, we need to ask if this actually implies his absence from believers. One author, Philip Church, has recently suggested that 'the dualism in Hebrews is more eschatological than spatial'.[89] He interprets in quite novel ways a number of texts that speak of Christ's heavenly location. So, the typical translation of 4:14 is that 'we have a

---

[84] See also 1:10–12 (quoting Ps. 102:25–27) and 12:26 (quoting Hag. 2:6).

[85] See also 12:25 and 9:24.

[86] As Ellingworth (1993: 476) notes, there seems to be no distinction in the Greek between the singular and plural of *ouranos* (as is the case with other contemporary authors; cf. Paul in 2 Cor. 5:1–2).

[87] Ibid.

[88] Ibid.

[89] Church 2017: 435.

great high priest who has *passed through* the heavens', suggesting that Christ has completed a heavenly journey. However, Church suggests that the verb here (*dierchomai*) should be rendered 'going about' and so understands the verse to speak not about a previous journey but his current ministry: we have 'a great high priest ministering in the heavens'.[90] He argues this on the basis of an intertextual echo with 1 Samuel 2:30 and 35 where the work of a priest is to '*go in and out* before [the Lord] for ever'. Second, in Hebrews 4:14 the verb is a perfect participle, and Church suggests that this better suits a reference to current activity rather than an antecedent action.

The strength of Church's interpretation is that he connects Hebrews 4:14 to the only other verse in the Greek Bible which uses this verb in a priestly context. Further, as he notes, 'the description of Jesus in Heb. 4:15 is more appropriate as a description of a priest ministering in heaven than of a priest who has passed through the heavens'.[91]

Nevertheless, on balance, Church's rendering of the verse is unconvincing. First, although matters of tense and aspect are still the subject of (considerable) debate, perfect participles are used in Hebrews to express antecedent action – perhaps most strikingly in the next verse (4:15), where the author describes how Jesus *has been tempted* (*pepeirasmenon*) in every respect as we are, and yet remained sinless.[92] To render this perfect participle as a present – 'is being tempted' – would be nonsensical. So, although Church is correct to say that a perfect participle *can* have a contemporaneous time referent, it is an overstatement to say that 'if the author had antecedence in mind in 4:14 one would expect an aorist participle'.[93] Second, and more fundamentally, although the verb *dierchomai* can have the meaning 'move about', and does so in the priestly context of 1 Samuel 2, when it is used, as here, with a direct object, that is, with no preposition (*enōpion* in 1 Sam. 2), the verb virtually always means 'pass through'.[94] It would seem, then, that Hebrews is

[90] Ibid. 372.
[91] Ibid. 378, n. 34.
[92] Cf. other perfects used to refer to antecedent action: Heb. 2:9; 5:14; 7:20.
[93] Church 2017: 374.
[94] Judg. 11:20; 1 Sam. 14:23; 2 Sam. 17:22; Mic. 2:13; Jer. 48:32 (32:32 LXX); Luke 19:1; Acts 14:24; 15:3; 19:1, 21; 1 Cor. 16:5. Cf. Jdt. 2.24; 10.10; 13.10 and 1 Macc. 11.62. The one exception is Josh. 18:4 (the men 'go up and down the land') and possibly Deut. 2:7 (where it could refer to their 'wandering about' the desert, but the reference to forty years indicates that this is about to finish and so the ESVUK's rendering 'go through' the desert may be closer to the mark).

presupposing Jesus as having undergone a journey through the heavens.[95]

Hebrews 7:26 seems to indicate that this journey results in Jesus' moving beyond the heavens when it describes him as 'a high priest, holy, innocent, unstained, separated from sinners, and *exalted above the heavens*'. The most straightforward way to understand this is to see 'heavens' referring to the visible, created heavens. Christ's exaltation means that he is above the highest part of the universe. The image of exaltation is expressed in terms of spatial separation (cf. Eph. 4:10 'above all the heavens').

Moffitt's application of Janet Soskice's work on metaphor is helpful here.[96] Soskice distinguishes between a metaphor and an analogy. A metaphor generates a new perspective on a subject. Moffitt gives the example 'the brain is a computer'. Here we explain the brain by appealing to something external to it ('a computer'). An analogy, on the other hand, 'is a model whose subject is also its source'.[97] Moffitt gives an example of a child playing with a toy aeroplane. To tell the child 'to be a good pilot, and land the plane carefully' is to speak 'in a way that while recognizing differences also recognizes that the application of certain terms is fitting or appropriate to an object or state of affairs'.[98] Moffitt applies this difference to Hebrews' understanding of the heavenly tabernacle in relationship to the earthly tabernacle. The relationship, argues Moffitt, is analogical rather than metaphorical. That is, there is an essential continuity between the structure of the two spaces. This does not mean that there has to be a *literal* heavenly tabernacle, any more than a child is flying a *literal* plane. Nevertheless, there is more continuity than when we operate with a metaphorical construct.

As such, even if we do not understand Christ to be located *literally* 'exalted above the heavens', an analogical understanding allows us to see this as an expression of *spatial separation*. Certainly, Hebrews 7:26 describes Christ as 'separated from sinners'. Now, this could be a qualitative, moral separation. And that would certainly fit the description of Jesus in the first half of the verse: 'holy, innocent, unstained'. However, it is also possible to read this separation with the second half of the verse: 'exalted above the heavens'. In fact, given the

---

[95] Barnard 2012: 116, 'although Hebrews does not express Christ's otherworldly journey in narrative form, a narrative of ascent is clearly presupposed'.

[96] Moffitt 2016; Soskice 1985.

[97] Moffitt 2016: 261.

[98] Ibid. 262.

transitional point in the sentence, it may be that both ideas are in view.[99]

Although Christ is 'exalted above the heavens', he is still 'in heaven'; that is, with God. Hebrews brings this out in its description of Christ 'seated at the right hand of the throne of the Majesty in heaven' (8:1) and as appearing in heaven itself (9:24). The conceptuality here resonates with Jewish apocalyptic literature. As such, as Moffitt points out, Jesus has not left the universe in a Platonic (or Philonic) sense and been 'absorbed into the ultimate realm of the divine that exists outside the cosmos'. Instead, he has 'been invited to ascend to the highest place in the heavens, the place above all the other heavens where the heavenly holy of holies and the heavenly throne of God are'.[100]

Christ's location with God does imply separation but also accessibility. Believers are exhorted to 'draw near to the throne of grace' in order to 'find grace to help in time of need'. That is, although Christ is seated at the right hand of the throne 'in heaven' which is 'far above the heavens', he remains accessible to believers. Although the conceptual language is different, what we have in Hebrews, in other words, is similar to what we have seen in the Gospels – Christ is both absent and present.

Conclusion

The exaltation of Christ is a function of his glorification. To sit at God's right hand is an attribution of the greatest honour. However, the ascension and exaltation of Christ also lead to his absence. Mark's Gospel has a very sparse account of the resurrection, but the statement of the angel to the two Marys is appropriate: 'He has risen; he is not here' (16:6). The resurrection, ascension and exaltation of Jesus lead to his relocation and attendant absence from believers.

[99] So Koester 2001: 367.
[100] Moffitt 2016: 274.

Chapter Six

The body of the exalted Christ

Introduction

In the last chapter we considered the absence of Christ and in the next chapter we will see that (particularly for Paul) this is a *bodily* absence; that is, it is predicated on the fact that he possesses a distinct, individual body. In this chapter we will consider the 'middle step'; that is, the nature of that individual body.

There are three passages in the NT that provide us with insight into the nature of the individual body of the risen Christ: (1) Luke's description of the encounter between Jesus and the disciples in Luke 24:36–43, (2) John's description of Jesus' interaction with Thomas in John 20:24–29 and (3) Paul's extensive discussion of the resurrection and resurrection bodies in 1 Corinthians 15. The last will make up the bulk of this chapter since in it Paul directly addresses the question of what kind of body those who have been raised will possess (15:35). We will see that as Paul provides an answer to this question, what he says about the resurrection body applies both to believers and to Christ. Having considered 1 Corinthians 15 in some detail, we then more briefly consider two related passages in Paul that concern the bodily nature of the exalted Christ – Romans 8:29 and Philippians 3:20–21.

A physical body (Luke 24; John 20)

Luke 24:36–43

On the surface Luke 24:36–43 reads as a straightforward account of a resurrection appearance of Jesus in which he demonstrates that he is not a 'spirit' or 'ghost' since 'a spirit does not have flesh and bones as you see that I have', by having the disciples touch him (24:39) and by eating a piece of fish in front of them (24:43). It is, then, particularly a demonstration of the *physical* nature of his resurrection body. However, scholars have questioned this.

Why does Jesus deny that he is a 'spirit'? It is relatively common to understand Jesus to be denying that he is a 'ghost' (cf. NIV). In other words, Luke has included this account of Jesus' resurrection appearance to critique 'ghostly' understandings of his resurrection form. However, it has been suggested that the use of the Greek word *pneuma* to refer to a ghost, that is, an appearance of a dead person, was unattested in antiquity before the second century AD.[1] As Smith has argued, Luke's 'aim of excluding a "ghostly" interpretation of the resurrection appearances would have been better served had the author used one of the customary terms for "ghost"'.[2] Smith cites Paige, who has shown that 'not a single Gentile, non-Christian writer prior to the late second century ever used [*pneuma*] to signify a "demon," "ghost," or "spirit" of any sort'.[3] So, if Luke is not critiquing a 'ghostly' understanding of the resurrection, what (if anything) is he critiquing?

Smith argues for the suggestion that Luke is actually critiquing Paul's understanding of the resurrection body in 1 Corinthians 15 and particularly his contention that it was a 'spiritual body' (15:44) and that Christ himself had been transformed into a 'spirit' (15:45) because 'flesh and blood cannot inherit the kingdom of God' (15:50).[4] Although Paul and Luke agree on both the continuity of Jesus' identity and the *bodily* nature of his resurrection, Smith suggests that they disagree on the constituency of that body.[5] Although Smith explores other possible areas of tension between Paul and Luke (e.g. Paul's correlating his own 'visionary' experience with other post-resurrection appearances in 1 Cor. 15:5–8), he sees this as the fundamental point of difference between them.

A number of aspects suggest that Smith's suggestion is not correct.[6] First, Smith leans heavily on Paige's contention that *pneuma* was not used by any Gentile, non-Christian writer to refer to a 'ghost' or a 'demon' or a 'spirit' before the second century.[7] This may well be the case, but it is unquestionable that Luke himself uses the word in this way. So, for example, in 8:29 and 9:42 *pneuma* is used in parallel with 'demon' (*daimonion*). The question of the semantic range of

---

[1] Smith 2010: 756.
[2] Ibid.: *phantasma, skia* or even *psychē*.
[3] Paige 2002: 433, cited in Smith 2010: 756.
[4] Smith 2010: 767.
[5] Ibid.
[6] Smith's (2010) suggestion is not new, and has been made by other interpreters. However, Smith's is one of the strongest and most recent articulations of this position.
[7] Paige 2002: 433, cited in Smith 2010: 756.

pneuma is complex, and Smith himself does acknowledge some of these complexities, but it does seem as if Luke is using them in more distinctly 'Christian' ways and so it is not unreasonable to understand Jesus in 24:39 to reject the idea that he is a disembodied spirit akin to a 'ghost'.

Smith acknowledges the fact that the disciples respond with fear and are startled (24:37), troubled and doubting (24:38), and suggests that the response of the disciples approximates 'to a cultural commonplace, that of seeing a ghost'.[8] However, he suggests that this does not explain Luke's theological and apologetic concern. But surely, if the word itself *and* the response both allow for and even suggest that the disciples think they see a ghost, this is the simplest way to understand Luke.

One important parallel is found earlier in the Gospel in 8:55. Jesus has just healed Jairus' daughter and we are told that 'her spirit [*pneuma*] returned, and she got up at once. And [Jesus] directed that something should be given to her to eat'. It is possible to make too much of the parallels between this girl and what later happens to Jesus.[9] However, for our purposes it shows that Luke is happy to speak of death leading to a disembodied spirit and to use the word *pneuma* to communicate this. In this case the girl being given food does not seem to be for the purpose of proving the reality of her recovery (it is rather an act of kindness and concern on Jesus' part); nevertheless, it does suggest that this scene anticipates, to some degree, what will later happen to Jesus. The response of the girl's parents is one of 'amazement' (the same word used of the response to the news of Jesus' resurrection in 24:22). Luke in chapter 24 is showing that the risen Jesus is a complete person – spirit and body – just as this little girl was.

But what of the parallel language between Luke and Paul and the fact that in Luke Jesus rejects the idea that he is a 'spirit' and affirms that he has 'flesh and bones', while Paul affirms that the risen Christ is *not* 'flesh and blood' (1 Cor. 15:50), that he has a spiritual body (15:44) and that he himself is a 'life-giving spirit' (15:45)? A full answer will have to wait until my treatment of 1 Corinthians 15 below, but perhaps to oversimplify it: Luke is concerned to show the *continuity* of the resurrection body with physical materiality – underlining the *certainty* of Christ's resurrection (cf. 1:4), while Paul (as we will see)

[8] Smith 2010: 772.
[9] A few commentators note but do not develop them; e.g. Bock 1996: 804; Nolland 1989: 422.

is concerned to show the *radical transformation* that Christ's risen body has undergone and which makes him fit for a new realm and reality.[10] To posit a contradiction on the basis of their use of lexemes that have a wide range of meaning is to miss the force of their respective concerns.

For Luke, the risen Jesus possesses a distinct, physical body. He can be touched and he can eat. He cannot be reduced to a mere disembodied spirit.

John 20

In John 20 we have similar descriptions of the body of the risen Christ as we have just seen in Luke 24. We have the somewhat enigmatic description of his encounter with Mary, where Jesus tells her not to touch him (on this see chapter 5), but we also have Jesus showing the disciples his hands and his side (20:20) and then actually asking Thomas to touch his hands and his side (20:27). Here, as with Luke 24, the risen Christ is presented as having a body that is located and can be handled. However, as with Luke 24, this understanding has been called into question.

Even though John presents Jesus as being able to be touched, Sandra Schneiders argues that for John, 'Jesus' resurrection is *bodily but not physical*'.[11] Thomas refuses to believe the testimony of the other disciples concerning Jesus' resurrection (20:25); that is, as Schneiders puts it, 'the testimony of the church'.[12] He is refusing the 'new structure of faith' and so wants to 'return to the dispensation of pre-Easter faith'; that is, 'to relate to Jesus in the flesh'.[13] When Jesus encounters Thomas the following week, he does not actually acquiesce to Thomas's demands. Rather, he says to him, 'Bring your finger and *see my hands*' (20:27).[14] As Schneiders notes, 'One does not "see" with one's finger.'[15] No, the 'invitation is not to see physically but to grasp what cannot be seen with the eyes of flesh'.[16] Jesus' wounds are not 'a proof of physical reality but the source of a true understanding of the meaning of Jesus' revelatory death'.[17] This is

[10] This is not to deny that Luke communicates discontinuity too. The risen Christ can appear (24:36) and disappear (24:31).
[11] Schneiders 2008: 154, emphasis added.
[12] Ibid. 168.
[13] Ibid.
[14] Schneiders' translation.
[15] Schneiders 2008: 168.
[16] Ibid.
[17] Ibid.

further expounded, Schneiders argues, in the next part of Jesus' discussion with Thomas when he tells him to put his hand into his side. Again, this is not to establish the physical nature of Jesus' body. Rather, Jesus' side is the place 'from which had issued the lifegiving blood and water, symbol of the gift of the Spirit in baptism and eucharist which Jesus had handed over in his death and had focussed in the gift to the community a week earlier when Thomas was absent'.[18] Thomas responds not by touching, but by confessing, 'My Lord and my God!' In other words, Schneiders argues:

> Jesus says to Thomas not what the Lukan Jesus says to his disciples who disbelieve their eyes through startled joy: 'Feel me and see that I have flesh and bones, that I am not a ghost,' but rather, 'Thomas, grasp in faith what my saving death means and appropriate in faith the fruits of that death, the Spirit poured forth from my open side.' He is saying in effect what he said to Simon Peter at the last supper, 'Unless you enter by faith into the new dispensation inaugurated by my glorification you can have no part with me.'[19]

In the narrative of John 20, then, Schneiders argues we move from Mary's approaching Jesus as if he were still in his pre-Easter state – wanting to touch him. She is told not to touch him, but to go to his 'brothers and sisters' (20:17); that is, the new covenant community. This community is created as the risen Lord Jesus encounters the disciples and breathes the Spirit on them (20:19–23). Thomas is then rebuked for his faithless (*apistos*, 20:27) refusal to believe the witness of this newly constituted community. It is 'embodied sacramental symbolism'[20] that convinces Thomas to believe. Thomas, as all believers after him, comes to faith 'through an experience of signs, material mediations of spiritual reality', which are *not* the 'visible flesh of the pre-Easter Jesus but the sacramental body of the Lord which is, and is mediated by, the church'.[21]

There are a number of significant problems with Schneiders' reading of John's resurrection narrative. For a start, there is lack of precision regarding what she is rejecting. She starts by proposing that Jesus' resurrection is '*not* physical but *is* bodily',[22] but finishes by

[18] Ibid.
[19] Ibid. 169.
[20] My summary of Schneiders' argument.
[21] Schneiders 2008: 173.
[22] Ibid. 154, emphases original.

103

arguing that Jesus 'is no longer in the flesh (i.e. he is no longer mortal)'.[23] If flesh is understood as that which is mortal, we would have no problem in agreeing that the risen body of Christ is not fleshly – we will see that this is essentially what Paul maintains in 1 Corinthians 15. However, she further makes the qualification that his body is 'material in the sense of being a principle of individuation but not in the sense of being a principle of physicality'.[24] Her rejection of the physical nature of Christ seems to turn on the idea that Christ is no longer 'subject to the conditions of time, space, causality' but is 'now acting through his ecclesial body' so that we 'experience his real presence in our lives and in our world, through our participation in the life of the ecclesial community'.[25]

I have deliberately spent time outlining Schneiders' conception of the resurrection body in John because it so helpfully crystallizes the issues. Here is a conception of the resurrection that is resolutely *bodily* but equally definitively *non-physical*. For Schneiders, Jesus' ongoing physicality would imply *constraint* – not simply in terms of mortality but also in terms of *availability*. If Jesus rose *physically*, he would not, Schneiders implies, be *available* and would be unable to act in the world: 'if Jesus is merely physically resuscitated, if he is still in the flesh, then he cannot be mediated by a community from which he would be not only distinct but separate'.[26] What she is positing then is a Christ who is *fully present*.

However, Schneiders' reading of John 20 stumbles both exegetically and theologically. Exegetically, as we have seen, she argues that the point of the encounter with Thomas is *not* that Jesus can be touched. She concedes that the 'glorified Jesus can self-symbolize quasi-physically if that is necessary'.[27] However, in the interaction between Jesus and Thomas, John is clearly emphasizing that the purpose of the encounter is to underline the *physical* nature of Jesus' resurrection body. Schneiders, as we have seen, suggests that John's use of the language of 'seeing' injects a note of non-physicality into the encounter. However, John carefully matches Thomas's demands with Jesus' responses. So, in 20:25 he tells the other disciples, 'Unless I *see* [*idō*] in his hands the mark of the nails, and *place* [*balō*] my finger into the mark of the nails, and *place* [*balō*] my hand into his side, I

[23] Ibid. 174.
[24] Ibid. 175.
[25] Ibid. 174, 175, 176.
[26] Ibid. 175.
[27] Schneiders 2013: 95.

will never believe.' When Jesus meets him a week later, he tells him, 'Put [*phere*] your finger here, and see [*ide*] my hands; and put [*phere*] out your hand, and place [*bale*] it in my side. Do not disbelieve, but believe' (20:27). The instruction to 'see' is not an indication that this is only a 'quasi' physical encounter. Rather, it is a response to Thomas's statement 'Unless I see . . . I will never believe.' Thomas wants to see *and* to touch; Jesus responds by telling him to do just that. The main exegetical argument that Schneiders uses to establish the non-physical nature of the risen Jesus' body does not hold.

Further, the risen Jesus *is* physical in the sense that he is *constrained* by his physical body. In the last chapter we saw that for John, the exalted Jesus is *absent*. Yes, the Spirit *mediates* his presence, but Jesus himself remains *bodily* absent. As Jesus prays, 'I am no longer in the world, but they are in the world' (John 17:11). There is separation, and an inherent *unavailability* of Jesus to believers. John, like Luke, maintains the physical, discrete nature of the body of the risen Christ.

A heavenly body (1 Cor. 15:35–41)

Perhaps more than any other chapter it is 1 Corinthians 15 that helps us understand the nature of the body of the exalted Christ. The whole chapter concerns the resurrection, but the nature of resurrected *bodies* comes into focus in 15:35. Here Paul asks, 'how are the dead raised?' and 'with what kind of body do they come?'

These questions have often been scrutinized in order to determine the underlying theology of Paul's opponents.[28] However, Asher has convincingly argued that Paul is not actually addressing opponents.[29] Rather, demonstrating that Paul's argument is not adversarial but didactic in style, he suggests that he is actually attempting to reconcile the Corinthians to one another by correcting the views of one group that was misunderstanding the nature of the resurrection.[30]

Asher suggests that the problem the dissenters have is not the *bodily* aspect of the resurrection. Rather, they seem to think that Paul's view of resurrection would violate the 'strictures of cosmic polarity', namely the idea that a *terrestrial* body could ascend to and inhabit the *celestial* realm.[31] The problem they have is a failure to understand

[28] Asher 2000: 32–35.
[29] Ibid. 36–48.
[30] Ibid. 48.
[31] Ibid. 82.

how to relate the resurrection to a cosmic polarity, where the earthly and heavenly realms are understood as opposites.

Paul, according to Asher, is arguing that his teaching on the resurrection 'can be comprehended within a cosmological system where the celestial and terrestrial realms are understood as opposites'.[32] That is, his idea of resurrection 'is compatible with the locative aspects of this cosmology'.[33] In relating the resurrection to the ideas of locative (vv. 39–44a) and temporal (vv. 44b–49) polarity, Paul's aim is to show that 'the resurrection of the dead is spatially compatible with the principle of polarity and that this principle also allows for the succession of opposites over time and ultimately an eschatological resurrection'.[34]

Asher's argument, then, is that the Corinthian dissenters did not struggle with the idea of a *bodily* resurrection but with the idea that an *earthly* body could be raised to the *heavenly* realm. Key to this is Asher's contention that it is Paul himself, and not the Corinthians, who introduces the issue of the body into the question of verse 35. That is, he argues, the Corinthian dissenters were not actually disputing the idea that there could be such a thing as a bodily resurrection.

It does seem, with Asher, that assumptions about cosmic polarity lie at the root of the misunderstanding Paul is addressing. However, I would argue, it is precisely when this is combined with their understanding that Paul held to a *bodily* resurrection that it causes them problems. This, I think, is the simplest way to understand verse 35. Paul is correcting their idea that there can be such a thing as a resurrected *body* that is fit for a *heavenly* habitation. It seems that the Corinthian dissenters are confused in thinking that Paul means that *earthly* bodies will be resurrected in their *current* form to dwell in heaven. They seem to be combining the thoughts of cosmic polarity and resurrection of untransformed earthly bodies.

Understanding the body of Christ as a *heavenly* body provides an answer to the seeming presupposition behind the question that human bodies in their current form are unable to inhabit a resurrected existence. To demonstrate that it is, in fact, possible to have a body that is fit for celestial existence, Paul answers the question by first arguing that just as a seed is different from the resulting plant, the resurrection body is different from the earthly body (15:37). It is

[32] Ibid. 91.
[33] Ibid.
[34] Ibid. 99.

the *power of God* that determines the form of the body that comes from the seed (15:38). From this, Paul notes that in the universe there are different forms of flesh and different forms of body,[35] and this also applies to the resurrection body. That is, the body that is sown is different to the body that is raised. The idea of a 'heavenly body' is just as possible as an 'earthly body' (15:40).

And so the argument does proceed, as Asher argues, in terms of polarity. Paul assumes an earthly–heavenly polarity, employs the language of 'body' in a philosophically neutral manner in verses 35–57 and these verses centre on the polarity between heaven and earth. The key aspect of verse 40, then, is that there are *earthly* and *heavenly* bodies, not simply that there are a wide *variety* of bodies in the cosmos. That explains why when Paul expands on his observations in verses 42–44a, he does so *only* in terms of earthly and heavenly bodies.[36]

So, the variety of bodies described in verses 39–41 can actually be analysed in terms of location. In verse 39 we have the terrestrial bodies made up of flesh, namely humans, animals, birds and fish, while in verse 41 we have the celestial bodies, the sun, moon and stars, each of which possesses a different type of glory. This distinction turns on verse 40, where Paul divides the cosmos into two regions – heaven and earth.[37] In other words:

> Paul does not use vv. 39–41 as an analogy to show that the God who can create a variety of bodies can also create a resurrection body. Rather, he uses these verses to lay the foundation for his following argument that the resurrection of the dead can be comprehended within a scheme where bodies are arranged between two polar spheres of habitation.[38]

It is this locative polarity between heaven and earth that is fundamental to his argument. Different bodies then are 'classified as coordinates by their location (celestial or terrestrial) and by their characteristics: composition (as in the terrestrial flesh) and radiance (as in the celestial *doxa*)'.[39] This principle of polarity means that a

---

[35] As Thiselton (2000: 1267) notes, for Paul *sarx* is 'a polymorphous concept' and hence 'heavily context dependent and variable' and probably here has a reference to the 'substance' of the body.

[36] Asher 2000: 102–103.

[37] Ibid. 103–104.

[38] Ibid. 102–103.

[39] Ibid. 105.

body is suitable only for its particular environment. This is underlined in verse 50 ('flesh and blood cannot inherit the kingdom of God'), where Paul underlines that 'the ascension of a terrestrial human form or substance to the celestial region' is impossible.[40]

Within this schema of cosmic locative polarity the clear distinction between the earthly and heavenly realms is maintained. While Paul's purpose is not to outline a *spatial* separation, in establishing a cosmic locative polarity the former idea is not an entirely foreign concept. Within a scheme that assumes a clear cosmic polarity between heaven and earth, the idea of Christ's body dwelling in heaven is commensurate with his bodily absence from believers on earth. Christ has a heavenly body and dwells in heaven. Believers with their earthly bodies continue to remain on earth.

A spiritual body (1 Cor. 15:42–44)

The earthly–heavenly contrast is not the only one that Paul employs in this chapter. In verses 42–44 Paul continues to use a number of contrasts (perishable–imperishable; dishonour–glory; weakness–power) climaxing in verse 44: if there is a *natural (psychikos)*[41] body there is also a *spiritual (pneumatikos)* one. This affirmation together with the statement in 15:50 that 'flesh and blood cannot inherit the kingdom of God' has led to strands of interpretation that understand the body of the risen Christ to be something other than a physical body.

In a recent article James Ware has traced three lines of interpretation of 1 Corinthians 15 in the early Christian period.[42] A line running from Irenaeus in the second century to Augustine in the fifth understood the resurrection to be a transformation of *this* body into an imperishable body. That is, the resurrection body 'is *this* body restored and improved in a miraculous manner'.[43] A second line associated with Gnostic theology essentially denied any kind of literal resurrection. However, a third line associated with Origen in the third century held to a literal resurrection but understood the *substance* of the resurrection body to be of ethereal matter as distinct from the body of the flesh. Ware shows how this third line of interpretation did not gain any real traction until the late twentieth

---

[40] Ibid. 153.
[41] See below for a defence of this translation.
[42] Ware 2014. The following section is a summary of this article.
[43] Dahl 1962: 7, cited in Ware 2014: 811.

century, when a number of scholars, including Dale Martin and Troels Engberg-Pedersen, began to make similar arguments.[44] Although there are significant differences between these proposals, in essence they understand the resurrection body to be an '*ethereally material body* composed not of flesh but of the corporeal substance of *pneuma*'.[45]

There is not space here for anything other than an overview of the issues.[46] Four points suggest that Paul is not conceiving of the resurrection body being transformed into a non-physical, ethereal body composed of *pneuma*. First, at the most simple level, this interpretation assumes that Paul would have been confident that the Corinthian church were all familiar enough with Stoic metaphysics to follow the nuances of his argument. Given the 'mixed' nature of the first century, with both Stoic materialism and Platonic immaterialism, a question can at least be raised against the idea that to convince the Corinthian dissenters Paul would have adopted a basically Stoic ontology of the body.[47] Second, the contrast in verse 44 between a *psychikos* body and a *pneumatikos* is not between *physical*[48] and *spiritual* but *natural*[49] and *spiritual*. The earlier use of *psychikos* in 2:14, where Paul describes how the *psychikos anthrōpos* cannot accept 'the things of the Spirit of God', suggests that Paul is not operating with a material–non-material contrast.[50] Rather, in a similar way to Jude 19 (division being caused by *psychikoi* who do not have the Spirit) it seems that he is understanding *psychikos* as 'natural'; that is, pertaining to the nature of this world. Third, as Ware has shown, in 15:36–49 the subject of the verbal pairs is the same. In other words, it is not one body that dies and then another one that is raised. It is the *same* body that dies and then is raised: the same body that is 'sown in dishonour' is raised in 'glory'. This means that it is the body of the flesh which is subject to resurrection and transformation. And so Martin's assertion that Paul 'does not believe in a resurrection of *this* body' does not hold.[51] No, 'mortal flesh, far

[44] Martin 1995; Engberg-Pedersen 2009, 2010, 2011.

[45] Ware 2014: 816, emphasis original.

[46] For a detailed response to Martin see Orr 2014: 68–72; for a detailed response to Engberg-Pedersen see Orr 2014: 72–81 and Barclay 2011.

[47] Barclay (2011: 408) asks the question from a slightly different angle.

[48] E.g. RSV, NRSV.

[49] E.g. Fee 1987: 785, NIV, ESVUK.

[50] As far back as Deissner (1912: 34) scholars have pointed out that given a *sōma psychikon* does not consist of 'soul', we would not expect a *sōma pneumatikon* to consist of 'spirit'.

[51] Martin 1995: 130, cited in Ware 2014: 825, emphasis original.

from being excluded from this divine, saving event, is the subject of that event'.[52] Finally, and most critically, the nature of the change in 15:36–54 refers 'not to the substance of the body but to *qualities, states,* or *conditions* of the body: corruption, incorruption, dishonour, glory, weakness, power, mortality, and immortality'.[53] Paul is not then positing a reconstitution of the body into a different *pneumatic* substance but *transformation* of this body so that it is 'adapted to the eschatological existence under the ultimate domination of the Spirit'.[54] Or as Rabens puts it,

> [b]y calling the resurrection body [*pneumatikos*], Paul conveys that the natural body will be transformed, animated and enlivened by God's Spirit (cf. Rom. 8:11 and parallels). It is the most elegant way Paul can find of saying both that the new body is the *result* of the Spirit's work (answering 'how does it come to be?') and that it is the appropriate *vessel for* the Spirit's life (answering 'what sort of a thing is it?').[55]

The body of this risen Christ is not 'natural' but 'spiritual'. However, as we saw with both Luke and John, it is not thereby non-physical. Rather, it is a body transformed into imperishability and so rendered suitable for eschatological existence.

A discrete body (Rom. 8:29)

Towards the end of Romans 8, the apostle assures his readers that everything works for the good for those who love God and are called according to his purpose (8:28). In 8:29 Paul unpacks this purpose on two levels: soteriological and Christological. In the first clause, Paul describes how those whom God foreknew he predestined to be conformed to the image of his Son. He then explains that the purpose of this eschatological[56] conforming is that God's Son might be the firstborn among many brothers. Thus God's transformation of believers leads to the exaltation of his Son.

[52] Ware 2014: 825.
[53] Ibid. 831, emphases original.
[54] Fee 1987: 786.
[55] Rabens 2010: 96, emphases original.
[56] Although in 2 Cor. 3:18 Paul views this transformation as a presently occurring process, the close parallels between our text and Phil. 3:21 and 1 Cor. 15:49 suggest that the final, eschatological transformation is in view here. So Moo (1996: 535), who notes that 'eschatology is Paul's focus in this paragraph'.

This passage is not without complexity and debate. First, the description of believers as conformed to 'the image of his Son' could be understood epexegetically; that is, 'conformed to the image, which is his Son'.[57] Alternatively, it could be understood in a simple possessive sense; that is, 'conformed to the image which his Son possesses'.[58] In other words, are believers conformed to Christ who is the image of God, or are believers conformed to the image of Christ? On one level the difference is immaterial.[59] Certainly Paul speaks of Christ as the image of God (2 Cor. 4:4; cf. Col. 1:15) and so to be conformed to Christ is, necessarily, to be conformed to the image of God. However, in the parallel text, 1 Corinthians 15:49, Paul specifically refers to believers bearing the image of Christ. That is, 'just as we have borne the image of the earthly man, so shall we bear the image of the heavenly man [i.e. Christ]' (NIV). Believers will bear this image as their mortal bodies are clothed 'with immortality' (15:53 NIV). As such, in this context, bearing Christ's image in 1 Corinthians 15:49 means being conformed to his glorious body.

It would seem, then, that the image refers to the exalted body of Christ. This fits the generally agreed idea that image does not simply refer to a replica or reproduction but is a form that expresses the essence or being of something.[60] As such, Christ's resurrected body perfectly expresses his immortal, glorious, powerful, spiritual character (1 Cor. 15:42–44). This fits with Philippians 3:21, where believers are awaiting the transformation of their humble bodies into the form (*symmorphon*) of his glorious body. These parallels then seem to indicate that Romans 8:29 is speaking of believers being conformed to Christ's image, which is more specific than simply 'participating in the glory of the resurrected Lord'.[61] Rather, the 'image' of Christ is his resurrected body, and as such our bodies will be conformed to his body. In other words, Paul is assuming the resurrected bodily nature of Christ, which can be *distinguished* from the resurrected bodies of believers.[62]

---

[57] So e.g. Dunn 1988a: 483. Byrne (1996: 272) argues that the complete phrase is 'tautologous' unless it is read epexegetically.

[58] So e.g. Murray 1960: 318–319.

[59] Which may explain why this question is so frequently overlooked by commentators – a fact that Kim (1982: 233) notes in passing.

[60] E.g. Conzelmann 1967: 100.

[61] Lohse 2003: 252.

[62] Even if we were to interpret the genitive epexegetically and understand a reference to Christ as the image of God, we would then have a pointer to his role as the last Adam and hence his humanity. The parallel with 1 Cor. 15:49 is especially important.

Second, there is the question of whether the language of conforming (*symmorphos*) has a participatory aspect. So, for example, in an important article, Kürzinger argues that it is important to note that Paul says *symmorphos* and not *homo-morphos*.[63] The important *syn-* prefix indicates that what is in view is not a mere 'likeness' to Christ but an actual participation in or incorporation into Christ.[64] That incorporation or participation is involved in this verse is certainly not a new idea[65] and Kürzinger does not deny that a 'likeness' arises from this participation. However, the *syn-* prefix combined with the participatory theology in Romans (e.g. 6:6, 8) leads him to conclude that the idea of 'likeness' is not the *primary* aspect of Paul's thought here.[66] However, a *syn-* prefix does not in itself *necessitate* an idea of participation.[67] Kürzinger correctly notes that *syn-* and *homo-* compounds do not have to be synonymous.[68] However, given, as Kürzinger himself notes, *homo-morphos* does not seem to appear in any extant Greek source,[69] it seems difficult to lay too much weight on the absence of the prefix. That is not to rule out participation; rather, it is to question whether, on the basis of this prefix, one can say that the idea of 'likeness' is *secondary*. Further, both the immediate context and the Pauline parallels indicate that the idea of believers bearing the likeness of Christ is actually the primary thought here. So, Paul's immediately following description of Christ as the firstborn[70] among many brothers and sisters functions as the climax of God's plan. The eschatological position of honour of Christ in the midst of his brothers is the dominant thought. As such, the idea of *differentiation* and *distinction* rather than *participation* is stressed.

So, the picture we have in this verse is of the Christ in the midst of his brothers and sisters who have been conformed to his resurrected body. There is similarity but it is not possible to think of Christ and believers fused into one indistinguishable corporate entity. No, Christ stands out as firstborn. He occupies the place of rank as he is

---

[63] Kürzinger 1958: 295.

[64] Ibid.

[65] The idea goes back at least as far as Athanasius (*Against Arians* 4.61).

[66] Kürzinger 1958: 297.

[67] Cf. BDAG 961–962.

[68] Kürzinger 1958: 295.

[69] It does not seem to appear in either the Thesaurus Linguae Graecae or Perseus databases.

[70] As Kürzinger (1958: 297) notes, this term indicates 'more than temporal precedence'. Michaelis (1968: 877) shows that, on the basis of the use of the term in other Jewish texts, Paul is viewing Christ as like his brothers 'but above them in rank and dignity, since he remains their Lord'.

surrounded by other humans who are like him. Even in their eschatological state, then, there can be a distinction between believers and Christ that centres on their bodily nature. The idea of spatial distance is not present in this text but the *necessary* bodily distinction between Christ and his siblings is. Though less explicit, the picture we have here of the exalted Christ fits with what we have seen in 1 Corinthians 15, namely that he remains a human being with a body in distinction from other believers.[71]

A glorified human body (Phil. 3:20–21)

In Philippians 3 we have another example in Paul that the exalted Christ possesses a discrete body. In contrast to the 'enemies of the cross of Christ' (3:18), who are thinking of 'earthly things' (3:19), Paul and his readers' 'citizenship is in heaven'. Heaven is the location from where believers are waiting for their Saviour. That is, 'if Christ is to come from heaven, then he is envisaged as being there until that time'.[72] Paul's use of the verb 'to wait' (*apekdechomai*) fits with the concept of Christ's currently being absent. The verb is used by Paul in other eschatological contexts: in Romans 8:19 creation waits for the revealing of the sons of God; in 8:23–25 Paul widens this waiting not just to creation but to believers themselves; and in Galatians 5:5 believers are said to wait for the hope of righteousness. Perhaps the clearest parallel is in 1 Corinthians 1:7, where the Corinthians are said to be waiting for the revealing of Jesus Christ (cf. Heb. 9:28, where the readers are told that Christ is coming to save those who wait for him). Believers then wait for Christ, who is absent.

Their waiting here has a specific focus, namely that when he comes the Lord Jesus Christ will 'transform' their bodies of humiliation into the form of his glorious body. Jesus does this by his ability 'to bring all things under his control'. This last phrase is an allusion to Psalm 8:7 [LXX]. However, unlike Paul's use of this verse in 1 Corinthians 15:27, where God is the subject of the action of subduing all things, here the power is attributed to Christ.[73] We thus have a tantalizing combination of Christ as the fulfilment of humanity's dominion over creation and the one who bears the divine power to

---

[71] Schmithals (1988: 301), in particular, argues that the Christological difference and distinction between Christ and believers must not be lost here. The redeemed do not merge with the redeemer 'but rather become conformed to his image'.

[72] Lincoln 1991: 101.

[73] Kreitzer 1987: 153.

bring about this dominion. Right at the heart of his work of subjection and his identity as the one who subjects is his possession of a glorious body.

Here then we have Christ fulfilling humanity's role in subduing all things under God. The exalted Christ's possession of a (glorified) body means that he can be distinguished at a bodily level from believers. He is not collapsed into them but retains his own distinct identity. The exalted Christ remains a human being with a distinct human body. However, it is a glorious body and it will be the prototype for the body of believers to be transformed into. Christ remains a human being and brings humanity into glory.

Conclusion

In this chapter we have seen that Luke, John and Paul all conceive the exalted Christ possessing a discrete, distinguishable body that cannot be collapsed into the Spirit or the church. Even given the close relationship we have seen between Christ and the Spirit and Christ and the church, Christ retains his individual particularity at the *bodily* level. The risen corporeity of Christ must not be configured in a supra-individual way so that any distinction between Christ and believer is elided to such an extent that the believer's body becomes 'a material part of Christ'.[74]

John and Luke stress the physical nature of Christ's resurrected body. Despite the language of a 'spiritual body' in 1 Corinthians 15:44, we saw that there is not a contradiction between Paul and the Gospel accounts. Paul stresses the *transformed* nature of the body of the exalted Christ, but nevertheless maintains its physical nature. Romans 8:29 complements what we see in 1 Corinthians 15, suggesting as it does that Paul understood Christ's body to be both discrete and localized. Philippians 3 stresses the ongoing humanity of the exalted Christ and his role in bringing humanity into glory.

Christ's possessing an individual body is not merely *accidental* to Paul's theology; it is *essential*. And not merely for our eschatological salvation but for the very exaltation of the Son – who will remain as 'firstborn' over and among his many brothers and sisters for eternity (Rom. 8:29).

---

[74] Engberg-Pedersen 2010: 1.

Chapter Seven

The location of Christ: Paul and the bodily absence of Christ

Paul: the bodily absence of Christ

Does Paul really have a concept of the absence of Christ? The frequently occurring and widely discussed Pauline motif of the believer's *union* with Christ surely calls the very idea of the *absence* of Christ into question. How can Christ be absent from believers when Paul so frequently speaks of believers being 'in Christ'? We will see in this section that Paul does indeed assume and articulate the absence of Christ. In Philippians 1 Paul expresses his desire to 'depart' and be 'with Christ', suggesting, as we will see, that he recognizes an absence between the believer and Christ. Further, when we look at the idea of Christ's coming from heaven in 1 Thessalonians, we see that, for Paul, Christ is located in heaven. Only when he comes from there will believers be 'with' him 'for ever' (1 Thess. 4:15–17). Further, in 2 Corinthians 5 we will see that it is the individual body that the exalted Christ possesses which explains his absence. Because the exalted Christ retains a distinct and distinguishable individual body, he is not omnipresent but located in one place – and so absent from believers. Finally, we consider Romans 8:34 where we consider the relationship between Christ's absence, exaltation and ongoing bodily nature.

Christian experience and the absence of Christ (Phil. 1:21–26)

In Philippians 1:23 the apostle expresses his desire to depart and be with Christ, which is 'far better' than remaining 'in the flesh'. The fact that Paul feels he needs to 'depart' (i.e. die)[1] to be 'with Christ'

---

[1] The verb *analyō* occurs only here in Paul (though cf. *analysis* in 2 Tim. 4:6). Paul probably employs it because it enables him to avoid making the bald statement that he actually desires *to die*.

suggests that he considers himself, in some sense, currently to be separated or absent from Christ. How seriously are we to take this statement as an expression of genuine absence between Paul and Christ? For a start, the desire to be with Christ *at death* seems to contradict other statements in Paul that tie this hope to the final resurrection or parousia of Christ (e.g. 1 Thess. 4:17). Second, can we speak of a real 'absence' between Christ and the believer when for Paul in this letter the believer is so patently 'in Christ' now (cf. Phil. 1:1; 2:5; 4:7, 21)?

It is generally agreed that these verses are part of a unit that stretches from 1:18 to 1:26.[2] In this section Paul opens with a question ('what then'?) in response to the previous section (1:12–17), where he has recounted how his (negative) experiences (imprisonment 1:13–14; rivalry from other preachers 1:15–17) have served the advancement of the gospel (1:12). The affirmation in 1:18 that Paul rejoices because the gospel is being preached matches (thematically at least) the earlier affirmation that what has happened to him has increased the advancement of the gospel (1:12). Paul affirms that he will continue to rejoice (1:18) because what has happened will turn out for his vindication (*sōtēria*, 1:19)[3] through the prayers of the Philippians and the help of the Spirit of Jesus Christ. His expectation is that he will not be put to shame but will always have the boldness so that Christ will be glorified in his body (1:20) – whether through life or death.

Mention of life and death leads Paul to reflect on his respective attitudes to each. In 1:21–24 Paul ties his argument around alternating expressions of life and death (1:21a to live; 1:21b to die; 1:22 to live in the flesh; 1:23 to depart; 1:24 to remain in the flesh).[4] Verse 1:21a, however, stands as an 'overarching headline' that gives Paul's discussion its orientation: for Paul, 'to live is Christ' but 'to die is gain'. While to continue living 'in the flesh' will actually mean fruitful labour, he is genuinely torn[5] between life and death. The latter will mean departing and being with Christ (1:23), which is better by far, but the former is actually more necessary for the Philippians. Thus,

---

[2] So Snyman 2005: 93.

[3] It seems clear that given he allows for the possibility of his death (1:20), something other than mere release from prison is in view when he speaks of *sōtēria*. So Croy 2003: 519.

[4] Gnilka 1976: 70.

[5] Silva (2005: 73) is surely right to argue that Paul is not just giving 'a sustained contrast between life and death for its mere stylistic impact'; *pace* Croy 2003: 6, who argues that Paul is using a rhetorical device of 'figured perplexity'.

inasmuch as the choice depends on him, he will remain 'in the flesh' for the sake of the Philippians (1:25).

How then does this idea of being with Christ *at death* match other statements in Paul that tie this hope to the resurrection or parousia? Some scholars are pessimistic that these ideas can actually be reconciled.[6] Others suggest that any apparent differences are simply caused by the different situations that Paul addresses. So Lincoln suggests that the apparent differences between Philippians 1 and, for example, 1 Thessalonians 4 are explained by the fact that in the latter case the issue at hand is the relationship between those who are dead and those who are alive at the parousia. Paul, in 1 Thessalonians 4, does not discuss the state of those who are dead but this is precisely his concern in Philippians 1.

Bockmuehl argues that perhaps the best solution is to view the dead as passing 'into a kind of time beyond time, where judgment and resurrection and full knowledge of the risen Christ are seen to be a present reality, even while they are still anticipated on earth'.[7] According to these kinds of interpretations[8] Paul is not expressing any current absence from Christ. Rather, he is effectively collapsing the *experience* of time passing between his death and the final resurrection. Others, however, reject the 'systematic imbalance' of this sort of *'timeless eternity'* idea[9] and argue, rather, that Paul holds to a form of conscious existence in an 'intermediate state'.[10]

Whether or not we use the *term* 'intermediate state', the *idea* it represents is surely the simplest way to understand Paul's words in this passage.[11] Further, there is no *necessary* tension between the idea that this 'intermediate state' is more *preferable* than remaining 'in the flesh' and the idea that it will not be until Christ's parousia that the *fullness* of eschatological blessing will occur. Paul expresses the supremacy of the latter idea in this very letter (3:20–21).

The idea of Paul – or indeed any believer – wanting to die and be 'with' Christ even as Paul anticipates the eschatological consummation does not stand in contradiction with the latter expectation. However, how do we understand Paul's expression of the necessity of *dying* in

---

[6] E.g. Hawthorne 1983: 59: 'No completely satisfactory resolution to the problem posed by these seemingly contradictory views has as yet been given, and perhaps none can be given.'

[7] Bockmuehl 1997: 93.

[8] Cf. Fee 1995: 149.

[9] Schreiber 2003: 343.

[10] Ibid. 340.

[11] Ridderbos 1975: 506; cf. Lincoln 1991: 106.

order to be 'with' Christ? Surely Paul's 'present existence "in Christ" makes it *unthinkable* that he would ever – even at death – be in a "place" where he was not "with Christ"'?[12] In what sense is it 'far better' to die and be 'with' Christ? In what sense is to die 'gain' (1:21)?

Some commentators seek to understand how Paul could understand death as gain by considering similar sayings in antiquity. After a survey of such literature, Palmer concludes that for Paul death is gain '*not because of any closer union with Christ*, since [*to live*] is *already* [*Christ*]', rather it is gain 'as in the commonplace of Greek literature, because it brings release from earthly troubles'.[13] In that sense, what Paul says is of a piece with his non-Christian contemporaries. What is more, Paul is in a *better* situation because death does not cut him off from Christ but involves his going to Christ (1:23). However, according to Palmer, going to Christ is not the *essence* of Paul's desire to die. Rather, the heart of his desire is freedom from earthly troubles.[14] However, as Croy has pointed out, Palmer's thesis falls on two fronts. First, it misses the fact that nowhere does Paul in Philippians actually *bemoan* his existing condition. Far from it, as we have seen: he rejoices in his troubles because through them the gospel is being preached (1:18).[15] Second, Palmer's thesis 'deprives the expression "depart and be *with* Christ" of any meaning beyond being "*in* Christ"'.[16]

But we return to our fundamental question: How is this being with Christ better than his current existence 'in Christ' (cf. 1:1; 4:21)? Some commentators are content to speak in quite general terms. Lincoln argues that Paul's 'relationship of union with Christ cannot be broken by death but will continue in *an even more intimate* way where Christ now is, that is in heaven'.[17]

Three aspects of this text suggest that Christ's absence is a bodily absence. First, as we have seen, departing to be with Christ is contrasted with Paul's current bodily existence (vv. 22, 24). Paul's absence from Christ arises from his ongoing bodily existence. Second, we can note Paul's use of the word 'desire'. Commentators note that this is usually a negative word for Paul (Rom. 1:24; 6:12; 7:7–8; 13:14; Gal. 5:16, 24; 1 Thess. 4:5; cf. Eph. 2:3; 4:22; Col. 3:5; 1 Tim. 6:9;

---

[12] Fee 1995: 149.
[13] Palmer 1975: 218, emphasis added.
[14] Ibid.
[15] Croy 2003: 522.
[16] Ibid. 523.
[17] Lincoln 1991: 104, emphasis added.

2 Tim. 2:22; 3:6; 4:3; Titus 2:12; 3:3). In fact there is only one other use in Paul which is not negative and that is in 1 Thessalonians 2:17.[18] In this verse Paul expresses his desire to come to the Thessalonians. Collange describes this verse as an *exception* in Pauline usage, whereas it is possibly the most important parallel use to Philippians 1. It would seem that Paul can use this more frequently negative word to express the noble desire to be in bodily presence with someone. In 1 Thessalonians 2:17 Paul is expressing the desire for *bodily* presence with the Thessalonians, which would suggest that in Philippians 1:23 his desire is for the *bodily* presence of Christ. Third, we note that Paul does not simply say that he desires 'to depart *and be closer* to Christ' but 'to be *with* Christ'.[19] As such, Paul's use of the phrase 'with Christ' which may more frequently refer to a participation in Christ-events here refers to a 'quasi-physical proximity to Christ himself'.[20]

Philippians 1:23, then, suggests that for the apostle Paul even though believers are united with Christ and 'in him' (Phil. 1:1), this does not override or negate the painful experience of absence from Christ.

The parousia and the absence of Christ (1 Thess. 4:15–17)

In this section we will examine the motif of the *coming* of Christ and how it contributes to the idea of the current *absence* of Christ. Rather than survey all the texts in Paul that speak of Christ's *coming*, we will focus on 1 Thessalonians with its high concentration of the word parousia. In this letter the themes of Christ's coming and his current absence are most closely related.

Paul speaks explicitly twice in 1 Thessalonians of Christ's coming *from heaven*. In the first instance he speaks of how the Thessalonians have turned from idols to the 'true God' and are now awaiting his Son 'from heaven' (*ek tōn ouranōn*, 1:10). In the second (4:14–17), Paul describes Christ's coming from heaven in more detail. Here we are told that the Lord will 'descend' from heaven (*ap' ouranou*) and be united with believers both dead and alive so that they will be with him for ever (4:16–17). The Lord himself will descend; those who have died in him will rise first, followed by those who have remained alive,

---

[18] E.g. Collange 1979: 64.

[19] This is a point made by Campbell (2012: 222, n. 25).

[20] Ibid.

and both will meet him 'in the air' (4:16–17). The result is that they will all be with the Lord 'for ever' (4:17 NIV).

While these references to heaven evoke a number of questions among commentators, many simply comment that in referring to Christ in heaven, Paul is here assuming Christ's exalted status rather than assuming anything about his *location*.[21] However, Luckensmeyer argues that the fact that the expected deliverance comes *ek tōn ouranōn* 'confirms the saving action of God' and means that 'heaven' here should be understood as a 'circumlocution for God'. It 'does not refer to a physical locality but a dynamic point of departure'.[22]

However, it seems fair to note that the fact that Christ will come *ek tōn ouranōn* at the very least 'presupposes that in the interim he is *in* heaven'.[23] Moreover, to conceive of Christ in his relation to believers and to heaven itself purely in dynamic terms underplays an important motif in 1 Thessalonians – Christ's current absence from believers. Paul does not *simply* describe Christ as 'the One who comes'. No, he is the one for whose coming from heaven believers are *'waiting'* (1:10). His identity here is defined not only by his future 'coming' but also by his current absence that requires believers to wait for him. To speak of heaven, as Luckensmeyer does, purely as a 'dynamic point of departure' collapses the future into the present and minimizes the present *static* period of waiting. The one for whom believers wait is currently located in heaven.

However, Andrew Perriman has suggested that the OT antecedent imagery should strongly shape how we understand this passage. The idea of the Lord's descending occurs frequently in the OT (e.g. Exod. 19:11, 20; 34:5; Num. 11:25; Deut. 31:15 LXX). The details in Paul's passage also echo OT passages. For example the 'trumpet call' echoes Isaiah 27:12–13; the reference to archangels may allude to the 'great Angel' Michael in Daniel 12:1 (LXX). As such Perriman suggests that this 'compressed narrative' takes on 'much greater complexity and depth when we empty the box of Old Testament allusions out on to the table and begin to sort through it'.[24] Two passages in particular seem to lie behind Paul's passage: Isaiah 31:4–7 and Micah 1:3 (both LXX).[25] In both cases, Perriman notes, the Lord 'does not "descend"

---

[21] Best 1972: 196; Fee 2009: 49; Kim 2002: 93.

[22] Luckensmeyer 2009: 97.

[23] Lincoln 1991: 186, emphasis original.

[24] Perriman 2005: 154.

[25] Isa. 31:4 speaks of the Lord's coming down to march against Zion and its inhabitants; in Mic. 1:3 he descends to 'tread upon the high places' of the land.

arbitrarily or for no particular reason; he descends into the turmoil of history to deal with a situation that actually threatens either the security or the sanctity of his people'.[26]

Accordingly, Perriman argues that if Paul is reusing this prophetic idea, it is because he is conceiving not of 'a remote end-time state of affairs but an actual (present or impending) situation that requires a similar intervention'.[27] The details in the text are not 'incidental' or added for 'dramatic effect' but

> [a]long with the wider setting of the eschatological descent of God to judge and defend, they characterize the *parousia* of the Lord as an event *for the purpose* of safeguarding the integrity of the suffering people of God (communities such as the church in Thessalonica) and of ensuring that *all* in Christ, including those who have died since they abandoned their idols and turned to the living God, will accompany the Lord 'in clouds' in order to be acknowledged before God and vindicated in the world.[28]

As a result of their abandoning of idols and turning to the 'living and true God', the Thessalonians 'faced considerable hardship, but they were assured of eventual gain because God would intervene to save them' in the same way that he had delivered Israel from her enemies in the past.[29]

Perriman's observations regarding the OT allusions are uncontroversial and, indeed, helpful. However, it would seem that he allows the background of the text to crowd out the foreground. As a result he downplays the *Christological* focus of the passage. The idea that the hope that Paul is holding out is the idea of vindication from enemies is not absent from the context (cf. 5:3). However, the climax of this immediate passage is precisely the idea that believers will be 'with the Lord [Jesus] for ever' (4:17 NIV). It is *this* hope that the Thessalonians are to encourage each other with (4:18). Thus Perriman downplays the fact that the Thessalonians faced not just opposition from outsiders, but the destabilizing idea that those who died were somehow separated from Christ (4:13). Paul reassures them that those who have died in Christ will come with him when this final meeting takes place (4:14).

---

[26] Perriman 2005: 155.
[27] Ibid.
[28] Ibid. 156.
[29] Ibid. 157.

The focus of Christ's parousia for Paul in *this* passage is not his vindication of believers but his reunion with them. Until that parousia Christ and believers remain absent from one another. It is only when he comes that they will be 'with' one another in the fullest sense.

Locating Christ in heaven fits with the fact that in 1 Thessalonians being 'with the Lord' is a purely *eschatological* hope lying *only* in the future. Following the coming of the Lord (4:15) and the subsequent events (4:16–17), believers will meet the Lord in the air and 'only then' (*kai houtōs*)[30] be with the Lord for ever. While the motif of being 'with' Christ or 'with' the Lord, like the related 'in Christ' language, resists simple categorization,[31] it seems fairly clear that, in this instance, Paul means something like being 'in the company of' the Lord.[32] As such, in 1 Thessalonians Paul's locating Christ in heaven involves his conceiving Christ *in some sense* as absent from believers. Only when he comes will he be 'with' them.

Paul's first letter to the Thessalonians, with its emphasis on the coming of Christ, indicates that heaven is a 'place of absence' for Christ and not simply a state of exaltation. Though believers are 'in Christ' (2:14; 5:18; cf. 4:16), he is also conceived as *absent* from them in heaven so much so that Paul can say that they will be with each other only at his parousia. Christ's future coming, then, implies his current absence from believers. As Tilling notes, when Paul writes that 'the Lord is near' (Phil. 4:5 NIV), whether he is thinking spatially or temporally, 'near' is not 'here'. Paul

> [d]oes not yet live with the Lord in the eschatological sense indicated in these verses. He is not yet 'with the Lord', in the presence of the Lord, in the eschatological sense for which Paul hopes. Christ is absent from the apostle while he lives in the body.[33]

Christ's current bodily absence (2 Cor. 5:6–9)

In 2 Corinthians 5:6–8 Paul reflects on the current location of believers relative to Christ,[34] namely that as long as they are 'at home in the

---

[30] For a defence of this translation see van der Horst 2000: 524.

[31] See the brief survey in Harvey 1992: 329–340.

[32] Campbell (2012: 223) argues that the reference here is to a 'quasi-physical accompaniment with Christ rather than a conceptual or spiritual participation with him'.

[33] Tilling 2012: 163.

[34] In 5:6 and 8 the references to 'Lord' clearly refer to Christ, following as they do the distinct references to God and the Spirit in 5:5.

body', they are 'away from the Lord'.[35] Verse 8 repeats the thought of verse 6 in negative terms so that there is an antithetic parallel between

| While we are at home | in the body | we are away | from the Lord (v. 6b) |
| We would rather be away | from the body | and at home | with the Lord (v. 8). |

Paul's statement in 5:6b provokes an exasperated reaction in many commentators. The language of being 'at home' (*endēmeō*) and 'away' (*ekdēmeō*) suggests that a spatial absence from Christ is in view.[36] But, as Thrall asks, '[h]ow can the Christian living [in Christ] (cf. 5:17) be said to be absent from Christ's "presence"'?[37] Murphy-O'Connor labels the verse 'one of the most problematic statements in the Pauline letters' given that it seems to contradict

> one of the most basic tenets of Pauline theology, namely, that the whole being of believers is infused with the grace of Christ (2 Cor.12:9), which has reconciled them with God (2 Cor.5:19), and which progressively transforms them into the image of Christ (2 Cor.3:18).[38]

Before examining these verses in detail, we need to sketch the context. In a letter where Paul spends considerable time discussing his suffering as an apostle (e.g. 2 Cor. 1:3–11), chapter 5 performs an important role in showing that this suffering is not the ultimate reality. Already Paul has affirmed that although he is outwardly wasting away, inwardly he is continually being renewed (4:16). Paul develops this idea in the present section, by specifying the hope that he has as he faces death. The beginning of chapter 5 (5:1–5) swirls with interpretative complexity. In verse 1 Paul seems to be encouraging the Corinthians in the face of death – the destruction of our earthly bodies[39] – that they can be encouraged by provision of a 'building' from God. This could be referring to some kind of individual or

---

[35] Neither *endēmeō* nor *ekdēmeō* appears anywhere else in the Greek Bible, but their respective meanings of 'being at home or in one's country' and 'leaving one's country or being abroad or in exile' are fairly well attested elsewhere (cf. BDAG 300, 332).
[36] Tilling 2012: 162.
[37] Thrall 1994, 1: 386.
[38] Murphy-O'Connor 1986: 214.
[39] So most commentators.

corporate temporary dwelling before the parousia. However, it is perhaps more likely that Paul is speaking of the resurrection body. As Harris argues, given that the 'earthly tent-house [*oikia*]' of 5:1a refers 'primarily, if not solely' to the physical body, the parallelism would be destroyed if 'the second, antithetical [house; *oikia*] referred to anything other than some form of embodiment'.[40] Further, as he notes, the parallels with the description of the 'spiritual body' in 1 Corinthians 15:44 are strong. Like the body in 1 Corinthians 15:44, the body in 5:1 is envisaged as being of divine origin ('from God'; cf. 1 Cor. 15:40, 48–49), spiritual ('not made with hands'; cf. 1 Cor. 15:44, 46), permanent and indestructible (cf. 1 Cor. 15:42, 52–54), and heavenly (cf. 1 Cor. 15:40, 48–49).[41]

Paul could well be assuming in 5:2–4 a post-mortem bodiless existence for believers (an 'intermediate state') as they wait for the resurrection body.[42] Though they are confident that they will receive their resurrection bodies, this 'intermediate period' would be a period of 'groaning' and 'nakedness' (5:2–3) as they long to be clothed with their resurrection bodies. Paul reminds the Corinthians in 5:5 that it is God himself who has prepared them for this reception of the spiritual body and given the Spirit 'as a pledge'.[43] There is an obvious parallel to Romans 8:11, where Paul points to the Spirit as a reason for confidence that believers' bodies will be raised and where this resurrection (cf. 8:18–22) is expected at the parousia of Christ.

Paul then moves on to discuss how believers are to view life in the body. In response to the starkness of 5:6b ('while we are at home in the body, we are away from the Lord'), a number of attempts are made to 'reconcile' it to Paul's wider theology. So, for example, Murphy-O'Connor argues that the slogan of 5:6b reflects the views of a group within the Corinthian church who devalue bodily existence (cf. 1 Cor. 6:12–20; 15). He argues on the basis of the fact that Paul's language here of *endēmeō* and *ekdēmeō* is unique not only in his own writings but also in the entire Greek Bible. The introductory phrase 'we know that' parallels 1 Corinthians 8:1a and 4, where the same verb is used

[40] Harris 2005: 372.

[41] Though 'we have' (*echōmen*) in v. 1 is a present-tense form, it most likely has a future time-reference. There is no compelling reason to understand Paul as teaching anything different from what he teaches in 1 Cor. 15 – the reception of the resurrection body at the *parousia* of Christ. Gillman (1988: 454) shows that the only shift is 'from the use of more literal, abstract, and anthropological terminology in 1 Cor. 15:50–55 to a rather intricate development of metaphorical language in 2 Cor. 5:1–4'.

[42] Without actually using the term.

[43] Harris 2005: 392.

to introduce the Corinthian slogans and 'expresses only recognition, not acceptance of the sentiments expressed'.[44] Accordingly, Murphy-O'Connor argues that the conjunction *de* that introduces 5:8 is adversative[45] not resumptive[46] and so suggests that 5:8 is a counter-statement to 5:6. That is, in 5:8 Paul reformulates the static opposition (seen in the Greek) of 'in [*en*] the body' and 'away [*apo*] from the Lord' into the dynamic form of 'away [*ek*] from the body' and 'to [*pros*] the Lord'. That is, he introduces 'the idea of motion, which links the two states' and thus 'refutes a dichotomized perception of reality in favour of a unified one'. So, rather than 'a chasm between the present and the eschaton, there is a difference *only of degree*'.[47] Paul then dismisses the slogan as irrelevant in verse 9, where he makes clear that the only thing that matters is pleasing the Lord: 'whether we are at home or away, we make it our aim to please him'.[48]

The main problem with Murphy-O'Connor's proposal is that in 5:6 'we know' parallels 'we are of good courage', which introduces Paul's own view suggesting that the knowledge is not something that Paul is conceding but actually affirming.[49] In other words in 5:6–8 Paul suggests that the confidence that believers have from knowing that they are looking forward to the resurrection body (5:1–5) *and*[50] the knowledge of their present separation from the Lord (5:6) means they can be confident and actually prefer to be away from the body so that they can be with the Lord (5:8). This desire to depart from the body creates a surface contradiction with 5:3 where Paul says that we do not desire to be found in a bodiless state. However, as Ladd points out, is this not 'precisely the kind of psychologically sound tension that a man could express when caught in the grasp of strong ambivalent feelings'?[51] That is, while Paul does not want to be found naked, that is, disembodied, he knows that if he is, it will be better because he will be with the Lord.

In what sense, then, are believers currently 'away from the Lord'? Plummer is typical in arguing in quite general terms. So he argues that

[44] Murphy-O'Connor 1986: 217.
[45] Ibid.
[46] E.g. Furnish 1984: 272; Plummer 1915: 152; Thrall 1994, 1: 389.
[47] Murphy-O'Connor 1986: 218, emphasis added.
[48] Ibid.
[49] Thrall 1994, 1: 386.
[50] The *kai* in 5:6 is conjunctive ('we are of good courage *and* we know'); so Furnish 1984: 253. Other translations ('although', NRSV; 'but', Harris 2005: 394) seem to make the knowledge of our present distance from the Lord a *problem* rather than an *encouragement* in the face of death.
[51] Ladd 1968: 106, quoted in Osei-Bonsu 1986: 94.

Paul 'does not mean that while we are in the body we are absent from the Lord' since 'our union with Him both in life and in death is one of his leading doctrines (4:10, 11; 1 Thess. 5:10)'.[52] Rather, the apostle 'is speaking relatively'. That is, the 'life of faith is less close and intimate than the life of sight and converse'. Or, Barrett comments, 'Paul cannot mean that in this life the Christian is separated from Christ; he has used too often such expressions as "in Christ".' Rather, because Christ reigns in 'heaven, and so long as the Christian lives on earth in this age he cannot be in the full sense with Christ as he will be when he departs'.[53]

Furnish suggests that 'orientation (commitment) is involved here, not location' and so Paul's thought here is not to be compared with that in Philippians 1:23.[54] In the present context Paul is dealing with the question of loyalty and the direction of one's life. In line with this, Furnish argues that in verse 8, rather than the usual translation of *eudokoumen mallon* as something like 'we would prefer' (e.g. NIV), the phrase should be rendered 'we are resolved instead'.[55] Thus Paul is not expressing a desire to die and be with Christ (cf. Phil. 1:23), but rather he expresses his determination not to be orientated to his body but to the Lord instead. The specifics of Furnish's arguments have been answered by a number of commentators.[56] However, as Tilling notes, even if one did accept his rendering of the phrase, 'it is not necessary that one should exclude the notion of the risen Lord's real absence by setting "orientation" against "location"'.[57] Similarly, Thrall is more specific in speaking of a 'spatial' separation, indicating a lack of 'fellowship'.[58]

However, it may be that there is nothing particularly significant in Paul's statement regarding separation from the Lord given that, at least on the surface, Paul's expression does not seem to be unique. This is most clear in the *Testament of Abraham* 15.7, where we have Michael telling Abraham, 'Make disposition of all that you have, for the day has come near in which you will depart [*ekdēmein*] from the body and go to the Lord once for all'.[59] The thought of leaving the body to go to be with God/the gods can be found elsewhere. So, Lindgård lists

[52] Plummer 1915: 150.
[53] Barrett 1973: 158.
[54] Furnish 1984: 303.
[55] Ibid. 273.
[56] Thrall 1994, 1: 390.
[57] Tilling 2012: 161.
[58] Thrall 1994, 1: 386.
[59] Menzies 1896: n.p.

a number of parallels in antiquity including a passage where Seneca comments, 'When the day comes to separate the heavenly from its earthly blend, I shall leave the body here where I found it, and shall of my own volition betake myself to the gods.'[60] Feuillet notes this language resonates with OT ideas of 'sleeping with one's fathers' (e.g. Gen. 15:15) or 'being reunited with one's fathers' or 'one's people'.[61]

Is Paul simply reflecting a contemporary view of the necessity of death to be reunited with God? Paul's parenthesis in 5:7, where he seems to explain what he says in 5:6b, may help us. Paul describes this state of being away from the Lord in terms of what is normally translated 'walking by faith, not by sight' (5:7). There are a number of problems with this translation. First, 'by sight' renders *dia eidous*. Harris is typical in rendering it this way, despite acknowledging that in each of the other NT instances of *eidos* (Luke 3:22; 9:29; John 5:37; 1 Thess. 5:22) it has the meaning 'form' or 'appearance' and denotes the external appearance of something. He argues that perhaps Paul 'has used [*eidos*] in an unusual sense'.[62] As such, he suggests, Paul is contrasting 'seeing with believing'. However, *eidos* everywhere else in the Greek Bible[63] means 'form' or 'appearance'. The Greek text of Numbers 12:8 is sometimes pointed to as an example where *eidos* means 'sight'.[64] Here Moses is described as speaking with the Lord 'mouth to mouth'. This is further qualified as *en eidei* and not *di' ainigmatōn*. Typically this is rendered 'clearly, not in riddles' (NRSV), suggesting that *eidos* pertains to sight. However, *di' ainigmatōn* can be used in context to mean something like 'through a reflection' (cf. 1 Cor. 13:12). Thus the point here may be that Moses speaks to God 'in his real form', not 'in a reflection'. This is relevant for 2 Corinthians 5:8 since although the exact phrase *dia eidous* does not appear anywhere else in the Greek Bible, the comparison made with *di' ainigmatōn* in Numbers 12:8 may suggest that it means something like 'according to form'. The emphasis, then, is on the fact that 'we live

---

[60] Lindgård 2005: 191–192, citing Seneca's *Epistles* 102.24.

[61] Feuillet 1956 : 191.

[62] Harris 2005: 396.

[63] Not simply in the four other NT occurrences that Harris mentions (2005: 396): Gen. 29:17; 32:31–32; 39:6; 41:2–4, 18–19; Exod. 24:10, 17; 26:30; 28:33; Lev. 13:43; Num. 8:4; 9:15–16; 11:7; 12:8; Deut. 21:11; Judg. 13:6; 1 Sam. 16:18; 25:3; 2 Sam. 11:2; 13:1; Esth. 2:2–3, 7; Jdt. 8.7; 11.23; Prov. 7:10; Song 5:15; Job 33:16; 41:10; Wis. 15.4–5; Sir. 23.16; 25.2; 43.1; Isa. 52:14; 53:2–3; Jer. 11:16; 15:3; Lam. 4:8; Ezek. 1:16, 26; Sus. 1.7; (Theodotion) 1.31; Luke 3:22; 9:29; John 5:37; 2 Cor. 5:7; 1 Thess. 5:22.

[64] E.g. BDAG 280.3; Harris 2005: 396.

our lives in the sphere of faith, not in the presence of his visible form'.[65]

Paul's conviction of his desire to be with Christ translates into a desire to please him 'whether we are at home or away' (5:9); that is, whether in the body or not. There is a parallel with what we saw in Philippians 1. Despite the fact that being with Christ would be far better, he is convinced that remaining will be better for the Philippians and for the glory of Christ (Phil. 1:26).

This distinction between faith or physical form fits perfectly with the idea that Christ is *bodily* absent. Believers do not walk in the light of Christ's 'visible form'. Rather, they walk by faith. For Paul, then, being 'in the body' is to be absent from the Lord and it is to 'walk by faith' rather than 'according to the form' of the risen Christ. As long as believers are in this body they are separated from Christ. Their untransformed bodies prevent them from seeing Christ or from being with Christ, *where* he is. In other words it is not *simply* the unredeemed nature of believers' bodies that prevents them from being with Christ. The spatial language of 'being at home' and 'being away' from the Lord indicates that the risen Christ, as an exalted *human being*, with a localizable, discrete body is not currently *here* and so they are away from him.

Exaltation, absence and Christ's human body (Rom. 8:34)

In Romans 8:34 Paul locates Christ Jesus at the right hand of God. Among some of the earliest Christian interpreters Romans 8:34 and other 'right hand' texts created something of a problem.[66] The tendency was to baulk at the seeming literal reference to Christ's somehow being spatially located *with respect to* God. Thus there is a 'noticeable reserve' in the Eastern church to this idea, which, Hengel argues, may explain why it is missing from the Eastern confessions of the third and fourth centuries.[67] Similarly, the motif does not appear frequently in the writings of the Apologists. For Justin, though he quotes Psalm 110:1 frequently, 'the pre-existence of the Son in v. 3 and the indication of the priesthood of the Son in v. 4 were more important than the exaltation to the right hand of God in v. 1'.[68]

---

[65] Thrall 1994, 1: 397.
[66] For a comprehensive survey see Markschies 1993: 252–317.
[67] Hengel 1995: 124.
[68] Ibid. 126.

Hengel suggests that one gains the impression that 'Justin wants to avoid this motif because it demands an interpretation'.[69] Though the tension suggested by what this verse seems to imply regarding the localizability of God and Christ continues to be recognized by early interpreters,[70] there is also a significant strand of interpretation that sits more comfortably with regarding the idea simply as a metaphorical description of the exaltation of Christ.[71]

The reference to Christ at the right hand of God in Romans 8:34 may have more of a *conceptual* than a *local* significance in that it predicates an exalted status more than a location of Christ. It is certainly used elsewhere in the New Testament in this way.[72] However, it is also worth noting that another important issue that early interpreters wrestled with was whether Paul was here conceiving Christ as exalted to the right hand of God by very nature of his eternal sonship or as an exalted *human* being. Cyril argued the former,[73] while others such as Epiphanius of Salamis were clear that when he sat down at the right hand of God he did so as the *incarnate* Christ.[74] So, Augustine in his letter to Consentio is clear that the body of Christ in heaven is a body with 'bones and blood' like his body on earth (PL 33.205.2).

While this verse is not concerned about the nature of Christ's body, there are two aspects to the text that point to the humanity of Christ being in view. First, the description of the exalted Christ as the one who died and was raised maintains the continuity of identity between the historical Jesus and the exalted Christ. Second, at God's right hand Christ is interceding. The same word is used to describe the activity of the Holy Spirit in 8:26. However, in 8:34 the fact that Christ is not described as 'Son' but as 'Christ Jesus' may suggest that his humanity is primarily in view. Further, as I will argue in chapter 10, Paul's argument is being influenced by Isaiah 53 and would suggest that he is thinking of the exalted Christ in human terms analogous to the exalted Servant. Christ, then, is pictured as a human being in an exalted position at the right hand of God.

---

[69] Ibid. 128.

[70] E.g. Basil, *De Spiritu Sanctu* 6.15, who suggests that if we understand the reference to God's right hand in a bodily sense we need to understand him to have a *skaion* (left/negative) side (i.e. Basil seems to be playing on the negative sense of 'left').

[71] Cf. Augustine's Tractate on John 17 (Tract. 111 in PL 35.1925), where he counsels the reader to remove the image of 'bodies' from their mind.

[72] This is especially clear in Acts 2:33 and 5:31.

[73] See Reischl and Rupp 1848–60.

[74] Epiphanius of Salamis, *De Fide* 17.9, cited in Markschies 1993: 280.

Is the right hand of God a *location*? We have already seen the reserve with which many early exegetes treated this passage, though some were happy to see it in quite specific localized terms. So Augustine comments:

> [h]aving risen on the third day . . . he ascended into heaven; it is *to there* (*illuc*) that he raised his body; it is *from there* (*inde*) that he will come to judge the living and the dead; it is *there* (*ibi*) that meanwhile he sits at the right hand of the Father . . . He has ascended into heaven and he is not *here* (*hic*).[75]

Is this simply an example of early Christians operating with mythological categories? Ralph Norman has argued that ancient cosmology was more complex than suggested by the simple 'triple-decker universe' reduction. He notes how certain ancient writers operated with the concept of the 'great outside' which lies *beyond* the ultimate sphere (of the fixed stars) – a kind of 'spatial eschaton'.[76] This was not the 'place' where God dwells, and as such it is 'not the top of a triple-decker universe because it is not properly part of the universe at all'.[77] Nevertheless, though it was seen as *beyond* the material universe, it was still conceived as *spatially extended*. Thus the paradox of the New Testament's affirmation of the risen Christ's possessing a material body but existing in an immaterial heaven led Origen, for example, to conceive of the ascension in *mental* terms.[78] In reaction to Origen's speculation, the fifth ecumenical council denounced the view that the body of the risen Christ was only ethereal.[79] Norman notes how in the ensuing history of interpretation Christians accepted the 'paradox that the human body of Christ has been removed from the universe of space and time, has passed beyond the finite boundary of the cosmos, and is now located nowhere'.[80] As such, he argues that the contention that Christ is at the right hand of God can

---

[75] This citation of Augustine's Sermon 272 is from Norman 2001: 3–15, emphases added. This section is a summary of Norman's article.

[76] Norman 2001: 7, citing Plato *Phaedrus* 247c.

[77] Norman 2001: 7.

[78] Cf. his *On Prayer* 23.2, where he speaks of 'the ascension of the Son to the Father . . . as an ascension of the mind rather than the body' (cited in Farrow 1999: 97).

[79] Concilia Oecumenica (ACO), Canones xv (contra Origenem sive Origenistas), 4.1.249 (Schwartz and Straub 1971: 248–249). The idea that the Lord's body was 'ethereal' or 'spherical' (i.e. perfect according to Stoic philosophy) was specifically condemned.

[80] Norman 2001: 8.

be understood in a way that does not need to be demythologized, precisely because it was always understood in *acosmic* terms.[81]

Norman's analysis is questionable at points,[82] but his general point is sound. The location of Christ at the right hand of God should not be understood in cosmic categories that need to be demythologized. Nevertheless, in describing Christ in his humanity *with* God, Paul is operating in *spatial* and *locational* terms. The risen, exalted, human Christ is not here; he is with God – beyond the realm of this universe. He is not making a point about the *geographical* location of Christ but about his *bodily absence*.

Conclusion

Paul, like every believer, experiences the absence of Christ. He longs for the 'far better' experience of departing and being with Christ (Phil. 1:23–24) or of being 'away from the body and at home with the Lord' (2 Cor. 5:8). When he dies, he will be with Christ in a way that he is not while alive. We have seen that this wish cannot simply be explained by collapsing the experience of time between Paul's death and the parousia so that he simply wakes up at the resurrection. No, Paul's desire needs to be allowed to stand with its full Christological significance. Paul on death envisions himself going to be with Christ, whom he is not with now. His current experience is of being absent from Christ. Thus, though believers are 'in Christ', they are also absent from him.

This absence is further presupposed in Paul's teaching on the parousia. He sees believers currently waiting for Christ from heaven (1 Thess. 1:10). Only when he comes from there will they be fully united with him for ever (1 Thess. 4:17). Christ, then, in heaven is currently absent from believers.

Tilling's conclusion that the future hope of 'being with the Lord' should be understood as being in the Lord's presence rather than *something else* (i.e. possessing a heavenly body) is surely correct. As he notes:

> [t]o speak of Paul's deep travail in light of the painful reality of the 'spatial' absence of the risen Lord is not to dislocate interpretation

---

[81] Ibid. 14, n. 40, notes that while both Copernicus and Kepler reorganized the inner structure of the universe, the *boundary* of the universe was left in place.

[82] See e.g. Farrow 2011: 45–49. He argues that thinking of the ascension in 'acosmological' terms is not sufficiently 'eschatological'. Rather, he suggests that it should be conceived as a 'transformative relocation'.

into a dubious eisegesis of dry theistic theologising, but is rather to look into the passions and pains of the Apostle himself.[83]

In this chapter we have seen how Christ's current absence from believers is a function of this ongoing individual corporeity. Christ's body plays an essential role in his eschatological redemption of believers – it is not an accidental aspect of Paul's theology but a function of his location at God's right hand (Rom. 8:34). For Paul death or the parousia will mean being with Christ. In the intervening time, though, having an individual body that is distinct and distinguishable from the bodies of believers means that Christ is located elsewhere from believers. This other place is at the right hand of the Father (Rom. 8:34) in heaven (e.g. 1 Thess. 1:10). It is only when he comes at his parousia that he will be with them (1 Thess. 4:17). In the meantime, Paul expresses his longing to be with the Christ (Phil. 1:23) from whom he is absent (2 Cor. 5:6–8).

---

[83] Tilling 2012: 162.

Chapter Eight

The location of Christ: the epiphanic presence of Christ

Introduction

In Romans 8 Paul locates Christ simultaneously *in* the believer (v. 10) and at the right hand of God (v. 34). We have seen that the polarity between the presence and absence of Christ is repeated across the New Testament, which has led some interpreters to argue that precise 'conceptual clarity' regarding the exalted Christ may always remain 'elusive'.[1] As a result, interpreters have generally neglected to consider the possibility that these two aspects of the location of the exalted Christ might *mutually* interpret one another. The two are simply held in a straightforward tension or, perhaps more commonly, Christ's *absence* is relativized and simply interpreted in terms of his *presence*. That is, if the believer is 'in Christ' and Christ is in the believer, his heavenly location is understood more as a mode of his ubiquitous presence than any kind of significant absence.

To understand Christ's absence in the light of his presence is not incorrect and indeed recognizes the importance of the presence of Christ. However, too often, the reverse move is not made; that is, to understand the presence of Christ in the light of his absence. This has led to two unfortunate consequences. First, it has resulted in a truncated view of the absence of Christ so that the concept is regarded as of little or no relevance to what the NT says about Christ. Second, once the presence of Christ is used effectively to *relativize* his absence in this way, the latter motif is no longer used to interpret the former. Concerning the first of these consequences, we have already seen the significance of the absence of Christ for understanding the exalted Christ as a human being with a discrete, localizable body. This chapter will address the second consequence. Since the *absence* of Christ is

---

[1] Dunn 1998: 410.

133

significant for what the NT says about the exalted Christ, it is reasonable to assume that it should inform and balance our interpretation of texts that deal with the *presence* of Christ.

In this and the following two chapters we will consider Christ's presence in Paul. At each point we will consciously bring the *absence* of Christ to bear on our interpretation. In practice this will mean specifically thinking of Christ's presence as a *mediated* presence and attending to the nature of the mediation. Christ's absence prevents us from simply collapsing Christ into the medium of his presence – a tendency especially common when considering the Spirit's mediation. Moreover, we will see that Christ's absence actually highlights the depth and *transparency* of the mediation involved. Though Christ is absent, the mediation of his presence is so 'transparent'[2] that the absent Christ himself can operate in the world in 'real time'. He is not merely *represented* in the world, but is himself *active*. Thus, in interpreting Christ's presence in the light of his absence, it is hoped that the clarity which has proved to be so 'elusive' may be more firmly grasped.

At this point I need to make a brief comment on my terminology. I recognize that *presence* itself is a simple term that belies significant underlying complexity. In simple terms it can be defined as 'being in the world'.[3] However, as O'Collins notes, 'presence assumes a multiform diversity';[4] that is,

> [a] seemingly infinite variety of form and intensity characterizes the presences we experience; 'presence' is a radically analogous term and reality. We never face a simple alternative, presence or absence. It is always a question of what kind of presence and what kind of absence, or how someone is present or how someone is absent . . . Given the stunning variety and qualitative differences that characterize human presence, we should be ready to acknowledge an endless variety in the qualitatively different possibilities of divine presence and activity.[5]

In the course of the next three chapters I will not offer a full taxonomy of the presence of Christ but will examine distinct modes of Christ's presence in the world. The following two chapters consider the

---

[2] This concept of 'transparent' mediation has been used in media studies e.g. Benjamin 1999: 223–234.

[3] This working definition is suggested by Marcel 1950: 219.

[4] O'Collins 2009: 349.

[5] Ibid. 342.

particular form of his presence in the form of his *activity*; that is, his interaction and intervention, from two perspectives. Chapter 9 discusses his activity with the emphasis on his intervention on earth. Chapter 10 discusses his activity *in heaven*, where he responds to prayer and intercedes with the Father.

In this chapter we will consider a mode of Christ's presence where the emphasis is placed on him being present to the *senses*. I have termed this mode Christ's 'epiphanic' presence. Though an epiphany is perhaps more strictly a *visual* manifestation, we use it here in the broader sense as referring to any *manifestation* of the exalted Christ directed to the believer's senses so that he or she *experiences* him in some way.[6] In the epiphanic mode of Christ's presence the emphasis is not on Christ as the subject but as the object. Accordingly, in this mode of his presence, Christ is essentially *passive*. This does not mean, as we will see, that his epiphanic presence is weak or ineffectual. Rather, this 'passivity' highlights the fact that his presence is not a direct, unqualified presence but is *mediated*.

Though there are other passages we could consider, in this chapter we will concentrate on one extended section in Paul's second letter to the Corinthians. Second Corinthians 2:4 – 4:12 is part of a larger argument stretching to 7:4,[7] and commentators generally suggest that Paul's main concern is to defend or at least to commend his apostleship. However, Jane Heath notes the frequency of verbs and themes related to sense-perception.[8] Accordingly, she concludes that Paul's main concern in this section (and through to 5:12) is 'to teach people how to perceive Christ'.[9] Correct perception of the manifestation of Christ is essential because it anticipates our own manifestation before Christ's judgment seat on the last day (5:10). Whether or not this theme should wholly replace the idea of Paul's (at least implicit) 'defence' of his apostleship, Heath is certainly correct to see it as dominant to Paul's line of argument. In 2 Corinthians 2:14 – 4:12 we encounter a high density of images relating to the exalted Christ that we can term *epiphanic*. In this section the apostles are described as the 'aroma' of Christ (2:14–16) and the Corinthian church as a 'letter' of Christ (3:3). In 3:18 believers *behold* the glory of the Lord and are

---

[6] With Mitchell (2004: 186), we use this term in a very broad and non-technical sense.
[7] Commentators frequently note the references to Macedonia in 2:13 and 7:5 that bracket the section.
[8] Particularly the use of *phaneroō* (2:14; 3:3; 4:2, 10–11; 5:10).
[9] Heath 2013: 196; cf. Duff 2008: 775.

transformed by his Spirit. In 4:1–6 the combination of *auditory* ('the gospel . . . of Christ', 4:4; 'the word of God', 4:2 NIV) and *visual* imagery (unbelievers are blinded so that they cannot see 'the light of the gospel of the glory of Christ', 4:4) culminates in the striking image of believers seeing the very 'face of Christ'. Finally, in 4:7–12 we have the life of Jesus *manifested* in the bodies of the apostles and at work in the lives of the Corinthians. The language of manifestation (*phaneroō*) and working (*energeō*) underlines something that we will see throughout this section, namely the dynamic, powerful nature of this mode of Christ's presence.

In this section of 2 Corinthians we see that the mediation switches between Paul, the gospel, the Spirit and the Corinthian church themselves. It is not that these different 'entities' simply represent Christ but rather through them the risen Christ himself is encountered and experienced. At each stage we will see that the absence of Christ necessitates a *qualified* presence. As such, Christ cannot be confused with the medium of his presence.

The aroma of Christ (2 Cor. 2:14–17)

The first sensory description of the exalted Christ is not visual but olfactory (smell), where Paul describes himself[10] as the 'aroma' of Christ that brings death to 'those who are perishing' and life to 'those who are being saved' (2:15). He thus 'anticipates in olfactory mode what he goes on to present in visual mode' in 2 Corinthians 4:1–6, where he describes the gospel as veiled 'to those who are perishing', while others see in it the very face of Christ (4:4).[11]

Paul does use visual imagery when, with language evocative of the Roman triumph,[12] he pictures himself being led 'in Christ' by God in triumphal procession as a captive slave (2:14). It is as he is led in this way that 'the fragrance of the knowledge of [Christ]'[13] is made manifest (*phanerounti*) 'everywhere' through him (2:14). As well as being related causally, verses 14 and 15 are in parallel:[14]

[10] It is generally accepted that Paul is employing an epistolary plural here.

[11] Heath 2013: 197.

[12] Harris 2005: 242.

[13] Though 'the knowledge of him' could be a subjective genitive ('the fragrance that comes from knowing him'), e.g. NRSV, it is more likely epexegetic ('the fragrance that is the knowledge about him'; so Kuschnerus 2002: 103. The second genitive 'of him' refers to Christ rather than God given that Christ is mentioned immediately prior to this phrase, which parallels the phrase 'aroma of Christ' in 2:15.

[14] De Oliveira 1990: 21.

Verse 14	Verse 15
The fragrance of the knowledge of him	Aroma of Christ
Through us	We are
Everywhere	Among those who are being saved and those who are perishing

Thus the 'fragrance of the knowledge of [Christ]' spreads 'through us' because 'we are' the 'aroma' of Christ. It spreads 'everywhere'; that is, 'among those who are being saved and those who are perishing'. There then seems to be a ring arrangement between verses 15 and 16, with verse 16 expanding on the nature of the spread of knowledge to these two groups:[15]

A   among those who are being saved
B   and among those who are perishing
B' to one a fragrance from death to death
A' to the other a fragrance from life to life

Therefore, Paul functions as the aroma of Christ in a dual way. To one group he is the fragrance (*osmē*) 'from death to death'; to the other he is the fragrance 'from life to life'. This leads Paul to ask rhetorically, 'who is sufficient for these things' (2:16)? This question implies the difficulty of genuine apostolic ministry – a difficulty that stems from the fact that he does not, like so many, 'peddle' the word of God (2:17). Rather, in sincerity and as one 'from God' he speaks 'in Christ before God' (2:17 NIV).

The Christological shape of this epiphany is emphasized by the organic description of Paul as the aroma of Christ combined with the dynamic image of his speaking 'in Christ'. The resulting knowledge of Christ that is spread like a fragrance leads either to death or to life. Though Christ is absent and hence only present through the medium of his apostle, his presence is not merely a static representation. No, as Paul speaks he does so 'in Christ' and so the aroma of Christ himself is experienced. However, we need to probe more carefully the relationship Paul is presupposing between himself and Christ. To do so we briefly examine the background to Paul's language.

The two words *euōdia* and *osmē* are used together in multiple sacrificial contexts in the OT. This sacrificial use later developed in a

---

[15] As suggested by Kuschnerus (2002: 104).

spiritual or metaphorical direction. So, in the rest of the NT the language is employed in a spiritual sense. For example, in Philippians 4:18, Paul describes the gifts that the church have sent to him as a 'fragrant aroma' (*osmēn euōdias*). And in Ephesians 5:2 Christ's death on the cross is described as a 'a fragrant [*osmēn euōdias*] offering and sacrifice to God'. The use of sacrificial imagery is especially appropriate in our context since it fits the fact that Paul's own life of suffering, in some sense, parallels the sacrificial suffering of Christ.[16]

In 2 Corinthians, then, we see a pattern already present in the Psalms[17] and the Prophets[18] of a spiritualizing of OT sacrificial language.[19] However, the employment of this sacrificial language in a metaphorical way does not mean that it is simply cut off from its original cultic context.[20]

Granted that Paul may be employing this metaphor because of the appropriateness of its sacrificial resonances to his own ministry, we can address the question whether Paul is applying this imagery to his *preaching*, his very *existence* as an apostle or *both*? In other words, what exactly is the point of contact in this form of Christ's epiphanic presence?

McDonald sees Paul in this passage exalting his *preaching* to the extent that it is 'virtually sacramental, mediating the real presence of God to his children'.[21] However, Stegman notes that the use of *phaneroō* here in 2:14 parallels 4:10–11, where it is used by Paul to describe how the 'life of Jesus' is made manifest in Paul's own body.[22] As such, he argues that by using the metaphor of fragrance in 2:14 Paul wants to indicate that '*his very existence* is somehow revelatory of Christ'.[23]

Hafemann argues, however, that

> although the two aspects are distinct and ought not to be collapsed into one another, they nevertheless do interpenetrate and confirm each other as the essential hallmarks of the genuine apostolic calling. The apostolic message is embodied in the life of the apostle

[16] Cf. 4:10–12.
[17] See the discussion in Kuschnerus 2002: 121.
[18] E.g. Jer. 31:11 LXX; Ezek. 20:41.
[19] Kuschnerus 2002: 121.
[20] Ibid.
[21] McDonald 1983: 48–49.
[22] See below.
[23] Stegman 2005: 265, emphasis added.

itself, and in both cases this twofold apostolic activity takes place 'in Christ.'[24]

Hafemann is correct to emphasize the need to hold the two aspects together; nevertheless, the flow of Paul's argument in 2:14–17 puts the *focus* in this section on his preaching. We have seen that his concluding question ('who is sufficient for these things?') in 2:16b is expanded in 2:17 with a discussion of his *preaching* ('we are not, like so many, *peddlers of God's word*, but as men of sincerity, as commissioned by God, in the sight of God *we speak in Christ*'). Peddling or 'adulterating' (*kapēleuontes*) the word of God would seem to be the easy option. To preach sincerely means that one is part of the eschatological procession of verse 14 – and who is sufficient for that? As such, while Paul's suffering as an apostle is clearly here in the context, it is his *preaching* ministry that is the *focus* of that suffering. As Paul preaches 'in Christ', the aroma of Christ is experienced. His preaching is the point of contact with the epiphanic presence of Christ, the 'canvas' on which Christ himself is made manifest.

As the suffering apostle preaches Christ, he functions as an aroma of Christ. As his message is *heard* and the suffering by which he carries his message is *viewed*, then Christ is *manifested* and *known* (v. 16) The reaction of those encountering Paul's preaching is not simply a reaction to Paul as *any human being*, but is a reaction with eschatological consequences (death or life) pointing to the significance of the one whom Paul makes manifest. This image, combined with the fact that Paul speaks 'in Christ', points to the fact that Paul is more than simply a representative or substitute for an absent Christ but that he embodies Christ to such an extent that those who are encountering him are actually encountering a manifestation of Christ with the ensuing eschatological outcome of that encounter. Though Paul has been sent 'by God' (*ek theou*), he speaks 'before God' (*katenanti theou*) and 'in Christ' (*en Christo*, 2:17).[25] Where the suffering, preaching apostle is encountered, Christ, the one 'in whom' he speaks, is made manifest.

Christ is absent and cannot be encountered directly. However, in his apostolic existence and especially in his preaching, Paul mediates Christ's presence. He is not a static image or 'snapshot' of Christ but such a 'powerful place of Christophanic encounter' that he is the very

---

[24] Hafemann 1990: 46–47.
[25] Anticipating 13:5, where Christ speaks in him.

aroma of Christ.[26] The organic image of Paul as an *aroma* is reflected in the dynamic connection between him and Christ – he speaks 'in Christ'. He is not simply a static substitute for an absent Christ but one through whom people encounter the risen Christ – with the consequence of death or life.

The letter of Christ (2 Cor. 3:1–3)

It is not simply the apostle who mediates Christ. His presence is mediated by the Corinthian church, who act as an epistle authored by Christ for the world to read. Paul wants to distinguish himself from others who commended themselves and each other by operating with a system of letters of recommendation. Instead, Paul describes the Corinthians themselves as proof of his apostolic credentials.[27] He describes them as 'our letter' (v. 2), written not on paper but on his own[28] heart and known and read by everyone. However, Paul immediately qualifies this by stating that the Corinthians are shown (*phaneroumenoi*) actually to be a letter of Christ that has been 'delivered' by the apostles (v. 3). The letter is written not with ink but by the 'Spirit of the living God' and not on tablets of stone but on tablets of 'fleshly hearts'.

For our purposes the most pressing question is how to understand the phrase in 3:3, 'you are a letter of Christ'. How are we to understand the relationship between Christ and the church here? How does the church make Christ present? Is 'of Christ' (*Christou*) an authorial genitive or an objective genitive (Christ is the content of the letter)? Is the church sent like a letter from Christ into the world, or does the church display the character of Christ in the world? Until recently most commentators argued for an authorial genitive.[29] As is commonly pointed out, the *content* of the letter is not under question. It is 'the existence of the letter (as constituting Paul's credentials), rather than its contents, that is the point at issue'.[30] In particular, 'Paul wants to avoid giving the impression in v. 2 that either he or the Corinthians actually authored the letter: the letter was "from Christ"'.[31]

---

[26] Mitchell 2004: 189.

[27] Cf. 1 Cor. 9:1–2, where Paul describes the church at Corinth as the seal of his apostleship in the Lord. So Thrall 1994, 1: 222.

[28] On the textual variant, Metzger (1994: 509) argues that the external support for 'our' is 'overwhelming'.

[29] E.g. Furnish 1984: 182; Hays 1993: 127.

[30] Thrall 1994, 1: 224; cf. Furnish 1984: 182.

[31] Harris 2005: 263.

However, a number of German scholars have begun to swing opinion towards the objective genitive. That is, Christ is not the author of the letter but its content. That leaves the question of who is the actual author of the letter and here there is variation. Kuschnerus contends that God is the author. In 2:14 God is the subject of the Christ-revealing event. Similarly, the OT texts that Paul is alluding to (Jer. 38:33 LXX; Ezek. 11:19; 36:26) all refer to God as the one who writes and who gives the Spirit.[32] In contrast, Rabens argues for the Spirit as the author and the content as Christ.[33] Schröter, on the other hand, suggests that Paul himself should be regarded as the author. He has transformed and inscribed Christ on their hearts by turning them to him.[34]

Perhaps the variety of options suggested above simply reflects the complexity of this passage. Or perhaps it reflects the way that Paul views the different agencies of God, Christ, the Spirit and himself interacting. This 'letter of Christ' is in some sense delivered by the apostles and is inscribed by the Spirit of the living God. This leads to apostolic confidence through Christ to God (3:4) and an affirmation that their qualification to minister in this way comes from God (3:5), who has made them ministers of the Spirit. The language of agency permeates this passage. It would seem that this letter involves more than a single author taking a pen and writing. It involves multiple agents – Paul, God, the Spirit and Christ. However, while not denying the involvement of God, the Spirit and Paul himself in the creation of this 'letter', it seems most likely that when the Corinthian church is described as a 'letter of Christ', Christ is viewed as the author. The fact that 'letter of Christ' occurs so soon after 'our letter' (v. 2) suggests that Paul is clarifying or being more specific – the real author is Christ.[35] Further, given that the Corinthians stand in contrast to the 'letters of recommendation' that 'others' possess, it would seem to make sense that Paul is actually appealing to Christ as the author of *his* equivalent letter of recommendation.

It may seem that this is an image that simply highlights the *absence* of Christ. After all, one only sends a letter when one is physically separated from the recipient(s). However, we may have an instance

---

[32] Kuschnerus 2002: 163.

[33] Rabens 2010: 198.

[34] Schröter 1998: 249, n. 56.

[35] Lambrecht 2006: 41. In addition, the immediate context favours the authorial genitive. Paul needed to show that he himself did not write the letter since a letter of recommendation had to come from a third party – so Thrall 1994, 1: 242.

here where considering both the presence and absence of Christ is beneficial. In antiquity letters could also be understood as a mode of personal presence.[36] Certainly it seems that Paul understood his own letters to function in this way. Thus Paul's description of the Corinthian church as 'a letter of Christ' should be understand as the church functioning as a mode of Christ's epiphanic presence in the world. As any letter can effectively communicate the authority and the character of a person so that their voice is *heard* though they themselves are absent, so Christ is here revealed and made manifest through the Corinthian church. The Corinthian church communicates and displays the risen Christ to the world – with the result that Paul himself is vindicated. Though I have categorized this as a mode of Christ's *epiphanic* presence, as we have noted, it also highlights that the one who is being made present is also an agent. We see this more fully developed in the next section, but it is important to note in passing that even here where the dominant note is of Christ being *made* present, his agency is not entirely suppressed. To anticipate our conclusion to section 3, the Christ who is present through different media (Paul; the Corinthians; the Spirit) is not an inert *object* to be presented to the senses but remains an active agent.

The glory of Christ (2 Cor. 3:18)

Second Corinthians 3:18 is a crucial verse with respect to the epiphanic presence of Christ. Here Paul widens the scope of what the Spirit of the Lord does – nothing less than the glorious transformation of believers into the same image of Christ.[37] This transformation occurs as all believers with unveiled faces are enabled to 'see'[38] the glory of Christ. Here the exalted Christ is made manifest in his glory. The believer is able to gaze on the risen and exalted Christ. Naturally, this verse raises questions. Two in particular press themselves forward from this verse. First, what is the exact visual nuance and meaning of the verb *katoptrizō*; and second, exactly what experience does Paul have in view – how does this experience of 'seeing' the glory of the Lord occur?

Generally *katoptrizō* is either understood as 'seeing' or 'reflecting'. The extant usage of the word would suggest the former. In the active

[36] See the examples listed in Klauck 2006: 192–193.
[37] This image (*eikōn*) language points, as we have seen in chapters 5 and 6, to the ongoing humanity of the exalted Christ.
[38] We consider the translation of the verb (*katoptrizō*) below.

form, the meaning 'reflect' is possible (though rare), but in the middle form (as here) this meaning of the word is nowhere attested.[39] Further, the idea of 'transformation through vision' is a widespread concept in Hellenism, Judaism and Christianity – unlike the idea of 'transformation through reflecting'.[40]

On balance, then, we should understand *some kind of* 'seeing'. However, does Paul intend a 'visionary' experience or a more 'mental' beholding? Part of the answer to that question lies in understanding how the 'mirror' aspect of *katoptrizō* contributes to its meaning here. The rareness of the word prior to Paul suggests that the word should be understood to retain something of its original 'mirror' motif.[41] But what exactly does this motif contribute to the meaning of the word? It may be that Paul employs the word because he has a particular 'mirror' in mind; for example, the gospel,[42] Christ himself[43] or believers.[44] The gospel as mirror would imply a 'mental' beholding; Christ as the mirror would suggest some kind of visionary experience; while viewing other believers would involve natural sight. It may be, though, that rather than a particular mirror, Paul primarily employs the word to preserve a notion of mediation[45] and hence 'eschatological reserve'[46] in this vision of the glory of Christ. As such, perhaps the best understanding of the word is that of Rabens, who suggests that we understand *katoptrizō* here as 'contemplation' – an idea that encompasses *both* visual and mental beholding.[47] Not only does this idea have parallels in Jewish literature,[48] but for Rabens it 'is a welcome *via media*' between the dominant interpretations of the word. Following Hafemann and others Rabens thus suggests that 'beholding the glory of the Lord' takes place '*for one thing*, through the existential confrontation that is brought about by the preaching of the gospel of Jesus Christ'.[49]

A believer, then, does not gaze *directly* on the exalted Christ, but through the mediation of the gospel, he or she can truly behold the

---

[39] Cf. BDAG 535: *katoptrizō*. This verb is a hapax in both the NT and LXX.

[40] See Heath 2013: 160–161.

[41] See the references and discussion in Lambrecht 1983a: 248–249.

[42] Cf. Back (2002: 135–136), who notes the parallel between 3:18 and 4:4.

[43] Thrall 1994, 1: 384.

[44] Duff 2008: 773–774.

[45] Though the verb *katoptrizō* is not used in 1 Cor. 13:12, in this verse the notion of seeing via a mirror implies indirectness ('dimly').

[46] As Fee (1994: 317) notes, 'indirectly' does not mean in a distorted way but in contrast to eschatologically seeing the Lord face to face.

[47] Rabens 2010: 184.

[48] See ibid. 187–189 for a survey.

[49] Ibid. 190, emphasis added.

glory of the Lord and be transformed into the same image as the exalted Christ (3:18). Though the mirror language (*katoptrizō*) suggests the *mediated* nature of this vision of Christ, we should not downplay its power. Through this epiphany of Christ in the gospel, nothing less occurs than transformation of the believer from 'glory to glory'.[50]

Importantly, this transformation occurs *apo kyriou pneumatos*. This unusual phrase[51] probably means 'the Lord, the Spirit'[52] or 'the Lord who is the Spirit'.[53] This fits with the context of 3:17, where the agency of the Spirit is stressed. He is the agent of transformation and this Spirit is identified as the Lord. As in 3:17, Paul is not identifying the Spirit and *Christ*. Rather, he is assuming their shared status as 'Lord' (cf. 3:17c). The Spirit who is Lord thus enables transformation of the believer as she contemplates Christ, who is also Lord. Understanding the Spirit as Lord in this way highlights the ability of the Spirit to *mediate* Christ. Though not *identified* with Christ, in sharing the same status as 'Lord', the Spirit is a uniquely appropriate agent of mediation.

Thus the epiphanic presence of Christ is not simply a static contemplation of the character of Christ as one might view a picture in a book. No, as Christ is contemplatively encountered in the gospel his presence effects a glorious transformation in the life of the believer through the mediation of the Spirit with whom he shares the divine status of Lord.

The face of Christ (2 Cor. 4:1–6)

Perhaps the most dramatic image of the epiphanic presence of Christ occurs in 2 Corinthians 4:1–6, where Paul describes how through the gospel the very *face* of Christ is 'seen', thus revealing the glory of God. Here we have the concept of the epiphanic presence of Christ in its most focused form. The very face of the Christ who is absent can, *in some sense*, be grasped by the believer. This is obviously not a naked visual experience where Christ is physically regarded but a mediated epiphanic experience. Nevertheless, we will see that the mediated and non-physical mode of Christ's presence does not detract from the power of the experience in view.

---

[50] Most likely this simply refers to the transformation of believers from 'one degree of glory to a greater degree' (Lambrecht 2009: 145–146).

[51] See Thrall 1994, 1: 287.

[52] Barrett 1973: 110, 126.

[53] Martin 1986: 57.

Paul starts this section with 'therefore' (*dia touto*), indicating that Paul is likely building on what he has just said as do the strong verbal parallels with both 2:14 – 3:6[54] and 3:7–18.[55] Having reached the climactic statement of 3:18, it is significant that as Paul turns to describe *his own* ministry, he focuses on the proclamation of the truth of God's word in the gospel. Paul understands the transforming contemplation of the glory of Christ (cf. 3:18) to come through the gospel that he proclaims. Believers gaze upon Christ as he is made present in the gospel.

Since Paul has received this ministry as a recipient of God's mercy,[56] he does not 'lose heart' (4:1). In contrast (v. 2), he has renounced 'underhanded and disgraceful ways'.[57] He expands this with two phrases that relate to the execution of his ministry. He has neither acted in cunning nor tampered with God's word.[58] Rather, by an 'open statement [*phanerōsis*] of the truth' he commends himself to the conscience of every person 'in the sight of God' the ultimate judge. Here we have the existential impact of the gospel. As the truth of God's word is manifested, the consciences of human beings are confronted (concerning Paul's genuineness). But this confrontation is not merely between Paul and his hearers – it happens 'in the sight of God' (4:2) . This echoes the idea we have already seen that Paul speaks 'in the sight of God' and 'in Christ' (2:17) and with this preaching comes the life-bringing knowledge of Christ (2:14, 16). But this preaching also brings death (2:16) and in 4:3–4 Paul returns to this theme. If his gospel is veiled, it is veiled among those who are perishing due to the agency of the god of this age, namely Satan.[59] He has blinded the minds of unbelievers so that they are prevented from seeing (*augasai*) the light of the gospel (4:4).

Regarding the imagery and the context, two things are particularly important to note. First, Paul applies *visual* language to the *hearing* of the gospel. The gospel is *veiled* because unbelievers' minds are *blinded* so they cannot *see* (with their minds) *the light* of the gospel. Paul mixes his sensory imagery. This suggests that to understand 3:18 as referring to 'hearing' the gospel does not *necessarily* simply reveal

---

[54] See Lambrecht 1983b: 349.

[55] See Harris 2005: 320.

[56] Harris 2005: 323.

[57] So ibid. 324.

[58] Does this refer to the gospel or the OT Scriptures? On balance the mention of gospel in the following verses (Thrall 1994, 1: 301) and the parallel in 2:17 between 'the word of God' and 'we speak in Christ' suggest that the gospel is in view.

[59] Thus nearly every modern commentator.

the interpreter's 'ecclesial allegiances'.[60] Second, what is seen is the light of the gospel of the glory of Christ, who is the image of God (*ton phōtismon tou euangeliou tēs doxēs tou Christou, hos estin eikōn tou theou*).[61] There is general agreement concerning the relationships between the genitives in this construction. The first genitive (*euangeliou*, 'of the gospel') is a genitive of origin and represents the logical subject of the light; that is, the light goes forth from the gospel.[62] 'Glory' (*tēs doxēs*) is a genitive of content; that is, glory is the form or substance of the light[63] and it belongs to Christ (*tou Christou*).[64] Christ is here described as the 'image of God' (*eikōn tou theou*) – a description that, wherever its exact origin,[65] seems to point to the risen Christ in *human* and hence visible form. The gospel, then, manifests the exalted Christ who, in turn, is the image of God.

The medium of this revelation is *the gospel*. Here is the point of interface between the believer and the exalted Christ. Though this presence of Christ in the hearing of the gospel is a mediated event, Paul can compare this event to God's act of creation. Specifically, God's activity at creation of bringing light out of darkness is compared to his activity in illuminating (*elampsen*) our hearts so that we have the *light* of the knowledge of the glory of God 'in the face of Christ' (v. 6). Though there is debate concerning the exact scriptural allusion that Paul is making when he states that 'God is the one who said: "Light will shine out of darkness"' (v. 6), the allusion to creation is unmistakable.[66] Salvation is the work of the creator God and even the activity of the 'god of this age' cannot stand in his way.

That this work of God centres on the gospel is made clear as we examine the parallels between verses 4 and 6:[67]

Verse 4	Verse 6
The god of this world	God, who said, 'Let light shine out of darkness,'
has blinded	has shone
the minds of the unbelievers	in our hearts

---

[60] Heath 2013: 174.
[61] See Harris 2005: 330 for a brief discussion on the nature of these genitives.
[62] So Klauck 1987: 284.
[63] Ibid.
[64] Ibid.
[65] See ibid. 284–286 and Thrall 1994, 1: 309–310.
[66] Paul may be alluding to Gen. 1:3–4 and/or Isa. 9:2.
[67] De Oliveira 1990: 108.

to keep them from seeing the light	to give the light
of the gospel of the glory of Christ, who is the image of God.	of the knowledge of the glory of God in the face of Jesus Christ

In verse 6, then, 'the knowledge of the glory' parallels 'the gospel of the glory' in verse 4, with both following a reference to 'light'. This suggests that 'of the knowledge', like 'of the gospel', is a genitive of origin[68] and that 'the knowledge that produces illumination is nothing other than the knowledge of the gospel'.[69] This knowledge is defined by another chain of genitives. It is a knowledge of the glory[70] of God[71] in the face of Christ mediated through the gospel.

We see here the particular importance of the epiphanic presence of Christ. Christ as the 'icon' of God is the revelation of God in human form. The knowledge of God is revealed in the face of Christ. Thus with Christ removed from the earth the availability of this revelation seems compromised. However, through the gospel and the illuminating work of God in the heart, Christ is made manifest, his face can be comprehended, the icon of God grasped and the knowledge of the glory of God attained. The use of *katoptrizō* in 3:18 introduces an idea of mediation (but not distortion) to this encounter and the internal location ('in our hearts', 4:6) of this encounter underlines the bodily absence of Christ. However, we must not downplay the reality of the encounter. As in 3:18, where the believer is transformed 'from glory to glory', here this encounter with the risen Christ involves nothing less than God's work of recreation. In the gospel and by the Spirit the believer can encounter the risen Lord Jesus and experiences the same form of glorious divine power that Paul did on the Damascus Road.[72]

The life of Jesus (2 Cor. 4:7–12)

Though commentators usually consider 2:14 – 4:6 as a unit, for our purposes we will continue into the next section as we encounter

[68] So Harris 2005: 335.
[69] Ibid.
[70] An objective genitive.
[71] A possessive genitive.
[72] There is a strong possibility that Paul is comparing this epiphanic experience of Christ to his own conversion. See Thrall 1994, 1: 316.

another important image concerning the risen Christ. In 2 Corinthians 4:10 Paul states that as an apostle he is permanently carrying around the death of Jesus so that the life of Jesus may also be manifested in his body.

The suffering apostle *in himself* manifests the risen Lord. He is the very appearance of the incarnate Christ after his ascension.

Paul begins this section by referring back to 'this treasure' (v. 7) that 'we' have in our hearts – probably referring to the gospel itself.[73] In contrast to the treasure of the gospel, the containers, God's ministers, are 'jars of clay',[74] so that the glory goes only to God. Paul expands on how this embodied revelation takes place with a series of antitheses (vv. 8–9) that stress both the frailty of the vessel and the power of God. In each case the second element 'does not indicate a mere mitigation of the hardship; rather, it points to an actual divine deliverance; not simply a change of outlook on Paul's part, but God's intervention'.[75] Verses 10 and 11 then provide a 'christological inter-pretation' of the experiences described in verses 8–9.[76] These two verses are broadly parallel, both having a 'death-bearing' leading to a manifestation of the life of Jesus.

The parallelism[77] can be observed if we set the verses out as follows:

Verse 10	Verse 11
[We are]	For we who live are
always	always
carrying in the body the death of Jesus,	being given over to death for Jesus' sake,
so that the life of Jesus	so that the life of Jesus
may also be manifested	also may be manifested
in our bodies.	in our mortal flesh.

Specifically, in verse 10 the death-bearing is a continual 'carrying' of the 'death of Jesus' (*tēn nekrōsin tou Iēsou*)[78] in the body in order to

---

[73] So Harris 2005: 339 and Thrall 1994, 1: 321.

[74] The force of this metaphor is debated but Fitzgerald (1988: 167) is probably right to understand these 'earthen vessels' as 'the disposable bottles of antiquity, as in-expensive as they were fragile'.

[75] Harris 2005: 342.

[76] Kuschnerus 2002: 254.

[77] Ibid. 259.

[78] The Greek word *nekrōsis* is generally either understood as the 'process of dying' or the 'state of death' – both of which appear to be potential meanings (see BDAG 668).

'manifest' (*phaneroō*) the life of Jesus in the body. Verse 11 is linked with a 'for' (*gar*), suggesting it is an expansion of verse 10. Here the subject is identified as 'we who are living' and the carrying of the death of Jesus is more specifically described as being 'handed over to death for the sake of Jesus'. The reference to the manifestation of the life of Jesus remains the same but the location of this manifestation is changed from 'our body' to 'our mortal flesh'. Verse 12 serves as a summary of this argument but comes as a slight surprise.[79] Here Paul uses the same life–death parallelism but locates the apostles on the side of death ('so death is at work in us') and the Corinthians on the side of life ('but life in you').

Two issues particularly concern us. First, the meaning of 'the life of Jesus', and second, the specific way in which Paul relates to Jesus so that he can manifest this life in his body (v. 10) or mortal flesh (v. 11). On the first question debate turns on whether the earthly life of Jesus or his resurrection life is in view. At first glance the use of the name 'Jesus' and the parallel with 'the death of Jesus' suggest that the earthly life is in view. However, the pattern of death followed by life suggests the life of the resurrected Christ is intended.[80] Further, not only does Paul have no problem referring to the risen Christ by the name 'Jesus' (cf. esp. 1 Thess. 1:10); this life of Jesus is related to the power of God (4:7) that preserves Paul's body and spirit. This context of divine power active in the life of the treasure-holding vessel suggests that we should understand the 'life of Jesus' as a manifestation of divine power. Specifically, that 'it is God's power, taking shape in the form it took in the resurrection of Jesus, i.e. rescue from death, or its equivalent'.[81] Paul is happy to connect the resurrection life of Jesus with the power of God elsewhere (see esp. 2 Cor. 13:4; cf. Phil. 3:10). Stegman is more specific and argues that not only can the 'life of Jesus' be regarded as a form of the power of God, but also that it is 'an apt description of the transforming agency of the Spirit in 3:18'.[82]

The Spirit is not frequently mentioned in this particular section of 2 Corinthians. However, two very important texts in the context link

---

It may be unwise to build too much on the particular nuance of this word especially given that in 4:12 when Paul summarizes his argument he uses the more common word for 'death' (*thanatos*).

[79] Collange 1972: 159.
[80] Lim 2009: 112.
[81] Thrall 1994, 1: 335. Also Lim 2009: 112; Harris 2005: 347; Stegman 2005: 152; Furnish 1984: 256; Barrett 1973: 140.
[82] Stegman 2005: 251.

the Spirit and life. First, in 3:6 the Spirit is specifically identified as the one who gives life. Second, in 5:4 Paul refers to the time when death will ultimately be defeated by life and that God has prepared us for this by giving his Spirit as a guarantee (5:5). Here the Spirit is specifically tied to resurrection life. 'Paul's affirmation concerning the *all-surpassing power* that is from God, therefore, has an important *pneumatological substratum*.'[83] More broadly in Paul, we have this strong connection between the Spirit and life (e.g. Rom. 8:10; cf. 8:2, 6; 1 Cor. 15:45; Gal. 6:8). However, if this 'life of Jesus' is a pneumatic mode of divine power, it is Christologically shaped. It is not divine power in the abstract but the 'life of Jesus' mediated by the Spirit. Here we have the closest possible association between Christ and the Spirit. As such, the depth of the Spirit's mediation of Christ means that as the Spirit operates on the believer's body that body becomes the location of the epiphanic presence of Christ. The very life of Jesus is manifested in and at work in the body of the believer (vv. 11–12). Here we see clearly that the epiphanic presence of Christ has a dynamic effect and is not merely the presentation of an 'idea'.

Understanding the 'life of Jesus' in Paul's body as the resurrection power of God mediated by the Spirit leads us to my second question concerning the relationship between Paul and the risen Christ. Suggestions have included understanding the relationship to be one of 'imitation',[84] 'analogy'[85] or even 'realistic mystical participation'.[86] More recently, Jane Heath has suggested that Paul is portraying himself as an icon of Christ.[87] Though the specific *eikōn* language is not present in this section, it would seem that this is 'the point at which that [*eikōn*] of 3:18 and 4:4 becomes available to viewers at the level of shared sense perception'. Specifically, there is 'visual continuity between the images of Christ and Paul in their shared anthropological shape'.[88] This idea has parallels across his letters, in his call for his readers to imitate him as he imitates Christ (e.g. 1 Cor. 11:1) and where he 'emphasises the Christological character of his own role in encountering the community (1 Cor.2:1–5; 2 Cor.13:3–4)'.[89] It also fits with Paul's portrayal of himself earlier in this section as the 'aroma' of Christ.

---

83 Gräbe 2000: 251, emphases original.
84 Discussed as a possibility in Proudfoot 1963: 140–160.
85 Thrall 1994, 1: 332.
86 To summarize Schweitzer 1998: 17.
87 Heath 2008: 271–284.
88 Ibid. 275.
89 Ibid.

Heath argues that understanding Paul as an icon of Christ causes us to focus on different points than those normally raised in scholarly discussion on this passage, which focuses on questions of 'analogy', 'participation' and 'identity'. Particularly important is the fact that rather than focusing on the nature of the union between Christ and Paul (analogy vs. substantial), her approach raises questions concerning the generation of the image (thetic vs. substantial). The key concern is whether or not God has generated this image – a concern reflected in Paul's words 'to show that the surpassing power belongs to God and not to us' (v. 7b) and the divine passives 'being given over' and 'made manifest' (v. 11).[90]

Heath's presentation highlights a key aspect of this text. However, I have suggested that Paul has *already* 'made' the *eikōn* of 3:18 and 4:4 'visible' in the gospel. As such we need to consider the relationship of *Paul* as epiphanic medium to the *gospel* as epiphanic medium. Mitchell notes the fact that the 'epiphany currently on display in [Paul's] body actually signals the resurrection epiphany to come'.[91] As such:

it is precisely here that we can see how the visual and the verbal clearly come together in the Pauline gospel, for these two epiphanic events (death, life) correspond precisely with the two main episodes of narrative proclamation about Jesus which Paul calls 'the gospel'. The gospel that Paul orally proclaimed to the Corinthians, and all others he encountered, had a simultaneous visual counterpart in Paul's own physical self as *participating in and replicating* the dying ('co-crucifixion') and, by the logic of replication of the narrative, the promise of living ('co-resurrection') in the gospel story of Jesus.[92]

Mitchell further notes how this idea was later taken up in 2 Timothy 1:9–10. There Paul makes a parallel between 'the appearing [*epiphaneia*] of our Saviour Christ Jesus' and 'the gospel'.[93] As such, there is a 'clear parallelism and indeed an identification between the Christophany in the flesh of Jesus and that to be found in the apostolic teaching of Paul'.[94]

[90] Ibid. 282–283.
[91] Mitchell 2004: 190.
[92] Ibid. 190–191, emphasis added.
[93] Ibid. 200.
[94] Ibid. 200–201.

Thus it would seem that Paul 'saw himself as a one-man multi-media presentation of the gospel of Christ crucified' and that the 'message and the messenger were indivisibly united in representing to the audience an aural–visual icon of Christ crucified, which is the gospel'.[95] Thus the oral gospel had a visual counterpart in 'Paul's own physical self as participating in and replicating the dying ("co-crucifixion") and, by the logic of replication of the narrative, the promise of living ("co-resurrection") in the gospel story of Jesus'.[96]

In the description of Paul as 'aroma of Christ' we saw that the knowledge available through Paul was a result of his 'sincere' preaching of the word of God 'in Christ' (2:17). Paul, as a suffering preacher of the true gospel, brings death and life as Christ is encountered. The same idea is here in 4:10–12. As Paul suffers in preaching the gospel, the 'life of Jesus' is mediated by the Spirit to his (believing) hearers. As with the deep transformation in 3:18, this encounter with Jesus has profound effects, operating (*energeitai*) as it does at the level of their 'mortal bodies'.

Conclusion

What I have termed the *epiphanic* presence of Christ is the mediated presence of the absent Christ to the senses of believers. In this epiphanic mode of his presence Christ is portrayed as essentially passive. He does not act as the subject of his presence but is *made present* through the person of Paul and through the Spirit-carried preaching of his gospel. He is the object rather than subject of his presence. However, this objectivity does not mean that this is an inert mode of Christ's presence. Believers encounter him in a mediated but powerful way. The power of this encounter is revealed in the *effects* of this presence as believers come to know Christ (2:14), are 'known and read' by all (3:2), are transformed from glory to glory (3:18), experience God's recreating light (4:6) and have the Spirit-formed life of Jesus work even in their mortal bodies (4:11).

Considering Christ's epiphanic presence and his absence together helps us conceptualize both more clearly. Though Christ is absent, his influence is not removed from the world. His epiphanic presence has powerful epistemological, transformative and eschatological (death or life) effects in the world. In this section we have seen that even in

---

[95] Ibid. 189.
[96] Ibid.

the present the believer can encounter and experience the risen Lord in the most profoundly transforming way. However, though this mode of Christ's presence is so significant it does not override his absence. It is a mediated presence and though Christ himself is involved in the mediation (e.g. Paul speaks 'in Christ'; the Corinthians are a letter authored by Christ; the Spirit is the Spirit of the Lord), in this mode Christ's *agency* is not stressed. The dominant note is that Christ is experienced as an object of perception rather than as a subject of operation.

The different entities involved in the mediation of Christ's presence point to the complexity involved in this mode of his presence. Paul does not randomly switch between himself, the Spirit and the gospel. Rather, we have seen that the gospel and the apostle (and by analogy the Corinthian church) provide the external canvas upon which Christ is displayed. As the gospel is heard, Christ's glory and 'face' are seen (3:18; 4:4–6). As the apostle is heard preaching and seen suffering, the aroma of Christ is smelt (2:14–17) and the 'life of Jesus' encountered (4:7–12). This latter encounter, though, brings the role of the Spirit into focus. It is the Spirit who provides the 'depth' to this mode of Christ's presence. Believers do not simply encounter Christ as a cinema-goer observes a screen or a reader engages a text. Rather, the Spirit, who shares Christ's divine status as 'Lord', enables the epiphanic presence of Christ to penetrate to the very depth of the recipient's being (3:18; 4:10–11; cf. 4:2).

Chapter Nine

The activity of the exalted Christ on earth

Introduction: Christ as agent

In this chapter and the next we will examine Christ's presence with a slightly different emphasis. In contrast to his epiphanic presence, where Christ is powerfully but essentially passively portrayed to the senses, here Christ acts as an active agent.

Perhaps the most significant activity the exalted Christ undertakes is 'sitting' at God's right hand, since this indicates that his work of redemption is complete. As Hebrews puts it, 'when Christ had offered for all time a single sacrifice for sins, he sat down at the right hand of God . . . For by a single offering he has perfected for all time those who are being sanctified' (10:12–14). However, in this chapter and the next we will see that though his work of redemption is complete, the exalted Christ is still working to ensure that the gospel progresses and that Christians remain faithful.

In this chapter we will look at descriptions of Christ's activity that focus on its effect on earth. In the following chapter we look at where Christ is portrayed as acting from heaven. Although this is a slightly artificial distinction, it will bring to the surface important Christological implications, as we will see.

Christ and the progress of the gospel

In chapter 2 we saw how Beverly Gaventa helpfully observes Luke's motif of 'reidentification', where a character is introduced and then some aspect of his or her identity is clarified or reconfigured (e.g. Zacchaeus goes from being a 'chief tax collector' [Luke 19:2] to a 'son of Abraham' [19:9]). Gaventa shows that Jesus also undergoes this process of identity clarification. One of the categories she examines is that of Jesus as 'departed'. Acts opens with Jesus' ascension and so departure (1:9–11), and later Peter preaches that Jesus must remain in heaven until 'the time for restoring all things' (3:21). However,

Gaventa argues that this idea of Jesus as 'departed' is reconfigured in the text of Acts so that

> Jesus' departure does not mean that he is disconnected from or uninvolved with the story that follows. On multiple occasions, Luke communicates that Jesus is shaping, directing, and sustaining the witness. Furthermore, Jesus' various actions in the story provide a framework for understanding the witness of the apostles as Jesus' work rather than their own. That is, the apostles do not so much substitute for an absent Jesus as they exemplify his present, on-going activity. Indeed the terminology of 'absence' and 'presence' is somewhat misleading. When Luke says that Jesus is at God's right hand, he surely does not mean (as some commentators do) that Jesus cannot also be present among human beings.[1]

Gaventa argues that Acts 1:1 is to be taken at face value; that is, the Gospel describes the things that Jesus *began* to do and teach, and so Acts describes his ongoing activity.[2] Gaventa points out that arguably the most significant event in Acts, the outpouring of the Holy Spirit at Pentecost, is an activity of the risen Lord Jesus. Having been 'exalted at the right hand of God, and having received from the Father the promise of the Holy Spirit, *he* has poured out' what the crowd in Acts 2 have witnessed (2:33).[3] Gaventa argues that 'Jesus' ascension does not mean his absence; it simply means that his presence is no longer constrained by place and time'.[4]

We will see that Gaventa is correct to argue that Jesus' departure and absence do not prevent his involvement in the ongoing life of the churches or the mission of the gospel. However, at the same time we will see that his activity always remains activity *from* heaven or *through* agents (the Holy Spirit or the apostles). And so, although he *is* active, he remains absent. Or as Walton puts it,

> there is evidently a tension within Acts between the physical absence of Jesus from earth following his ascension, including statements about him as a figure of the past in evangelistic speeches, and Luke's presentation of the exalted Jesus as now *active from heaven* within the narrative.[5]

---

[1] Gaventa 2008: 161–162.
[2] Ibid. 163.
[3] Ibid. 162.
[4] Ibid. 163.
[5] Walton 2016: 124, emphasis original.

What Acts underlines for us is the ongoing involvement of Christ in the mission of the gospel as it progresses to the ends of the earth (1:8). As a focus, we will consider the apostle Paul in both Acts and his letters.

Christ appears to Paul

Acts recounts Saul's conversion three times and the issue of the identity of the exalted Christ is the initial focus of Paul's encounter with him. In response to the light from heaven (9:3; 22:6; 26:13) and the question 'Saul, why are you persecuting me?' (9:4; 22:7; 26:14), Saul asks 'who are you, Lord?' (9:5; 22:8; 26:15). The answer is simply 'Jesus, whom you are persecuting' (9:5; 22:8; 26:15).[6] The exalted Lord who speaks from heaven is none other than Jesus. Though he is absent in heaven he remains able to intervene on earth – appearing in a vision to Saul. He also appears to Ananias 'in a vision' (9:10), charging him to commission Saul as 'a chosen instrument of mine to carry my name before the Gentiles and kings and the children of Israel' (9:15). Paul later reflects on this commission by telling the crowd in Pisidian Antioch that Christ commanded him, 'I have made you a light for the Gentiles, that you may bring salvation to the ends of the earth' (13:47).

The Damascus Road is not the only time the exalted Christ appears to Paul. In chapter 22 as he recounts his conversion to the crowd in Jerusalem, he describes how, following his encounter with Ananias, he returned to Jerusalem to pray in the temple and fell into a 'trance' (*ekstasis*, 22:17). As he did so, Christ[7] appeared to him and told him to leave Jerusalem since his testimony would not be accepted (22:18) and that he would send him 'far away to the Gentiles' (22:21). Similarly, in Corinth, the Lord[8] encourages Paul by telling him, 'Do not be afraid, but go on speaking and do not be silent, for I am with you, and no one will attack you to harm you, for I have many in this city who are my people' (18:9–10).[9] Further, in chapter 23 as Paul is imprisoned in Jerusalem, Luke tells us that 'the Lord *stood by him and said*, "Take courage, for as you have testified to the facts about me in

---

[6] Jesus of Nazareth in 22:8.

[7] Paul addresses him as 'Lord' in v. 19. Clearly it is the risen Christ, as Paul goes on to say, 'I beat those who believed in you'.

[8] Walton 2016: 140, n. 69: that the Lord here is Jesus is 'suggested by the immediately preceding use, which speaks of believing "in the Lord" (18:8), a verb normally used in Acts with Jesus as object (when it has an object) (11:17; 16:31; 19:4)'.

[9] The implication being that the Lord has 'many people' who will come to believe in him if Paul continues his ministry.

Jerusalem, so you must testify also in Rome"' (23:11). Presumably this is another vision or a dream (Luke tells us this happened at night).

Christ works through Paul

Acts

Paul, then, is an 'instrument' (9:15) or medium of the risen Christ in Christ's ongoing activity. The beginning of chapter 14 describes Paul and Barnabas in Iconium, where 'they remained for a long time, speaking boldly for the Lord' (14:3). Luke immediately qualifies the reference to the Lord by adding 'who bore witness to the word of his grace, granting signs and wonders to be done by their hands'. That is, it is the Lord himself who 'bore witness' and the Lord who granted 'signs and wonders to be done'. However, he does so through Paul and Barnabas: the signs and wonders that Christ grants are 'done by their hands'.

In chapter 26, in his speech to Agrippa, Paul at one point summarizes the message of 'the prophets and Moses' as 'the Christ must suffer and that, by being the first to rise from the dead, *he would proclaim* light both to our people and to the Gentiles' (26:22–23). Gaventa labels this the 'most important (and probably the most overlooked) assertion about Jesus' activity in Acts'.[10] She observes that it 'points back to the words of Simeon at the beginning of Luke's Gospel: Jesus' birth means light for the Gentiles and glory for Israel (Luke 2:32)'.[11] However, she goes further and states that the 'risen Messiah is the one who preaches light'; that is, the 'preacher of light is *not Paul but Jesus himself*'.[12]

While it is true that Christ is presented as the agent of proclamation, it is not correct to say *in an absolute sense* that the preacher is *not* Paul *but* Jesus. Rather, as with 14:3, the dynamic is Christ speaking *through* Paul. Luke is showing us here that the 'mission is first and foremost the Lord's', but the risen Lord is continuing 'to work *through* his disciples to fulfil his saving plan'.[13]

Paul in his letters

We see the same dynamic in Paul's own reflection in his letters. He clearly understands his apostolic commissioning to be the result of the activity of the risen Lord. Fundamentally, Christ has made him 'his own' (Phil. 3:12). The very description 'an apostle of Christ'

[10] Gaventa 2008: 163.
[11] Ibid.
[12] Ibid., emphasis added.
[13] Peterson 2009: 672, emphasis added.

underlines that the exalted Christ has commissioned him (1 Cor. 1:1; 2 Cor. 1:1; Eph. 1:1; Col. 1:1; 1 Tim. 1:1; 2 Tim. 1:1; Titus 1:1). As such, his apostleship is 'not from men nor through man, but through Jesus Christ' (Gal. 1:1; cf. Rom. 1:5; 1 Cor. 1:17). He also clearly understands Christ's ongoing involvement in his work. So in Colossians 1:28 he reflects on his task of proclaiming Christ so that he might present 'everyone mature in Christ'. He then adds to this aim that he toils 'struggling with all his energy that he powerfully works within me' (1:29).[14] Paul works enabled and strengthened by the Lord Jesus. As Christ appears to Paul in Acts 23:11, Paul himself reflects that 'the Lord stood by me and strengthened me, so that through me the message might be fully proclaimed and all the Gentiles might hear it' (2 Tim. 4:17).

However, it is in Romans 15:18–19 that Paul reflects most clearly on the work of Christ in his own ministry. As Paul begins to draw his letter to the church at Rome to a close, he returns to many of the themes with which he started the letter, including the nature of his relationship with the church (cf. 1:11–15) – a church he has not founded but to which, nevertheless, he has written quite boldly (15:15). Paul's 'right' to write in this way stems, he argues, from his God-given role as a 'minister' (*leitourgos*) of Christ Jesus to the Gentiles (v. 16). This term, *leitourgos*, is sufficiently flexible that its precise nuance is hard to determine, though some kind of cultic aspect seems to be presupposed given the immediate context where Paul describes the nature of his role in priestly terms. He serves the gospel of God as a priest (*hierougounta*) so that the offering of the Gentiles might be acceptable, sanctified in the Holy Spirit (15:16). Paul can therefore boast in Christ Jesus of 'my work for God' (15:17). Paul can boast in this way, because he would not dare to speak of anything except what Christ has worked (*kateirgasato*) through him for the obedience of the Gentiles.

Paul expands on the nature of this work of Christ through him in a number of qualifying phrases: 'by word and deed', 'by the power of signs and wonders', 'by the power of the Spirit'. The first phrase ('by word and deed') seems to be a summary of Paul's entire ministry.[15] The reference to signs and wonders is often linked to the Exodus event[16] and seen as proof that Paul understands his ministry to be

[14] Moo (1996: 163), who notes the parallels with 1 Cor. 15:10 and Phil. 4:13.
[15] Cf. 2 Cor. 10:11 and Col. 3:17, where the author instructs his readers to do thankfully *whatever* they do 'in word and in deed'; cf. Jewett 2007: 910.
[16] A fixed formula for Paul (e.g. Moo 1996: 893), which points back to the Exodus (Exod. 7:3; Deut. 4:34; 6:22; 7:19; 26:8; 34:11; Neh. 9:10; Ps. 104:27 LXX).

an 'eschatological fulfilment of God's great past salvation of his people'.[17] However, in the first instance we must not miss the testifying or validating function of this phrase in this context.[18] These signs and wonders underscore Paul's claim that Christ is, in fact, working through him.[19] The final qualifying phrase *in the power of the Spirit*[20] is the most intriguing.

For our purposes, two questions are important to consider. First, what is the relationship between Christ and the Spirit in this activity? Some understand the connection quite generally: the work of Christ is simultaneously the work of the Spirit.[21] Jewett, however, argues specifically that the 'genitive construction indicates that the *source* of the power is the Spirit, while the parallel expression in the preceding verse shows that Christ is the *agent* in such exhibitions of power'.[22] However, it seems better to see Christ as the agent and the Spirit here not as the source but as the 'medium through which and the mode in which the exalted Lord is present and active in his minister'.[23]

Second, how are we to understand the relative involvements of Christ and Paul? Jewett takes an extreme position when he states that the 'accomplishments to be touted are "in Christ" and, as the next verse will show, they have been performed by Christ *rather than* by Paul himself'.[24] However, this overstates Paul's portrayal of Christ here. Rather, with Dunn, we should note 'the balance of [*Christos di' emou*]: anything achieved has been done by Christ; but the agency is Paul's'.[25]

Both qualifiers ('through me' and 'by the power of the Spirit') highlight the absence of Christ since they underline the fact that he does not act *directly* or in an *unmediated* way. Crucially, however, he is portrayed here as the *subject* ('what *Christ* has accomplished through me'). Paul is not *simply* a substitute or representative working on *behalf* of an *absent* Christ. No, he is a minister, *through whom* Christ works. The fact that Christ works in this mediated way reflects the fact of his bodily absence. However, the mediation is almost

---

[17] Schreiner 1998: 768.
[18] Jewett 2007: 910.
[19] Käsemann 1980: 393.
[20] The genitive *pneumatos* is most likely subjective: 'the power exercised [through me] by the Spirit' (Moo 1996: 893).
[21] So Kollmann 2000: 82–83; Lohse 2003: 395–396; Schreiber 1996: 206.
[22] Jewett 2007: 911, emphases added.
[23] Fatehi 2000: 172.
[24] Jewett 2007: 909, emphasis added.
[25] Dunn 1988b: 862; cf. Schreiber 1996: 205.

transparent – it is Christ *himself* who is working through Paul.[26] Believers who are impacted by Paul's apostolic ministry are actually being worked on by the exalted Lord Jesus himself. Christ's absence does not entail inactivity.

Christ works through the church

Christ works not just through Paul and the apostles but through the church. In Ephesians 2:17 Paul states that it was Christ who (cf. 2:13) 'came and preached peace to you who were far off [Gentiles] and peace to those who were near [Jews]'. It is frequently observed that 2:17 alludes to passages in Isaiah.[27] So, in 40:9 a herald evangelizes Zion and Jerusalem; in 52:7 the herald 'evangelizes a report of peace';[28] in 57:19 the Lord himself comes and proclaims 'peace, peace, to the far and to the near'. These aspects are all here in Ephesians 2:17 in Paul's description that Christ 'came and preached peace to you who were far off and peace to those who were near'; that is, to both Israel and the nations. What does this preaching of Christ refer to? Some see it as a reference to Christ's earthly ministry.[29] From the perspective of the Gentile readers, however, Christ came to them 'through the agency of the apostolic mission'.[30] Nevertheless, as Lionel Windsor insightfully points out, 'it is important to note that the apostles themselves are not at the forefront at this point in the letter'.[31] The issue Paul is dealing with at this point in the letter is the united body of Jew and Gentile (2:15–16). As such:

> In some way, therefore, the entire 'body' of Christ is caught up in this apostolic mission. In and through this united-yet-diverse body, Christ 'comes' and 'preaches' (v. 17). In other words, the nature of the church as a body called from both Israel and the nations is inextricable from the gospel-preaching mission.[32]

As we saw with the epiphanic presence of Christ, Christ's dynamic presence, his activity to cause the gospel to progress is a mediated presence.

---

26 It is this fact that leads to the overstatements of Jewett et al. above.
27 The following is a summary of Windsor 2017: 148.
28 Windsor's translation of the LXX (2017: 147).
29 E.g. Moritz 1996: 44–45, cited in Windsor 2017: 148.
30 Windsor 2017: 148.
31 Ibid.
32 Ibid.

Christ and the perseverance of Christians

In this section we will consider a number of texts that describe the work of the exalted Christ in causing Christians to persevere and stand.

1 Corinthians 1:7–8

At the beginning of his first letter to the Corinthians, Paul gives thanks to God for the Corinthians (1:4–9). Included in this thanksgiving section, he expresses his confidence that as they wait for the 'revealing of our Lord Jesus Christ' (1:7), they will be sustained 'to the end, guiltless in the day of our Lord Jesus Christ' (1:8). There is a question as to who will do this sustaining: 'you are not lacking in any spiritual gift, as you wait for the revealing of our Lord Jesus Christ, *who* will sustain you to the end, guiltless in the day of our Lord Jesus Christ'.

Does the 'who' (*hos*) refer to God or to Christ? The straightforward fact that the relative pronoun immediately follows a reference to Jesus would suggest that he is being referred to. However, Fee, who acknowledges that 'our Lord Jesus Christ' is the 'most natural antecedent', gives three reasons to read the antecedent as 'God': first, God is the implied subject of all the passive verbs in the paragraph; second, God is the implied subject of the prior occasion of the verb 'confirm' in verse 6 (i.e. he did it in the past [v. 6] and will do it in the future [v. 8]; third, in the climax of the paragraph in verse 9 Paul praises *God* for his faithfulness. Judith Gundry-Volf also notices the parallel in 2 Corinthians 1:21, where Paul reminds the Corinthians that God is the one who confirms them.[33]

However, the previous reference to God is back in verse 4, and so despite the strong theological reasons for regarding God as the one who 'sustains' or 'confirms' believers, the *grammar* suggests that Christ is the one Paul is referring to.[34] Perhaps we should not be dogmatic one way or the other but rather understand that 'Paul's language here concerns the promises of God-in-Christ'.[35]

In other words, we may not have a description of the *distinct* work of the exalted Christ. Nevertheless, it is correct to see Christ as being

---

[33] Gundry-Volf 1990: 78, n. 215; cf. Thiselton 2000: 101 for a list of those who take this position.

[34] Thiselton (2000: 101) helpfully summarizes the issues: 'Linguistic arguments favour *Christ*; theological arguments favor *God*', emphases original.

[35] Ibid.

involved in the 'confirming' of believers. What does Paul mean by 'sustaining' or 'confirming' them? The verb *bebaioō* is used in verse 6, where Paul says that the 'testimony about Christ was confirmed among you'. The idea is that the testimony about Christ was 'shown to be true' or 'established as true' among them. Taken this way, the verb in verse 8 could be saying that they will be 'confirmed as completely blameless' on the last day; that is, their blamelessness will be established on the last day. Alternatively, we could read it as saying they will be 'sustained to the end, guiltless[36] in the day of our Lord Jesus Christ' (cf. ESVUK). Here the idea is slightly different, with the emphasis not so much on the certainty of the outcome as on God's ongoing work of maintaining them as guiltless. There is not a great deal of difference between the two ideas – the Corinthians, with their proclivity to boast (cf. 4:7), need to be reminded that their final stance on the last day depends entirely on Christ (or God's acting in Christ). Perhaps the reference to their 'waiting' (1:7) pushes us slightly to see the emphasis on the Lord's *ongoing* sustaining.

Romans 14:4

Romans 14:1 – 15:13 is an extended discussion by Paul on how the 'weak' and the 'strong' are to relate to one another. Although these two groups are typically identified as Jewish (or former Gentile 'God-fearers') and Gentile Christians, this is overly simplistic (cf. 15:1, where Paul views himself as 'strong').[37] Nevertheless, his discussion of 'food' (e.g. 14:2–3), 'days' (14:5–6) and what is 'clean' and 'unclean' (14:14) 'best fit[s] a social context in which the observance of Jewish food laws and Sabbaths caused a strong difference of opinion'.[38] Critically, however, Paul does not address them as Jews or as Gentiles but as believers, 'welcomed by Christ and servants of a common Master, since it is on this basis alone that their varying behaviour might be justifiable, and on this basis that the dispute can also be resolved'.[39]

Paul begins by addressing the issue of food. Some believe they can eat everything, while the weak person 'eats only vegetables' (14:2). The critical issue for Paul is not whether a person is strong or weak (though Paul suggests that the strong are in the preferable position; cf. 14:14; 15:1), but how he or she relates to others. The strong are not to 'despise' the weak and the weak are not to 'pass judgment' on the

---

[36] 'Blameless' or 'irreproachable' (BDAG 76).
[37] Barclay 2015: 510.
[38] Ibid. 511.
[39] Ibid. 512.

strong (14:3). Paul expands on this final thought by asking the weak, 'who are you to pass judgment on the servant [*oiketēs*] of another'? He then tells them, 'it is to his own master that he stands or falls'.

The expression 'to his own master' is a dative and could be a 'dative of advantage'; that is, expressing the idea that it is in the interest of the master to ensure that the servant stands.[40] However, most commentators see it as a 'dative of reference'; that is, expressing the idea that the 'strong' will 'stand or fall' 'with reference to their own Lord, that is, by virtue of his decision'.[41]

Paul then moves beyond the analogy of the household to apply this principle to the (strong) Christian believer and his or her master. The believer 'will be upheld, for the Lord is able to make him stand'. The ESVUK translates the verb *stathēsetai* as a passive ('will be upheld'), which does seem to fit the emphasis of the passage.[42] Paul, then, identifies 'the Lord' as the one who is able to make the believer stand.

Two issues concern us. What does Paul mean by 'stand' and 'fall'? And who is the 'Lord' who is able to make believers stand?

On the first question, it seems fair to see Paul's using the imagery in the first instance as part of his master–servant analogy. That is, in a first-century household, a master is the one who approves (and hence causes to 'stand') or disapproves (and hence causes to 'fall') of a servant. However, Paul then moves beyond the analogy to speak of believers being made to stand before the Lord – and here it would seem that ultimate, eschatological vindication is in view.[43] It is wrong of the weak to judge the strong because they are taking the role reserved for their master; that is, of the Lord on the last day. 'It is the Lord, not the fellow Christian, whom the believer must please and who will ultimately determine the acceptability of the believer and his or her conduct.'[44]

On the second question, the identity of the Lord, at the end of verse 3 Paul tells the weak not to judge the strong, since 'God has welcomed him'. The reference to 'Lord', then, in verse 4 would seem naturally to refer to God. Further, Paul says in verse 12 that 'each of us will give an account of himself to God'. God is identified as the master to whom the servant must give account. However, in verse 9 Christ is

---

[40] Cranfield 1975, 2: 703.

[41] Schreiner 1998: 718, n. 14; see his list of others who take this view.

[42] Cranfield (1975, 2: 703) argues for a middle and Moo (1996: 841) for a passive but with an 'intransitive' sense. However, not only is a passive meaning more natural; the duplication helpfully underlines the point that Paul is making.

[43] So Moo 1996: 840; Jewett 2007: 843.

[44] Moo 1996: 840.

said to have 'died and lived again' so that he might 'be Lord [*kyrieusē*] of both the dead and the living'. Further, Jesus is identified as 'the *Lord* Jesus' in verse 14.[45]

As such, although some commentators are adamant that all the references to the Lord in this passage are to Christ,[46] others suggest that given the way 'Paul is inclined in this passage to oscillate between references to God and to Christ',[47] 'he may not have been intending to distinguish clearly in each case his referent'.[48] There does seem to be a very close relationship between Lord and Christ in the passage: As we eat/abstain in honour of the *Lord*, we give thanks to *God* (14:6), every knee will bow to the *Lord* (14:11a) and every tongue confess to *God* (14:11b).[49]

In the end this is not a passage where Paul delineates the work of the exalted Christ *as distinct from* the work of God the Father (as he does in Rom. 8:34 for example). The work of causing the Christian to 'stand', to persevere until the last day, is the work of Father and Son (and the Spirit). Nevertheless, for our purposes we can stress that the exalted Christ is involved in the work of enabling Christians to stand on the last day. The 'certainty of the promise rests not on the strong Christian's ability to stand but on the Lord's ability to make him stand'.[50]

Ephesians 5:29

Ephesians 5:22–33 has been the subject of considerable analysis, speaking as it does of the marriage relationship. We have examined the parallel between marriage and the relationship of Christ and the church. One aspect, however, that has been overlooked is Paul's comment in verse 29, following his comment that husbands should love their wives. He gives husbands the reason why they should love their wives: 'For no one ever hated his own flesh, but nourishes and cherishes it, just as Christ does the church'.

The word translated 'nourishes' (*ektrephō*) is used in Scripture (twenty-nine times across the Greek Scriptures) of providing food for someone (e.g. Gen. 45:11) or more specifically providing for a child

[45] Tilling 2012: 137.
[46] Fee 2007: 260.
[47] Cranfield 1975, 2: 702.
[48] Moo 1996: 840. Moo suggests that 'Lord' in v. 4 'probably' refers to Christ.
[49] Here Paul is citing Isa. 45:23; cf. Phil. 2:11, where he is much more Christologically specific.
[50] Cranfield 1975, 2: 740.

in order to raise it (e.g. 2 Sam. 12:3).[51] This latter sense is the sense of the only other NT use of the word when a few verses later, in Ephesians 6:4, Paul tells fathers, 'Fathers, do not provoke your children to anger, but *bring them up* in the discipline and instruction of the Lord'.

The second word, 'cherishes' (*thalpō*), is less frequent in the Greek Scriptures (occurring only six times) and generally it is used in the context of a mother caring for her children. In two places it is particularly the idea of the mother providing *warmth* for her young (Deut. 22:6; Job 39:14). This idea of warmth explains why the word is also used of the young virgin who served David in his old age – she slept next to him to provide him warmth (1 Kgs 1:2, 4). The final use of the word occurs in 1 Thessalonians 2:7, where Paul reminds the Thessalonians of how he and his colleagues were like a mother (or nurse) with her child.

It would seem these words evoke the imagery of a person who is dependent on receiving everything he or she needs (food, warmth) to grow and thrive. What is needed in a marriage relationship is different from what a child needs, but the imagery speaks of dependence. Applied to the church, Christ then gently provides everything the church needs to thrive.

The second clause reads literally 'just as Christ the church' (cf. AV).[52] However, most English versions imply that this is something that Christ currently *does* (e.g. RSV, NRSV, HCSB, ESVUK, NIV, NASB). This is a reasonable inference even though the emphasis in Ephesians is on the *past* activity of Christ in nourishing the church (cf. 5:25, 'Christ loved the church and gave himself up for her'). Inasmuch as the church needs to continue to grow (cf. 4:15) it seems fair to assume that it is Christ who undertakes to ensure that this happens.

2 Thessalonians 3:3

Towards the end of 2 Thessalonians, Paul reminds the Thessalonians that 'the Lord is faithful' and that he will 'establish' (*stērizō*) them and 'guard' them 'against the evil one' (3:3). Again, we are faced with the issue of identifying 'the Lord'. Paul attributes faithfulness to God in four other places (1 Cor. 1:9; 10:13; 2 Cor. 1:18; 1 Thess. 5:24). This is the only place he changes the subject to 'the Lord'. A number of ancient copyists changed the text to 'God',[53] and some modern

---

[51] See Hoehner 2002: 767.
[52] The AV, following the Majority text type, reads 'Lord'.
[53] See the discussion in Weima (2014: 628).

commentators, even if they think 'Lord' is original, see Paul attributing faithfulness to God.[54] However, while we have seen that 'Lord' does not always refer to Christ, in this context it seems fairly certain that it does. He is identified as Lord in the immediate context (2:16; 3:3) and given that this is a fairly typical construction for Paul, it would seem unlikely that he would change from 'God' to 'Lord' unless he was doing so intentionally.[55] It is Christ, then, who will continue to strengthen and guard the Christians at Thessalonica.

Christ and the discipline of Christians

1 Corinthians 11:27–34

In his analysis of Paul's description of the Lord's Supper in 1 Corinthians 11:17–34 Hans-Josef Klauck discerns four modes of Christ's presence.[56] First is the personal presence of the exalted Lord in 'his spiritual bodily existence', whereby he acts in his role as head of the table who summons his own to the meal and gives gifts to them. Second, his 'commemorative presence' reflects the fact that the exalted one who is spiritually present also bears the marks of his crucifixion. Third, the aspect of his 'proleptic eschatological presence' reflects the fact that this meal anticipates the eschatological meal as reflected in the important phrase 'until he comes' (1 Cor. 11:26). However, of most significance for Klauck is the motif of the *'real bodily presence'* on which he comments:

> The [principle of the] *real bodily presence* states that the body and blood of the crucified Christ are *really* present in the elements of bread and wine. The other modes of presence, encompassing the present, the past and the future, are also real, but they are compressed to a concrete point in his real bodily presence.[57]

Klauck's taxonomy of Christ's presence in this passage is helpful but his concentration on Christ's *'real bodily presence'* is problematic for two reasons. First, it is not at all clear that Paul is localizing Christ's

---

[54] Again, see Weima 2014: 592 for a short list.
[55] Fee 2009: 318–319.
[56] First presented at the conclusion of Klauck 1982: 373–374 and then developed in Klauck 1989: 313–330.
[57] Klauck 1989: 328, emphases added.

bodily presence *in* the bread and the wine.[58] At best the ontological import of Jesus' words 'this is my body' is elusive.[59] In fact, perhaps more significantly, the bread and the wine in this passage are fundamentally tied to the *absence* of Christ. The bread is to be eaten and the cup drunk *in remembrance of* Christ (11:24–25). The mode of this remembrance is expounded (in v. 26). As often as they eat and drink, they 'proclaim the Lord's death until he comes'. The connection between remembering and proclaiming suggests that the former takes place in the latter.[60] Certainly, the Lord's Supper itself cannot be reduced to a memorial meal for someone departed, and the mandate to remember Jesus cannot simply be understood as a command not to forget Jesus.[61] However, particularly the command to *remember* Jesus presupposes his absence. 'Remembering' in the Bible certainly involves *more than* simply 'not forgetting',[62] but it does not *exclude* that concept – and thus presupposes the absence of the person or thing that needs to be remembered. The need to remember in the biblical tradition occurs precisely because the person or thing to be remembered is not present to the consciousness. For example, remembering the poor (Gal. 2:10) certainly involves more than bringing them to mind. However, the very use of the word 'remember' rather than the more specific 'make a contribution' (Rom. 15:26) highlights the fact that they too easily slip from the consciousness and need to be actively 'remembered'. Even God needs to be 'remembered',[63] precisely because he too can slide from the consciousness of the believer. The need to 'remember' Christ occurs precisely because he is absent.[64] Further, the Lord's Supper is to be celebrated *until* he comes. This phrase, as well as defining the temporal limits of the celebration of the Lord's Supper, also points to Jesus' identity as the risen and exalted Lord.[65] The one whose death is proclaimed did not remain dead but is alive and will return one day. Thus, again, his absence is presupposed.[66]

---

[58] Klauck 1989 offers very little exegetical support for his contention.

[59] Dunn 1998: 621: 'exegetically the meaning of "This is my body" (11.24) is as open and as ambiguous as the earlier talk of "spiritual" food (10.3)'.

[60] Hofius 1993: 107.

[61] Ibid. 104.

[62] As both Hofius (1993: 104–106) and Thiselton (2000: 879) point out.

[63] With all that it entails (see the discussion in Thiselton 2000: 880).

[64] Thus Hofius 1993: 104.

[65] Powers 2001: 187.

[66] Hays 1997: 197; cf. Gunton 2001: 193: '*In that respect*, Paul is speaking of real absence, not real presence', emphasis original.

Second, Klauck misses what may arguably be the most significant mode of Christ's presence in this passage. Christ's bodily absence in heaven does not preclude his activity among Christian believers on earth. In fact in this passage we have one of the most 'intense' descriptions of his presence. Here Christ acts as an agent of judgment. The language of judgment permeates this passage:[67] eating and drinking in an 'unworthy' manner makes one 'guilty' of the body and blood of the Lord (v. 27). Thus people should 'examine themselves' (v. 28). To eat and drink without 'discerning the body'[68] is to eat and drink 'judgment' on oneself (v. 29). Because of this many of the Corinthians have become 'weak', or 'ill' or have even 'died' (v. 30). However, Paul states, 'if we examine ourselves, we would not be judged' (v. 31). Paul then makes a clarification: When 'we' are judged, it is 'by the Lord' and it is 'discipline' so that we are not 'condemned with the world' (v. 32). Thus the Corinthians are to reform their practice of the Lord's Supper so that when they come together it is 'not for judgement' (v. 34).[69]

Three things are important to note concerning this judgment. First, it is a judgment that occurs in the present, not the future.[70] Second, though the form of the judgment is serious enough to include death, this judgment is not an anticipation of the eschatological judgment that the world will face.[71] There is a clear distinction between both the object and nature of this judgment ('we are disciplined') while the world is 'condemned'. Third, and most importantly, this present judgment does not result from some magical property of the sacraments[72] or as a mere causal effect of the gluttony.[73] Rather, it is carried out directly by the risen Lord ('we are judged by the Lord', v. 32).[74]

A coming together that fails to discern the body (v. 29) means a coming together for judgment (v. 34). The Lord acts in judgment (cf.

---

[67] See Jamir 2017: 170–177.

[68] There is much debate concerning the referent of body in this verse, with the church and Christ's own body being the most common views. The immediate context, which speaks of Christ's own crucified body, tips us towards seeing this as a reference to the crucified body of Christ. Cf. Thiselton 2000: 893.

[69] In the first instance Paul's concern is on the nature of their *coming together* rather than on the presence, or otherwise, of Christ.

[70] *Pace* Thiselton 2000: 898. See the helpful discussion in Gundry-Volf 1990: 100–102.

[71] On how death could be a form of discipline see Gundry-Volf 1990: 103–112.

[72] Gundry-Volf 1990: 103.

[73] Fee rightly rejects this idea (Fee 1987: 544).

[74] The contexts of 11:26, 11:29 and 12:3 clearly indicate that 'Lord' here refers to Christ.

10:22, where he is provoked to jealousy by abuse of the Lord's Supper). Here is the risen Lord's acting in the present with tangible, dramatic effects (sickness and even death) in the midst of a congregation located on earth. Here Christ's presence is at its most 'dense'. However, even here the absence of Christ is not overridden. The context of the Lord's Supper emphasizes, as we have seen, the absence of Christ (11:24–26). Further, the fact that Paul needs to *tell* the Corinthians that their sickness is a result of Christ's judgment points to the fact that even though this is a direct action of the exalted Christ, it remains, in some sense, veiled and needs interpretation. Christ's presence in judgment is not unmediated. He works through sickness and death, which though not personal entities, are still forms of mediation. Christ is not present in a direct, unqualified way.

Revelation 2 – 3

When we consider John's vision in Revelation, we observe the same relationship between Christ's presence and absence. The description of Jesus as the coming one (*ho erchomenos*; 1:4; 1:8; 4:8), his promise that he is coming soon (2:25; 3:11) and the concluding prayer 'Come, Lord Jesus!' (22:20) all suggest that Jesus is *absent* from believers until his return. Moreover, Revelation locates him on the throne of God (e.g. 3:21) in heaven. However, John also describes Jesus as the one who is walking among the golden lampstands (i.e. the churches; 1:13; 2:1). Admittedly, John is seeing a vision and so, for example, we cannot overread the description of the risen Christ laying his hand on John (1:17).[75] Nevertheless, John locates the risen Christ *in the midst* of the churches. Moreover, even the *coming* language is not applied exclusively to his *future* coming. Thus, in three of the letters in the early part of the book he warns churches that unless they repent he will come to them. So, unless the Ephesians repent and do the things they 'did at first', Jesus 'will come to [them] and remove [their] lampstand from its place' (2:5). Likewise, the church at Pergamum is warned that unless they repent Jesus 'will come to [them] soon and war against them with the sword of [his] mouth' (2:16). Jesus tells the church at Sardis, 'I will come like a thief, and you will not know at what hour I will come against you' (3:3). He also promises the church at Laodicea, 'I stand at the door and knock. If anyone hears my voice

---

[75] E.g. Boring (1992: 706) perhaps overreads this imagery when he suggests that Jesus 'has his feet planted on the same soil where John stands, and places his hand on him (1:17)'.

and opens the door, I will come in to him and eat with him, and he with me' (3:20).[76]

Do the conditional comings in the letters refer to the parousia or to an imminent coming in judgment? There are several compelling reasons for interpreting the comings as a reference to the eschatological parousia, including the fact that everywhere else in the first three chapters where *erchomai* occurs, it refers to the final parousia (1:4, 7–8; 3:10–11).[77] Further, the parousia in Revelation is presented as imminent and, it is argued, the present tense of *erchomai* (2:5; 2:16) has the same force.[78] However, most commentators note that the local and conditional nature of the comings in the letters speaks against identifying them with Jesus' final parousia. Osborne, for example, settles for a both–and interpretation; that is, in 2:5 and 2:16[79] the coming language refers 'both to a present judgment upon the church and to the final judgment at the "parousia"'.[80]

However, that raises the question of what the relationship is between these local comings and Christ's final parousia. In his commentary Greg Beale presents a convincing case that Christ's 'coming' in 1:7 and elsewhere in Revelation should be understood as 'a process occurring throughout history' and 'the so-called "second coming" is actually a final coming concluding the whole process of comings'.[81] He argues this on the basis of the 'coming' language having its origin in Daniel's vision in Daniel 7:13: 'I saw in the night visions, and behold, with the clouds of heaven there came one like a son of man, and he came to the Ancient of Days and was presented before him'. Understood this way, the 'comings' in 'blessing and judgment throughout the course of time are but manifestations of [Christ's] exercise of [his] latter-day authority'.[82] Arguably the Synoptic Gospels use the Daniel 7:13 'coming' language in reference to Jesus' coming into the world (Mark 10:45; Luke 7:34; 19:10) and his judgment of Jerusalem (Matt. 10:23; Mark 13:26; 14:62).[83] And so,

---

[76] In two other places in the letters Christ refers to his coming (2:25; 3:11) but given their non-conditional character these are more easily understood as references to his final, future coming (so Beale 1999: 233).

[77] 2:16 would seem to be the obvious exception but even here Mounce (1998: 82) suggests that the final parousia could be in view.

[78] Osborne 2002: 118.

[79] Although for 3:3 (using the different verb *hēkō*) he suggests that 'this is not the second coming but a historical visitation in judgment' (Osborne 2002: 178).

[80] Ibid. 146.

[81] Beale 1999: 198.

[82] Ibid.

[83] Ibid. 233.

Beale concludes, the 'prophesied coming of the Messiah has begun to be fulfilled, is presently being fulfilled, and will be consummated at some point in the future'.[84]

The 'ambiguity' of the comings (i.e. present and/or future) seems to be a function and expression of John's already-not-yet eschatology.[85] There are parallels with the Lord's Supper, where 'believers experience in the present repeated anticipations of the judicial and salvific effects of Christ's final coming'.[86] Finally, as Beale suggests, the 'identification' of the Spirit and Christ at the conclusion of each letter implies that 'his salvific presence with his churches is through the Spirit and his threatened judgment will occur also through the Spirit's visitation'.[87]

Christ who speaks

Revelation 2 – 3

In Revelation 2 – 3 we have an interesting interplay between references to Christ and to the Spirit. Each of the letters in chapters 2 and 3 begins with an affirmation that the words of the letter are the words of Christ. Though he is not specifically named, he is identified each time (apart from 3:14) with a title that is connected to the vision of 1:19–20; for example, 'the words of him who holds the seven stars in his right hand, who walks among the seven golden lampstands' (2:1; cf. 1:12, 20). Yet each letter ends with a warning to 'hear what the Spirit says to the churches' (2:7; 2:11; 2:17; 2:29; 3:6; 3:13; 3:22). As with other passages we have considered, this interchange has led some to suggest that the risen Christ is to be identified with the Spirit.[88] However, most commentators agree that this is actually a reference to the exalted Lord's speaking through the Spirit.[89] John maintains a distinction between Christ and the Spirit. So, in 22:17 'the Spirit and the Bride' both say 'come', which would be nonsensical if Christ and the Spirit were identified.[90]

Koester suggests that the Spirit mediates the word of the risen Jesus in two ways. First, the Spirit enables *John* to receive the words of the

[84] Ibid.
[85] Ibid.
[86] Ibid.
[87] Ibid.
[88] Boring 1989: 89.
[89] E.g. Bauckham 1993: 96; or, more fully, Koester 2014: 270.
[90] Boxall 2006: 51.

risen Christ (1:9). Second, the Spirit enables *the readers* to receive the risen Christ's words through John's written words. 'Communication is complete when the word given to John in visionary form is received by the readers in written form.'[91]

2 Corinthians 13:1–4

In 2 Corinthians 13:3 Paul raises the issue of whether Christ is speaking through him. Here Paul continues to address an issue that he has already touched upon in chapter 10 (cf. 10:1, 11), namely the supposed distinction between his physical presence with the Corinthians and his letters written to them in his absence. The Corinthians seem to understand Paul to have double standards. He is humble when 'face to face' with them but bold 'when away' from them (10:1). In fact, some were saying that while his letters were 'weighty and strong', his 'bodily presence' was 'weak' and his 'speech' was 'of no account' (10:10). In defence, Paul affirms that what he says 'by letter when absent', he does 'when present' (10:11). Paul then spends the next chapter and a half (10:12 – 12:10) comparing himself to the 'super-apostles', concluding that even though he is 'nothing', he is not inferior to these super-apostles – since the 'signs' of an apostle were performed among them by him (12:12). Paul is about to make his third visit to the Corinthians (12:14; 13:1),[92] and as he prepares he does so in fear – fear that he will not find them as he wants them to be and that they will not find him as they want him to be (12:20). Paul expands his own fear in terms of finding the Corinthians beset by sins such as arrogance and disorder, and his being humbled before them by God over those who had sinned earlier but remain unrepentant of their impurity, sexual immorality and sensuality (12:21).

Paul continues these ideas into chapter 13 by warning them in the same way 'while absent' as he did when he was with them (13:2) that 'when' he comes[93] he will not spare those who sinned earlier or 'all the others' (13:2). Paul underlines the *continuity* in his stance towards them whether he is absent or present (cf. 13:10). Paul issues this warning 'since' they are demanding 'proof' that the exalted Christ is speaking through him (*en emoi*, 13:3).[94] Here, as we have already seen, is the strong connection between Christ and his apostle. Paul

---

[91] Koester 2014: 270.

[92] The previous visits were presumably the founding visit and the 'painful visit' (2:1).

[93] The Greek is *ean elthō*. The normal meaning of *ean* is 'if', but it can be understood as 'when' (see BDAG 268).

[94] Käsemann 1942: 37–43, 47.

does not simply speak as a representative for an absent Christ. Rather, the risen Lord speaks *through* (*en*) his apostle.[95] Thus 'the risen Christ encounters the hearer in the apostle'.[96]

What sort of proof were the Corinthians seeking? How could Paul have demonstrated that Christ was indeed speaking through him? Commentators suggest a number of possibilities, but most likely it is Paul's execution of his warning not to 'spare' them (13:2) which provides the proof that Christ is speaking through him.[97] Though this may not be the proof they are expecting,[98] it underlines the unity of Paul's stance towards the Corinthians whether absent from or present with them. This is confirmed as we see how Paul continues his argument.

Having noted that the Corinthians are seeking proof that Christ is speaking through Paul, he immediately defines Christ as 'not weak in dealing with you' but 'powerful among you' (13:3). Paul may ironically be restating a Corinthian slogan[99] or correcting the Corinthians' understanding of power.[100] However, it would seem most likely that Paul is building his argument – you seek proof that Christ is speaking through me, well first you need to know that Christ is not weak among you, but powerful. Here is a strong statement concerning the presence of Christ among his people. How are we to understand this presence (in the light of Christ's bodily absence; cf. 2 Cor. 5:6)? It is generally agreed that verse 4 substantiates verse 3. As such, Paul continues to correct this understanding of the 'power of Christ'. Yes, Christ is powerful among them, for indeed Christ was crucified 'in weakness' but he lives 'by the power of God' (13:4).[101]

Christ is 'powerful among' the Corinthians (13:3). Paul expands on this statement in two parallel clauses in 13:4:

A   For he was crucified in weakness,
B   but lives by the power of God.
C   For we also are weak in him,
D   but in dealing with you we will live with him
         by the power of God.

---

[95] Cf. 12:19, where Paul states that he has been speaking 'before God in Christ' for their upbuilding.
[96] Bultmann 2007: 306.
[97] Plummer 1915: 374; Thrall 2000: 882.
[98] Such as charismatic signs: Martin 1986: 455.
[99] Thrall 2000: 881; Harris 2005: 913.
[100] Cf. Calvin 1998c.
[101] Quite probably a reference to the Spirit; cf. Rom. 1:4; 8:11.

The parallelism is obvious but it is also important to notice the differences.[102] First, there is the perhaps unsurprising lack of reference to crucifixion in C. Second, in C in the Greek Paul adds the strictly unnecessary and hence emphatic pronoun 'we' (*hēmeis*).[103] Third, both Paul's weakness and his strength are 'christologically conditioned'.[104] That is, he is weak in Christ and he will live with Christ. But perhaps the most surprising difference is that in D Paul's living is qualified with respect to the Corinthians. He will live by the power of God 'in dealing with you'.

What does Paul mean by this statement 'in dealing with you we will live with him by the power of God'? His reference to living stands in parallel to the resurrection life of Christ. As such, this reference to living *with Christ* suggests to some an eschatological context.[105] Again, however, the reference to the Corinthians suggests that Paul has his upcoming visit to Corinth in view.[106] When Paul visits, he will live *with Christ* by the power of God *with respect to the Corinthians*. Is Paul simply pointing to 'his own inclusion in the story and character of Jesus'?[107] That is, 'because of the apostle's intimate relationship with Jesus' does he embody 'the same mode of human existence' as Jesus?[108]

Examining 1 Corinthians 5:4 may help us. In this chapter Paul tells the Corinthians he has found out a member of their congregation has been sleeping with his stepmother. Paul is outraged not only by this behaviour but also because the Corinthians have done nothing about it *and* continue to have a high opinion of their spiritual status (5:2). Paul is astounded that the Corinthians have not acted to remove this man from their congregation (5:2). As he writes from Ephesus (16:8), it does not seem as if Paul is in any position to do anything about this offence. However, Paul continues in verse 3 to tell the Corinthians that though he is 'absent in body', he is 'present in spirit', and that 'as if present' he has 'already pronounced judgement' (5:3) on the one who has sinned in this way that he should be excluded from the congregation (5:5).[109] Though currently in Ephesus, Paul is with them 'in

---

[102] See Lambrecht 1985: 261–262.
[103] Ibid. 261.
[104] Ibid. 262.
[105] E.g. Deissmann 1892: 126, cited in Hoffmann 1978: 303.
[106] Lambrecht 1985: 269.
[107] Stegman 2005: 209.
[108] Ibid.
[109] Paul's description of himself as 'absent in body' but 'present in spirit' has obvious parallels with Christ's own location.

spirit', meaning that when they are assembled his 'spirit is present' (5:4). Further, they are assembled together 'with the power of our Lord Jesus' (v. 4). The passage forms a strong parallel with Matthew 18:15–20. Without suggesting dependence one way or another, it does seem that these two passages reflect a very similar understanding of church discipline and may both reflect an earlier common tradition.[110] In the Matthew passage Jesus tells the disciples that the unrepentant offender is to be treated like a tax collector or sinner. This seems to be parallel to the sinner being 'handed over to Satan' in 1 Corinthians 5. Jesus further tells the disciples that if two or three are gathered 'in my name', then he is 'in their midst' (18:20). The assembling, then, is in the name of the Lord Jesus and Jesus is with the disciples. If 1 Corinthians 5:1–5 and Matthew 18:20 are to be read in parallel, this would suggest that the phrase 'with the power of our Lord Jesus' has a stronger sense than simply 'in [or with] the authority of the Lord Jesus'. Rather, in some sense, Jesus is actually understood to be powerfully present. The Lord *himself* is present in power.[111] It would seem that the 'absent in body / present in spirit' dynamic that Paul understood about his own location applies to Christ. He too is present *by the Spirit*.

Paul may be assuming a similar dynamic in 2 Corinthians 13:1–4. When he visits to discipline the Corinthians and is assembled with them, it will not simply be the Corinthians and Paul but the Lord Jesus himself who will be present too. He will 'live with Christ by the power of God' in his dealings with the Corinthians (13:4). However, in 1 Corinthians 5, though Christ is present, it is *Paul's* action that is emphasized. He is the one who passes judgment (5:3). In contrast in 2 Corinthians 13:3 we have seen the description of Christ as powerful among the congregation[112] but the nature of his powerful activity is not expanded. In our next section, however, we see a clear description of Christ's activity.

Conclusion

Christ's work of redemption is complete. Perhaps the most important activity of the exalted Christ for the Christian believer to grasp is his sitting at God's right hand indicating as it does his finished work. However, although the work of redemption is complete, the progress

---

[110] Rosner 1994: 89–90.
[111] Gräbe 2000: 74.
[112] Assuming this is not a Corinthian slogan.

of the gospel is not and nor is the *final* salvation of the Christian believer. We have seen how the ongoing work of Christ relates to both of these. It is Christ in Acts who continues to work and who through his apostles (particularly Paul) continues to cause the progress of the gospel. Furthermore, it is Christ who ensures that believers will stand and be established in him.

Chapter Ten

The activity of the exalted Christ in heaven

In this chapter I continue my treatment of the ongoing activity of Christ. I look at it from a slightly different angle in considering Christ's activity in heaven.

Christ's acting as God from heaven

In a number of places across the NT believers relate to the exalted Christ the way that first-century Jews would relate to God. Chris Tilling has helpfully shown how these reports of prayers to Christ indicate a high Christology was held by Paul,[1] but we will see that this divine Christology is assumed beyond Paul. For our purposes, though, these prayers underline the expectation that the exalted Christ who is absent in heaven is nevertheless able to work profoundly in the lives of believers. Here, then, is not so much mediated activity on the part of Christ (there is no mention of the Spirit in these contexts) as divine activity. That is, the risen Christ's acting as God.

So believers are described as praying to the exalted Christ and asking him to intervene. In Acts 1:15–26 Peter speaks with a gathering of the church and suggests that following Judas' defection they should choose a replacement so that another might 'take his office' (1:20). In the end they do this by casting lots to choose between Joseph and Matthias, but not before praying, 'You, Lord, who know the hearts of all, show which one of these two you have chosen' (1:24). That the 'Lord' here likely refers to the Lord Jesus can be seen in the fact the only two other times the title 'Lord' is used in this context, it clearly refers to Jesus (1:6, 21). Similarly, Stephen prays to the Lord Jesus as Stephen dies at the end of Acts 7. His prayer echoes the prayer of Jesus himself to the Father on the cross (Luke 23:34, 46) in asking the Father to receive his spirit and to forgive those who have carried out his unjust execution (7:59–60).[2]

---

[1] Tilling 2012: 73.
[2] The apostles also pray to God the Father and address him as 'Lord'; see Acts 4:24, 29.

179

The Thessalonian correspondence contains a number of examples of prayers addressed to the Lord Jesus. In the first letter Paul prays that 'our God and Father himself, and our Lord Jesus, [would] direct our way to you' (1 Thess. 3:11) and then prays that the Lord would 'make you increase and abound in love for one another and for all, as we do for you, so that he may establish your hearts blameless in holiness before our God and Father' (1 Thess. 3:12–13). In the second letter he reverses the order of addressing God and Jesus[3] and prays, 'may our Lord Jesus Christ himself, and God our Father, . . . comfort your hearts and establish them in every good work and word' (2 Thess. 2:16–17). Later in the letter he prays that 'the Lord' would direct their 'hearts to the love of God and to the steadfastness of Christ' (3:5). The phrase 'the steadfastness of Christ' most likely refers to the perseverance that Christ displayed in his earthly life.[4] So, Paul is praying that the Lord Jesus will enable the Thessalonian believers to display the same patience that Jesus himself displayed. This flows from the description of the activity of the Lord Jesus as the one who 'is faithful' and who will 'establish and guard [them] against the evil one' (3:3) and is appropriate for the context of the Thessalonian church's suffering (1:5).

In the Corinthian correspondence Paul also prays to Christ. In 1 Corinthians 16:22 we have perhaps one of the earliest prayers used by Christian believers and it is addressed to Christ – 'Maranatha'; that is, 'come, Lord'. As Tilling notes, this is a significant prayer since in praying for Christ to come it implies his absence as well as, simultaneously, his ability to hear and answer the prayer.[5]

In 2 Corinthians 12 Paul recounts his struggle with a thorn 'in the flesh, a messenger of Satan' (12:7). Three times he pleaded with the Lord for this thorn to be removed (12:8) but received the reply, 'my grace is sufficient for you, for my power is made perfect in weakness' (12:9). There is little doubt that 'the Lord' here refers to Jesus,[6] especially as Paul reflects that he will 'boast all the more gladly of my weaknesses, so that the power of Christ may rest on me' (12:9). That is, the one who answers Paul's prayer and makes his power perfect in weakness is here specifically identified as Christ.

Again, the implication is that Paul prayed to the risen Christ because he believed that Christ had the ability to do something about

---

[3] Wanamaker 1990: 141: 'This suggests that the order was not fixed and that Christ was placed on the same honorific plane as God.'

[4] Ibid. 279; Weima 2014: 599.

[5] Tilling 2012: 194.

[6] So the majority of commentators.

the thorn.[7] This and the other examples of Christ as the object of believers' prayers is an important piece of evidence regarding the NT's Christology. The clear inference of Christ's being prayed to is that he was regarded as God. This is particularly the case in 2 Corinthians 12:7, where Paul prays to Christ with respect to a messenger of Satan. In the OT and Jewish theology more widely God is the one who is 'sovereign over Satan'.[8] Paul's prayer is addressed to Christ but is asking for 'something that only God could do for him'.[9]

There are a number of other instances in the NT where the author portrays Christ's acting as God from heaven.

We see it in Jesus' acting to enable people to respond to the gospel. So, in Acts 16:14 we read of the Lord's opening Lydia's heart to enable her 'to pay attention to what was said by Paul'.[10] Similarly, when Paul confronts Bar-Jesus / Elymas, the magician who was opposing his ministry, he tells him that 'the hand of the Lord is upon you, and you will be blind and unable to see the sun for a time' (Acts 13:11). Immediately the magician is blinded. Again, we have an example of the Lord's working from heaven. In Acts 18:21 as Paul sets sail from Ephesus, he tells the Jews he has been speaking to that he will return to them 'if God wills'. This attribution of sovereign will to God is typical across the Bible (cf. 2 Kgs 8:19; 13:23; Pss 115:3; 135:6; Prov. 21:1; Rom. 9:18; and esp. Rom. 1:10). However, in a number of places this sovereign will is attributed to the Lord Jesus. So, in 1 Corinthians 4:19 Paul warns the Corinthians that he will come to them soon 'if the Lord wills'. Similarly, at the end of the letter he tells them that he will come to them 'if the Lord wills' (16:7). Of course these could be alternative ways of referring to the will of God (cf. 1 Cor. 1:1); however, the context in both cases and Paul's regular usage suggest that they are both references to Christ.[11] These verses suggest that Christ is 'present and active' 'over/in the seemingly contingent course of historical events'.[12]

A similar dynamic is found with the concept of the Lord's rescuing believers. When Peter recounts his release from prison, he testifies that

---

[7] Tilling 2012: 148.

[8] Keener (2005: 240), who points to Job 1:6 – 2:6; cited in Tilling 2012: 148.

[9] Fee 2007: 576.

[10] 'Lord' here likely refers to Jesus given the reference to Lydia's already being a worshipper of God (16:14). As she responds to Paul's message she now becomes 'faithful to the Lord' (16:15), suggesting a change and that her devotion is now specifically Christian.

[11] Cf. 1 Cor. 4:5 and 16:22, and the discussion in Tilling 2012: 142.

[12] Tilling 2012: 138.

'the Lord' is the one who 'delivered' (*exaireō*, Acts 12:11) and 'brought him out' (*exagō*, 12:17). These verbs were typically applied to God in the OT, particularly in the context of the Exodus (e.g. Exod. 3:8; 18:4). The related verb 'rescue' (*ryomai*) is used of Paul to describe how the Lord rescued him from persecutions (2 Tim. 3:11)[13] and from 'every evil deed' (2 Tim. 4:18).[14] Again, this verb is typically used of God's rescue (Exod. 6:6; 12:27; etc.) throughout the OT and of God in the NT (e.g. Col. 1:13). Although it is used of the future deliverance that Jesus will bring (cf. Rom. 11:26; 1 Thess. 1:10), when Paul speaks of his present deliverance from danger in 2 Corinthians 1:10, it is God who delivers him. Again, we have an expression of the risen Christ's acting in a divinely sovereign way.

Similarly, in Acts 9:34 healing is attributed to Jesus ('Peter said to him, "Aeneas, Jesus Christ heals you; rise and make your bed"'), an activity that is typically attributed to God in the OT (e.g. Gen. 20:17; Exod. 15:26; Num. 12:13; Deut. 32:39; 2 Kgs 2:21; Pss 6:2; 103:3; Hos. 6:1; Isa. 30:26; Jer. 17:14). Of course Jesus' healing activity was a feature of his earthly ministry and proof of his divine status.

Prayer to Jesus, the expectation that things happen only according to his will, his ability to rescue believers from trial and to heal are all of a piece with what the OT attributed to God. His ongoing activity here, then, is a function not so much of his acting in a mediated way but of his divine status and his ability to act as God. As Hebrews puts it, Christ is 'the radiance of the glory of God and the exact imprint of his nature, and he upholds the universe by the word of his power' (1:3). His divine identity obviously continues beyond his exaltation and so we are not surprised to see him acting in a way that is in line with the way that God was expected to act.

Christ's interceding

In this section we examine the intercession of Christ. Although this is referred to only twice in the New Testament (Rom. 8:34; Heb. 7:25),[15] the concept of Christ's intercession has played a significant role in a number of doctrinal controversies in the history of the church.

---

[13] Observe the immediate reference to Christ Jesus in 2 Tim. 3:12, suggesting the reference to 'Lord' here is to Jesus.

[14] Again, this seems to be a reference to Christ given the following reference to 'his heavenly kingdom'.

[15] There are related descriptions; cf. 1 John 2:1; Heb. 9:24.

In the third and fourth centuries some used it to 'prove' the inferiority of the Son to the Father.[16] In reaction, others asserted that it was not 'a proof . . . of inferiority' but an accommodation[17] to more clearly show the depth of God's love for us.[18] When Arianism, of a kind, was later revived in the anti-trinitarianism of the late sixteenth century, we again see similar debates turning on the intercession of Christ. Calvin, for example, argued that 'those err very grossly, who imagine that Christ falls on his knees before the Father to pray for us', since this would 'detract from the celestial glory of Christ'.[19] Calvin understood that Christ's 'death and resurrection stand in the place of eternal intercession, and have the efficacy of a powerful prayer for reconciling and rendering the Father propitious to us'.[20] Calvin, thus, understands intercession more broadly as mediation and thus as a summary of the entirety of Christ's work. So, in discussing Romans 8:34, he argues that 'God justifies us through the intercession of Christ' (*Institutes* 3.11.3[21]). In contrast, Luther, who predated the anti-trinitarian controversies, sees Christ's intercession as unqualified prayer on our behalf. The content of this prayer is simply '"Father, I have suffered for this person; I am looking after him"' and as such '[t]his prayer cannot be in vain'.[22] So, the idea of Christ's interceding has had a doctrinal impact far beyond its textual frequency of being found only in Romans 8:34 and Hebrews 7:25.

Word study

In non-biblical Greek the broad semantic range of *entynchanō* referred to an encounter. Within this range, the word frequently has a verbal communicative focus – often used of making a petition, either for complaint or advocacy. In a religious context it can mean to 'pray for' someone. Less frequently, the verb can also mean 'to find oneself somewhere', 'confer' and even 'read'.[23]

In the LXX *entynchanō* can mean 'appeal' (Dan. 6:13), 'read' (2 Macc. 2.25; 6.12; 15.39) and 'pray' (Wis. 8.21; 16.28). In Jewish Hellenistic writing the verb is 'used in various senses for human

---

[16] Tait 1912: 149.
[17] Chrysostom 1841: 269.
[18] Ibid. 270.
[19] Calvin 1998a.
[20] Calvin 1998b.
[21] Calvin 1989, 3: 39.
[22] Luther 1967: 236.
[23] For examples of each of these and further discussion see Bauernfeind 1972, 8: 243.

relations'. So, for example: 'to encounter', 'to meet (admit) envoys', 'to approach' someone with a request, 'to pray for', 'to raise a complaint', 'to have an audience with someone'. It can also mean 'to read'.[24] Outside Romans 8 and Hebrews 7 the verb is used twice in the NT. In Acts 25:24 the Jewish community 'petition' or 'appeal to' Festus, while in Romans 11:2 Elijah 'complains' against Israel.

Though the word can have broader meanings ('read', 'encounter'), by far the most common idea (especially in reference to God) is that of verbal communication. However, although these results would suggest a reference to prayer, the question of a figurative understanding of *entynchanō* in Romans 8:34 and Hebrews 7:25 remains open. These NT authors could be using *entynchanō* in a figurative sense that may have been clear to their original readers. So, we may have an instance of ellipsis, where *entynchanō* was understood to mean intercede '*by his very presence*'[25] or was an umbrella term for a wider range of cultic activities.[26] Alternatively, we may have an example of metonymy, where *entynchanō* is understood in the broader sense of 'intervenes'.[27] Obviously, we need to examine the word in the contexts of the two verses.

Romans 8:34

Towards the end of Romans 8 Paul reflects on the certainty of God's love for Christian believers, but he then considers the reality of opposition – Satanic or otherwise: 'What then shall we say to these things? If God is for us, who can be against us?' (8:31). Given the repetition of themes found in 5:1–11 in 8:31–39, it would seem best to see 'these things' as referring to what Paul has taught in the entire preceding section of the letter.[28] As such, Paul's summary of Romans 5 – 8 is expressed simply as 'God is for us'. As part of a conditional sentence this summary statement repeats the lesser to the greater argument Paul has already employed in 5:9–10: if God is now reconciled to us, how can anyone else stand against us?

His lesser to the greater rhetoric is expanded in the following verse: 'He who did not spare his own Son but gave him up for us all, how will he not also with him graciously give us all things?' (8:32). God's

[24] Again, for examples of each of these and further discussion see Bauernfeind 1972: 243.
[25] e.g. Westcott 1892: 191, emphasis added.
[26] Spicq 1952: 69.
[27] Kurianal 2000: 36.
[28] Moo 1996: 539.

gracious activity in the past in the giving of his own Son gives confidence of his future 'easier' action of giving all things needed. The scope of 'all things' has been understood as either the broad idea of sharing in God's sovereignty over the universe[29] or the more narrow idea of everything that we need to secure our final salvation.[30] On balance, it would seem that given the parallel with 5:1–11, and in the light of 5:9–10, the idea of everything that believers need to secure our final salvation is especially in focus.

Paul then begins a series of rhetorical questions and answers. There is considerable debate about the punctuation. Talbert suggests that verses 31–34 break down into a transitional question (v. 31a) followed by three rhetorical questions (vv. 31b, 33a, 34a). He suggests that Paul answers each question with an implied 'No one!' and then gives supporting evidence (vv. 32, 33b, 34b).[31] However, it could be that each question is answered with a rhetorical question. This is certainly the case in verse 32, but verse 33b ('God who justifies?') and verse 34b ('Christ Jesus who died . . .?') could also function as rhetorical questions. Thus each answer would have the same force, pointing out the good that God and Christ have done, and so the absurdity of thinking they could oppose us. Verse 33 highlights the absurdity of God's bringing a charge against the ones he himself justified. Verse 34 similarly implies the absurdity of thinking that Christ who died and was raised for us, and now intercedes on our behalf, would also condemn us.

The relevance of this is that Christ's intercession is a general description of his activity and his orientation *for* believers, rather than strictly answering the question of condemnation. That is, on this reading, Paul is not asking, 'Who can condemn us?', and implying, 'No one *can* condemn us because Jesus is interceding for us.' Rather, he is asking, 'Who will condemn us? Jesus? That would be absurd – he died, rose and is interceding for us.' The implication of this reading is that we do not necessarily need to understand intercession in purely forensic terms; that is, in matching and answering condemnation.

Paul continues his description of Christ as he 'who is at the right hand of God, who indeed is interceding for us'. The first clause is generally recognized to be an allusion to Psalm 110 [LXX 109]:1.

What is the nature of the relationship between Christ's intercession and place at God's right hand? Fay sees a reference to Psalm 110:1

---

[29] Dunn 1988a: 502; Jewett 2007: 538.

[30] So e.g. Moo 1996: 541; Cranfield 1975, 1: 437.

[31] Talbert 2002: 226.

alone and argues that it is purely this throne-room setting that informs the use of the intercession motif. Jesus 'continues to intercede for [his people] as vice-regent'.[32] He notes that Paul does not appeal to the metaphor of the high priest anywhere else in Romans.[33] Moo, on the other hand, argues that Christ is 'acting as our High Priest'.[34] Similarly, Eskola argues that Paul is using this priestly motif as a 'counterpoint' to the judicial discourse.[35] Hengel also argues 'on the basis of the unique connection between resurrection, sitting at the right hand and intercession other than in Hebrews', that the reference to intercession here is dependent on the reference to the priesthood of Melchizedek in Psalm 110:4.[36] He argues that the parallel in Hebrews 7:25 makes this assumption probable. This priestly connection may support a figurative understanding of intercession; that is, it is functioning as an umbrella term for a range of priestly activities rather than as a specific reference to ongoing prayer.

However, two features I think suggest that what is in view is not a metonymic understanding of intercession, but that Paul envisages ongoing prayer on the part of Christ: first, an allusion to Isaiah 53:12, and second, the parallel reference to the intercession of the Spirit earlier in the chapter. Very few commentators have seen a significant link between Christ's intercession in Romans 8:34 and that of the Suffering Servant in Isaiah 53:12. For instance, neither of the two (fairly) recent studies on Paul's use of Isaiah in Romans raises the possibility of a link.[37] Some commentators do note the possibility of an allusion or echo of Isaiah 53:12 but no one that I have found develops the link.[38]

There are a number of reasons that might suggest that Paul, in fact, did not intend any connection to be made with Isaiah at this point. The conclusion of Isaiah 53 in the MT is 'and makes intercession for the transgressors'. However, the LXX has 'and he was delivered because of their iniquities'. There are good reasons for following the MT and seeing the LXX as a particularly 'free' translation at this point.[39] Certainly the Targum of Isaiah sees the idea of intercession as key to Isaiah 53. In the targum the Servant is specifically identified as the

[32] Fay 2006: 340.
[33] Ibid. 340–341.
[34] Moo (1996: 543), who does not make reference to Ps. 110:4.
[35] Eskola 2001: 186.
[36] Hengel 1995: 159.
[37] Wagner 2002; Shum 2002.
[38] Cranfield 1975, 1: 439, n. 2; Dunn 1988a: 504.
[39] Seeligman 2004: 128; 165, n. 35.

Messiah, and, as well as verse 12, intercession is introduced in verses 4, 7 and 11.[40]

However, the question remains as to whether Paul is actually referring to Isaiah 53:12 in Romans 8:34, especially given that there is a connection of only one word – and in a different language.

In both Isaiah 53:12 and Romans 8:34 intercession is positioned climactically. The intercession of the Servant in verse 12 is in contrast to the rest of the song, when he is silent (cf. Isa. 53:7) and passive.[41] In fact, he 'does nothing and says nothing but lets everything happen to him'.[42] When he does speak, we might expect that he would protest his innocence, but, rather, he intercedes for the guilty. This is surprising and the surprise 'is accented by its position as the final clause in the song'.[43] This climactic accent on intercession in Isaiah 53:12 is matched in Romans 8:34. A number of commentators have recognized the climactic nature of the series in Romans 8:34 with the focus building to intercession.[44]

In the surrounding context of Romans 8 a number of references to Isaiah 53 have been noted. Paul's contention in verse 32 that God did not 'spare' his own Son but gave him up for us all has been linked to Isaiah 53:6 ('the LORD has laid on him the iniquity of us all').[45] Further parallels have been noted between Romans 8:31b, 33–34 and Isaiah 50:8–9. As well as the linguistic and syntactical similarities between these two texts,[46] both deal with the inability of anyone to bring charges against those justified by God.[47]

As well as considering possible individual allusions, the cumulative effect must be taken into consideration. Accordingly, it is worth noting the use that Paul makes of Isaiah's prophecy as a whole in Romans. It is estimated that citations from Isaiah 'account for nearly half of Paul's explicit appeals to scripture in Romans'.[48] Further, arguably a proportionally higher number of citations and allusions

[40] Stenning 1949: 180; Chilton 1987: 103–105.

[41] Groves 2004: 85.

[42] Clines 1976: 64–65.

[43] Groves 2004: 85.

[44] Schreiner 1998: 462; Cranfield 1975, 1: 439; Moo 1996: 542; Jewett 2007: 541–542.

[45] E.g. Moo 1996: 540, n. 19; Schreiner 1998: 459; Cranfield 1975, 1: 436; Fitzmyer 1993: 532.

[46] Isa. 50:8: 'he who justified me draws near. Who is the one who contends with me?'

[47] Others who see a link here include Schreiner (1998: 462), Dunn (1988a: 503) and Jewett (2007: 541).

[48] Wagner 2002: 2. See also the list of allusions there and in Wilk 1998: 445. Note that neither sees a reference to Isa. 53:12 in Rom. 8:34.

seem to be taken from the Servant Songs of Isaiah 40 – 55, especially in Romans 1 – 8.[49]

Perhaps the strongest reason, though, for seeing an allusion to Isaiah 53:12 is actually the previous allusion in Romans 8:34 to Psalm 110. In Isaiah 53, because the servant 'poured out his soul to death', God will 'divide him a portion with the many' (v. 12). Further, 52:13, which introduces this Servant Song and speaks of the Servant's exaltation, is best understood as a reflection of what will happen after the suffering described in the chapter.[50] This exaltation may be more than simply receiving the praise of human beings. On the basis of the language in 52:13, which is reminiscent of the visions of God's exaltation in 6:1 and 57:15, Bauckham has argued that the Servant here is being exalted to the throne of God.[51] If this connection holds true, then it would seem that the exaltation of the Servant mirrors the very exaltation spoken about in Psalm 110:1. It seems that the early Christians made this connection since Psalm 110:1 is alluded to in combination with both Isaiah 52:13 (Acts 2:33; 5:31) and Isaiah 57:15 (Heb. 1:3).

So, I think the possibilities of the allusion are significant. We need to consider, then, how Isaiah understood the intercession of the Servant. While some commentators see the normal sense of intercessory prayer in view,[52] a significant number argue that the intercession here 'is accomplished not by prayer per se but rather by suffering'.[53] This 'silent' intercession fits the rest of the chapter, where the Servant 'does nothing and says nothing but lets everything happen to him'.[54] So, Westermann is adamant that intercession here 'does not mean . . . that he made prayers of intercession for them, but that with his life, his suffering and his death, he took their place and underwent their punishment in their stead'.[55] Is this a case where intercession and sacrifice are merged into one act?

Perhaps, though, a closer examination of the text leans us away from collapsing the Servant's intercession into his sacrificial death. In 53:12 the actions of the Servant are typically expressed using qatal forms but interestingly the final reference to intercession reverts to a yiqtol. Can we draw any significance from this change in verb form –

---

[49] See Shum 2002: 150.
[50] Bauckham 2008: 35.
[51] Ibid. 35–36.
[52] E.g. Baltzer 2001: 427.
[53] Ballentine 1984: 164, n. 12.
[54] Clines 1976: 64–65.
[55] Westermann 1969: 269.

particularly regarding whether the Servant intercedes during his humiliation, that is, even *by* his death, or whether he intercedes in his exaltation, that is, as a result of but distinct from his death? Some commentators see no significance in this change and translate the final verb as 'made intercession', suggesting that it happens in parallel with his bearing of sin or even that the Servant interceded by bearing sin.[56] However, it may be that this final line is a 'new, independent clause which forms an inclusio with 52:13' and thus is 'a new reference to the glorification of the Servant'.[57] This reading would explain the differences in the verb forms[58] and fits the climactic nature of this final clause. It would seem at least possible that the Servant's intercession is being presented as subsequent to his suffering death, a result of that death, but still distinct from it.

If we accept this allusion to Isaiah 53:12, we do not have to view intercession here as simply metonymy for Christ's death. The allusion could suggest that what is in view is intercessory prayer offered by the exalted Christ as he sits at God's right hand. In both cases we have a climactic series of events culminating with intercession, which follows atoning suffering and death and is possible *because of* that death but is not the same as that death. Rather, as I have argued, intercession is something subsequent to and distinct from atoning death in both cases. Obviously, the structure of Romans 8:34 on its own would point to this with its obvious sense of progression (death to resurrection to exaltation to intercession), but the allusion to Isaiah 53:12 helps confirm the significance of this structure. Christ is being presented as an exalted intercessor who intercedes by praying for his people.

The possible allusion to Isaiah 53:12 and the climactic position of the reference to intercession in the verse suggest that Christ's intercession be distinguished from his sacrificial death. The parallel with the Spirit's intercession in 8:26 further suggests that actual prayer is in view. While Paul can use the same word with different meanings in a close context,[59] the fact that *entynchanō* is such a rare word for Paul would count against this. Rather, the clear use in verse 26, where it refers to prayer, should act as a control for the more disputed use here.

---

[56] De Waard 1997: 197–198; Whybray 1978: 71; Westermann 1969: 269; Goldingay and Payne 2006: 330 '[t]he change is then no doubt partly for variation'.

[57] Koole 1998: 428.

[58] Ibid. 343: something which 'has not been given due attention by most exegetes and translations'.

[59] E.g. *nomos* in 8:2; see Moo 1996: 473–476.

If we do understand that prayer is in view, can we say anything concerning the content of the prayer? A number of factors push us to see a broad view of the goal of intercession here – that Christ is interceding for all that believers need in order to persevere. For a start, Christ's interceding for us mirrors the fact that God is willing to give us 'all things' (v. 32). The need for such intercession fits the context of the trials that believers face (v. 35). As we have noted, it mirrors the intercession of the Spirit who helps us in our weakness. The perseverance of God's people so that his Son may be 'the firstborn among many brothers' (v. 29) will not fail, because of the intercession of Christ and the Spirit in the face of all our weaknesses.

But within this broad framework of intercession, can we include intercession for our forgiveness? In other words, to put it somewhat crudely, does Paul envisage that every time believers sin, Christ prays for their forgiveness? Against this is the fact that Paul has spent three verses stressing how God is 'for us' and how the idea of his bringing any charge against us is absurd. This flows from the fact that he has given his Son up for us (v. 32), and that he has justified us (v. 33). To posit a wrathful stance towards us that needs to be met by Christ's intercession for forgiveness would go against the grain of these verses.

However, by far the most common goal of intercession in the OT was the aversion of God's wrath,[60] and if we accept the allusion to Isaiah 53:12 we should perhaps note that the Servant intercedes for 'transgressors'. Further, the juridical context of condemnation in these verses suggests that sin is in view. To fully answer this question would involve a wider study on the nature of ongoing forgiveness for the Christian (e.g. John 13:10; 1 John 1:9). Although there is no condemnation for those in Christ (8:1) and God is 'for us', the wrath of God in some sense remains a future reality (Rom. 5:9–10; cf. 2:16). That believers will be saved from that wrath is not in doubt given that God has done the 'harder' job of reconciling us (5:9), but salvation still needs to be realized. In a similar way, then, perhaps Christ's intercession includes an application of the benefits of our forgiveness.

In short, I have argued that Romans 8:34 presents Christ as exalted by God and praying for transgressors. As such he fulfils and surpasses the actions of the OT intercessors – none of whom could guarantee God's purposes in this way. This intercessory prayer of Christ mirrors both God's desire to give believers all things (v. 32) and the Spirit's own intercession for us (vv. 26–27) and shows the absurdity of Christ's

---

[60] Cf. Miller 1994: 266.

ever condemning us. As such, it highlights the central motif of this chapter that 'there is no condemnation for those who are in Christ Jesus' (v. 1).

Hebrews 7:25

In Hebrews 7:25 the author of the sermonic letter[61] to the Hebrews ties Jesus' ability to save those who come to God through him to the fact that he 'always lives to intercede for them' (NIV). At the heart of this book is the author's presentation of Christ as high priest. Although commentators differ on the structure of Hebrews, there is general agreement that the central section from chapters 5 (or 4:14) to 10 is broadly concerned with this priesthood of Christ.[62] Within that broad discussion, the author moves from the superiority of the Son as high priest (5:1 – 7:28)[63] to the superiority of his offering (8:3 – 10:18). Chapter 7, then, forms part of the author's argument concerning the superiority of Christ's priesthood. The author underlines the perfect nature of Christ's Melchizedekian priesthood in comparison to the earlier, Levitical and Aaronic priesthood. Within chapter 7, verse 25, with its promise that Christ is able to save 'to the uttermost' those who come to God through him, stands out.

The chapter naturally divides into two sections: verses 1–10, where the writer discusses the OT figure of Melchizedek, and verses 11–28, where this enigmatic figure is used to prove that the Levitical priesthood was never meant to be permanent since the fulfilment of Melchizedek's 'eternal' priesthood was still to come. Within verses 11–28 the sections verses 11–19 and 20–28 are respectively concerned with the insufficiency of the Levitical priesthood and the superiority of the new priesthood.[64] Verses 20–28 can be further broken down into 20–25, which consider the superiority of the new priesthood on the basis of its permanence (e.g. v. 24b, 'for ever'), and verses 26–28, which stand as a concluding summary that the Son has been made 'perfect' for ever (v. 28).[65] As such, verse 25 comes at the climax of the subsection 7:23–25, which underlines the permanence of Christ's priesthood.

[61] Lincoln 2006: 13–14.

[62] Guthrie 1994: 117; Lane 1991: cii–ciii; Lincoln 2006: 24–25; Ellingworth 1993: 50–52.

[63] Guthrie (1994: 82–83) notes the inclusio between 5:1 and 7:28 turning on the concept of the 'appointment' (*kathistēmi*) of priests.

[64] Lane 1991: 180.

[65] Ibid. 191; Kurianal 2000: 139.

Outside the concluding summary (vv. 26–28), in each of the chapter's sections the author orientates his discussion with respect to Psalm 110[LXX 109]:4:

The LORD has sworn and will not change his mind,
'You are a priest for ever after the order of Melchizedek.'[66]

So, in verses 1–10 the significance of Melchizedek is unpacked, particularly his greatness with respect to Levi, as the author discusses Genesis 14:17–20. The greatness of Melchizedek is established by the fact that Abraham, Levi's ancestor, paid tribute to Melchizedek. In verses 11–19 he argues that since Jesus is of the order of Melchizedek the priesthood has changed and that there can never be perfection through the Levitical priesthood.[67]

Finally, verses 20–25 are an examination of the phrase 'for ever' and especially how this applies to Jesus.[68] Unlike the former priests, whose death prevented them from continuing in their office, the fact that Jesus lives for ever means that he has a permanent priesthood. The section begins with reference to oaths in verses 20–22, particularly that Jesus is the recipient of the oath in Psalm 110:4, namely 'you are a priest for ever'. This is in contrast to the Levitical priests who were appointed without an oath. The writer has already associated God's making of an oath and eternal validity in 6:17,[69] and so is underlining the permanency of Christ's priesthood. This discussion of oaths leads to a consideration of covenants, which will be an important feature of the rest of the book.[70]

The structure of 7:23–24 is possibly chiastic,[71] but at the very least symmetrical[72] with 'because of death' in verse 23 matching 'because he remains' in verse 24. As such, although there is a strong comparison between the multiplicity of Levitical priests and the uniqueness of Jesus' priesthood,[73] this parallelism again relies on Psalm 110:4 and the fact that 'the author is more concerned at this point with the eternity of Christ's priesthood than with his uniqueness'.[74] However,

---

[66] Kurianal 2000: 47, 85.
[67] Ibid. 106.
[68] Ibid. 128.
[69] Peterson 1982: 113.
[70] Kurianal 2000: 128.
[71] Lane 1991: 189.
[72] Ellingworth 1993: 389.
[73] So Lane 1991: 188.
[74] Ellingworth 1993: 389.

perhaps this is not such a great distinction since 'the reason there were many priests is that every one of them was prevented from continuing in office by the simple fact of death'.[75]

Due to this permanency of Christ's priesthood, the writer concludes that Christ is able to save 'to the uttermost' those who come to God through him (v. 25). Although the verb 'to save' is rare in Hebrews (cf. 5:7),[76] the cognate noun is frequent.[77] The adverbial phrase *eis to panteles*, which I have rendered 'to the uttermost', has been widely debated. It has been understood temporally, meaning 'for all time' and thus as synonymous with *eis ton aiōna* (7:24b) and *pantote* (7:25b).[78] On the other hand, it has also been understood qualitatively, to mean 'completely' so that it refers to 'complete salvation'.[79] The only other occurrence in the NT is in Luke 13:11, where it is used qualitatively.[80] Some have argued that 'the very ambiguity of the phrase probably appealed to our author'.[81] As such, the 'salvation provided by Christ is everlasting precisely because it is complete'.[82] The phrase he 'always lives' has been largely read as causal, supplying the reason for the high priest's ability to save absolutely.[83] However, it could also be modal, 'indicating the manner in which he is able to save'.[84] Perhaps the fact that the participle *follows* the verb it is modifying may tip us in this direction.[85]

That brings us to the key issue of the reason that Christ can permanently save believers: 'he always lives to make intercession for them'. *Broadly* speaking, the interpretation of the key term *entynchanō* in 7:25 divides into two groups – those who understand it as prayer by Christ and those who understand it metaphorically. The figurative interpretation, as we have seen, takes different forms but has the common thread in seeing Christ's intercession as an umbrella term for something more comprehensive than simply prayer. So, Spicq specifically argues that intercession should be understood to include

[75] Lane 1991: 188.
[76] Ellingworth 1993: 391.
[77] Heb. 1:14; 2:3, 10; 5:9; 6:9; 9:28; 11:7.
[78] As noted by Koester 2001: 365.
[79] Ibid.
[80] Delling 1972: 66.
[81] Attridge 1989: 210.
[82] Koester 2001: 365.
[83] Attridge 1989: 210; Lane 1991: 190; Ellingworth 1993: 392; Kurianal 2000: 136; Koester 2001: 365.
[84] Lane 1991: 190.
[85] Wallace 1996: 629.

a diversity of sacerdotal activities.[86] Cody argues that the 'concept of intercession is valuable for laying weight on the role of Christ, eternally present before God, in bringing mankind to perfection'.[87] What is subsumed under intercession depends, by and large, on other doctrinal categories. Some who have argued for the perpetual nature of Christ's sacrifice have expressed this perpetuity through the doctrine of Christ's intercession.[88] This is not restricted to Roman Catholic or Anglo-Catholic theologians. Certain Protestants have stressed the continuation of Christ's sacrifice in the form of Christ's continuous representative standing before the Father,[89] which is then reflected in their understanding of intercession.[90] Others have stressed Christ's ongoing ministry as his application of the atonement and have tied this to his ministry of intercession. Tait expresses the difference between the non-metaphorical and metaphorical interpretations in that 'one takes its stand on the ordinary significance of intercession . . . the other starts from the study of the Levitical type, according to which *standing in the Presence* was everything, and words were nothing'.[91]

One of the strongest arguments that prayer is in view is the meaning of *entynchanō*, which, as we have seen, generally has the idea of approaching someone to communicate verbally. Further, the syntax of the clause may push us towards this active meaning. Crump has pointed out that the passive figurative sense would be better expressed by saying that 'Christ lives *as* an intercession' rather than that he 'lives to intercede'.[92] Negatively, however, as we have seen, the view that Christ is actually praying is often caricatured as implying that Christ 'is pleading with an ill-disposed Father to change his attitude toward us'.[93] However, John 17 as an example of Christ's earthly intercession is as far from the caricature of pleading with an ill-disposed father as one can get. In short, the active interpretation of Christ's continuing to pray does not *necessitate* a pleading Christ before an otherwise unwilling Father. Rather, 'Christ is seen to continue to do in heaven what he has already done regularly in his life here on earth'.[94]

---

[86] Spicq 1952: 69.
[87] Cody 1960: 198.
[88] E.g. Gore 1901: 253–254: 'His propitiation and his intercession are identical'; Miligan 1898: 160: 'The Intercession and Offering cannot be separated from each other.'
[89] Torrance 1976: 115.
[90] Ibid. 115–116: 'Jesus Christ remains in himself, in his very union with God the Father, the eternal pledge or surety of our redemption.'
[91] Tait 1912: 171–172, emphasis added.
[92] Crump 1992: 17.
[93] Hughes (1977: 270), who rejects this caricature.
[94] Crump 1992: 18.

However, perhaps the more fundamental objection to the active understanding of Christ's intercession is that it calls into question the effectiveness of the once-for-all nature of Christ's sacrifice. As Crump asks (rhetorically), 'how can our High Priest both have finished and be continuing his work? . . . why would he need to intercede for believers after offering the final sacrifice?' Hay, who dismisses 7:25 as a foreign element to the text, asks why Christ should 'need to intercede after offering an utterly adequate sacrifice'?[95]

Any understanding of intercession must recognize that Hebrews is insistent on the finality, uniqueness and unrepeatability of Christ's sacrifice. He has no need to offer sacrifices daily, since he has offered himself up once (7:27). Christ did not appear in heaven to offer himself repeatedly (9:25). No, Christ has been offered *once* (9:28; cf. 7:27) to bear sins. Unlike other priests, who repeatedly offer sacrifices (10:11), Christ has offered one sacrifice for all time (10:12). Christ's sacrifice need never be repeated because it is utterly effective. By his single offering he has 'perfected for all time those who are being sanctified' (10:14).

However, since Hebrews 'centres on the question of the future of the people of God',[96] when it discusses the concept of *salvation* it most often does so in terms of the 'final deliverance that will take place in the future'.[97] So, salvation is something that is inherited (1:14) and Christ will return a second time for the salvation of those who are waiting for him (9:28). This issue is focused by the so-called warning passages in Hebrews,[98] which have been the subject of seemingly endless discussion. Debates have tended to centre on the fate (Can they be restored?) and the identity (Were they really Christians?) of those who *fail* to heed the warning and what that implies for the doctrines of assurance, election and salvation.[99] However, in the first instance, as is being increasingly recognized, the warnings function as just that – warnings to be *heeded*.[100] They are spoken to Christians to rebuke them out of any complacency so that none of them will have an 'evil, unbelieving heart, leading [them] to fall away from the living God' (3:12). Since 'the promise of entering [God's] rest still stands', that is, is future, the author of Hebrews warns

[95] Hay 1973: 150.
[96] Koester 2005: 361.
[97] Ibid. 362.
[98] Heb. 2:1–4; 3:12 – 4:2, 11–13; 6:4–8; 10:26–31; 12:13b–17, 25–29.
[99] See the discussion on the wider issues involved in Schreiner and Caneday 2001: 19–45.
[100] See e.g. Schreiner and Caneday 2001: 44–45.

the readers of the real danger of failing to reach it (4:1). In the context of the warning passages, it is fundamentally faithful perseverance that the hearers are being exhorted to. Like the wilderness generation, it is lack of persevering in faith that will keep them from entering God's rest (3:12, 14, 19; 4:2). It is through faith that they inherit what is promised (6:12), through faith that they preserve their souls (10:39). At root it is not refusing him who speaks (12:25) but paying attention to the message of salvation that will keep them from drifting away (2:1–3). Persevering in faith involves holding fast the confession, not hardening one's heart (4:7) and making every effort to enter God's rest (4:11).

However, not everything lies in the future as far as Hebrews is concerned. Perhaps this is most clearly brought out in 10:14, where the author maintains that 'by a single offering [Christ] has perfected for all time those who are being sanctified'. As Peterson notes, the writer 'locates this perfecting *in the past with respect to its accomplishment and in the present with respect to its enjoyment*',[101] and as such the 'terminology of perfection is used by our writer here to stress the realized aspect of Christian salvation'.[102] How do we integrate these present and future perspectives?

Interestingly in 7:25 we have these two emphases combined: Christ's ability to save eternally and the need for continuing in faith or drawing near.[103] Crucially, *it is Christ's intercession that bridges the two.* It is Christ's intercession that guarantees the final salvation of those who come to God through him. F. F. Bruce argues that regarding the question of the nature of Christ's intercession, 'what better answer can be given than that he still does for his people at the right hand of God what he did for Peter on earth'?[104] In other words, just as Jesus prayed for Peter's faith not to fail (Luke 22:32), he continues to pray the same thing for believers. This fits with Jesus' prayer in John 17 that the disciples may be protected from the evil one (John 17:15). The prayers of Jesus, then, are for the perseverance in faith of the disciples. It is his ongoing prayer that sustains them in the faith.

In Hebrews this idea of Jesus' *continuing* to sustain and help believers is clearly present.[105] So, in 2:18 Jesus is described as being

---

[101] Peterson 1982: 152, emphasis original.
[102] Ibid.
[103] Notice how the concepts of 'drawing near' and faith are paralleled in 10:22 and 11:6.
[104] Bruce 1965: 154–155.
[105] For this section I am very grateful to Peter O'Brien for his insights through personal communication.

able to 'help' those who are being tempted. Similarly, in 4:16 believers are enjoined to go to the throne of grace so that they may receive 'help' in time of need. In both cases the immediate contexts (2:16 itself and 4:15) discuss temptation. The thought being expressed is that Jesus sustains believers in time of temptation *so that*, like Peter in Luke 22, they will persevere in their faith.

It would seem that what believers are *continually* in need of is help in the face of temptation. The severity of temptation is highlighted by the repeated warnings to persevere in the faith. As such, if Hebrews 7:25 *is* referring to Jesus' praying for us, this prayer seems to be that we would not fall in the face of temptation but would persevere. As we have seen, there is a 'now–not yet' tension with respect to the salvation of believers. In 7:25 it is Christ's ongoing intercessory prayer that undergirds the assurance that believers *will* be saved permanently.

This view of intercession reflects the great concern of the letter that believers persevere.[106] Does this prayer also include prayer for forgiveness? Ellingworth is circumspect and argues that 'the language is too general to determine whether prayer for help or for forgiveness is intended'.[107] While this should rightly make us cautious, perhaps we can explore the issue further. Intercession in the OT is primarily concerned with the aversion of God's wrath,[108] and we note that 4:16 exhorts believers to draw near the throne of grace to receive 'mercy', which would presuppose the need for forgiveness. Koester, therefore, argues that '[i]nsofar as people are tested and afflicted by other people or by the devil they need divine help to persevere (2:15; 13:3, 13), and insofar as they are sinful they stand under God's judgment and need forgiveness'.[109] However, 4:16 also exhorts the believer to approach 'with boldness'. Further, in Hebrews, ultimate freedom from sin is very closely tied to the efficacy of Christ's once-for-all sacrifice (10:2; cf. 9:22; 10:18). As mediator of the new covenant (8:6), Christ has inaugurated a new order, where God will 'be merciful toward their iniquities, and . . . will remember their sins no more' (8:12). The emphasis of Hebrews, then, would seem to suggest that this ongoing prayer of Christ results in the application of the *benefits* of our forgiveness rather than our forgiveness per se. Koester goes

---

[106] Peterson (1982: 114) sees the *goal* of that intercession to be the perseverance of Christians.
[107] Ellingworth 1993: 392.
[108] Miller 1994: 266.
[109] Koester 2001: 371.

too far in describing believers as 'under God's judgment'.[110] Rather, as Christ prays the benefits of forgiveness are applied, ensuring that believers will persevere and so will be saved.

The intercession of Christ in Hebrews 7:25, as in Romans 8:34, is his ongoing prayer for believers to persevere. In the context of the letter, this is not an excuse to relax but an incentive to persevere in faith.

Conclusion

In the light of my examination of Romans 8:34 and Hebrews 7:25, I have concluded that the intercession of Christ should be understood as intercessory prayer for believers with the primary goal being their ongoing perseverance.

Conclusion

We noted at the beginning of the last chapter that my division between the activity of Christ on earth and in heaven is slightly artificial; nevertheless, in attending to the latter we have noticed that NT believers relate to the exalted Christ as God and expect him to be able to act from heaven as God. The heavenly activity of Christ suggests a high Christology. At the same time we have seen that Christ is presented as not just receiving prayers but as praying. We saw that the goal of Christ's intercession in heaven is aligned with his intercession during his earthly ministry, namely the perseverance of believers.

[110] Ibid.

198

Chapter Eleven

Concluding reflections

Summary

We have examined the exalted Christ through the lenses of his identity, his location and his activity. In chapter 2 we looked at the identity of Christ by considering the relationship between the 'earthly Jesus' and the exalted Christ. We saw that there is both continuity (the Jesus who died is the Jesus who was raised and who ascended) and development. We saw that Jesus entered more fully into his identity as Lord, Christ and Son following his resurrection and ascension. It is not that he *became* these things in an absolute sense (as if they were not true of him below) but nor is it that his exaltation was a *mere* revealing of what was already true. Rather, the revelation of the fullness of Christ's identity is analogous to his role as 'Saviour'; although Jesus was genuinely the 'Saviour' before his death, it was through the cross and resurrection that he entered into his identity as Saviour. We also drew a parallel with believers, whom Paul views as already 'sons and daughters' of God (Rom. 8:14) but who do not enter into the fullness of their adoption until the resurrection (Rom. 8:23). In chapters 3 and 4 we considered the identity of Christ through the lenses of his relationship with the Holy Spirit and with the church. We saw that although some want to collapse the distinctions so that the exalted Christ is considered in some way *as* the Spirit or *as* the church, the NT maintains a distinction between Christ and the Spirit, and Christ and the church. Nevertheless, we also saw that considering Christ's relationship with the church underlines the fact that the exalted Christ's identity has a corporate dimension (even if this does not exhaust his identity).

In chapters 5–8 we investigated the location of Christ, considering the relationship between his ascension and absence (chapter 5) as well as his continuing possession of a distinct, individual, localizable, human body (chapter 6). It is a failure to understand this aspect of Christ's exalted state that leads to the tendency to collapse Christ into the church or the Spirit, but correctly grasping it underlines the ongoing human nature of Christ. Further, it is the body of Christ that explains the phenomenon of the absence of Christ (chapter 7). Because he possesses a distinct body, Christ cannot be present in an unqualified sense. Rather, his presence is a mediated presence (chapter 8). In my exegesis of 2 Corinthians 2 – 4 we considered what I termed the *epiphanic* presence of Christ, whereby Paul shows how Christ is *made* present through different media (the apostle, the church, the Spirit).

Chapters 9 and 10 considered the activity of Christ, although we could equally consider chapter 9 as a treatment of the *dynamic* presence of Christ; that is, his mediated activity on earth. We saw that his activity is particularly concerned with the progress of the gospel and the perseverance of Christians. Chapter 10 considered the activity of Christ *in heaven*. We saw that in responding to prayer and acting from heaven, Christ's functions align with those of God himself. In the second half of the chapter we considered his intercession and saw how that also had the goal of the perseverance of Christians to their final salvation.

Theological and pastoral reflections

The humanity of Christ

We have seen that the risen and exalted Christ remains a human being. His resurrected body is glorified, but it remains a distinct, individual, localizable *human* body. He did not shed or lay aside his humanity following his resurrection and ascension. Christian theology has, perhaps understandably, been more concerned to stress the deity of Christ. Although the early heresy of Docetism denied the humanity of Jesus and was opposed in the early church, it was generally concerned with Jesus as he lived on earth. Christ's *ongoing* humanity has not received much concentrated treatment. However, the ongoing humanity of Christ is important for a number of reasons.

First, the ongoing, eternal humanity of Christ underlines the dignity and uniqueness of humanity. Increasingly Western society is becoming intolerant of the idea that humanity is unique. As far back as 1975, the philosopher Peter Singer could speak of 'speciesism' to denote a prejudice against non-humans.[1] Singer's contention is that humanity is not distinct or unique, a position that frequently

---

[1] Singer 1975. Although he actually attributes the term to an earlier pamphlet produced by Richard Ryder.

undergirds, for example, arguments in favour of abortion or euthanasia, which question the inherent value of human life. As such, Christians need a firm grasp of the Bible's teaching on the uniqueness of humanity. The risen exalted Jesus – truly God and truly human – underlines God's *eternal* commitment to humanity. Humanity is valuable – eternally valuable – in the eyes of God and of greater value than any other species. Christians tend to turn to the doctrine of creation to understand the place of humanity, focusing on humans as the image of God. While this is right and helpful, it needs to be complemented with the fact of Jesus' *eternal* humanity. That the exalted Christ is a glorified human being shows us what humanity is meant to be and what redeemed humanity one day will be. Human beings are unique in God's eyes, and we know that because the Son of God became a human being and remains a human being for ever.

Second, the fact that Jesus retains a distinct, physical, human body means that, like him, *we* will retain our bodies for eternity. We will be transformed, we will be different but we will still retain our bodies. Our eternal future will be a physical, bodily future. It is very common for Christians to pit the 'spiritual' against the 'physical', as if the spiritual were somehow more holy than the physical, and to think of redemption in terms of escaping from our bodies. However, for many Christians the spiritual can appear vague and less substantial than our earthly existence, and so it seems less attractive. Images of eternity involve floating around on clouds playing harps. That is part of the reason that many Christians – at least in the more affluent 'West' – do not long for the new creation. We feel like we have so much more to experience in this life. Eternity seems 'lighter' and less substantial than our current existence on earth. However, in reality our eternal existence will be one of more *glorious* physicality. Christians long for the day when their bodies will be redeemed, when they will be transformed and glorified – not when they will be dissolved or turned into ethereal, spiritual substance. Jesus did not dissolve into spiritual nothingness. He retains his humanity and he retains a distinct, individual, physical body.

The location of Christ

As Christians, like Paul, we experience the absence of Christ. We do not have a full experience of what it means to know Christ and to have fellowship with him. Instead, we wait for the day when he returns or when we depart to be with Christ, 'which is better by far' (Phil. 1:23, NIV); we would rather be 'away from the body and at home with the Lord' (2 Cor. 5:8). This means that part of the Christian experience is grieving and longing as we wait to be united with our loved one.

There has been a recent move to critique an older evangelical piety that saw 'going to heaven when you die' as the ultimate goal of the Christian life. These critiques have pointed out that 'heaven' should not be the ultimate object of our longing. Rather, our ultimate gaze should be directed to the resurrection of our bodies and the new creation.[2] This is a helpful correction to a slightly imprecise understanding of 'heaven'. However, what the old evangelical piety got right and what evangelicals today could learn from is that this longing for 'heaven' was often, at its heart, an expression of longing for *Christ*. Heaven, as the place where Christ dwells, became the focus of the longing because *Christ* was the one longed for. The intense longing for Christ of past generations of evangelicals echoed Paul's own longing, and challenges the insipid worldliness of much contemporary (Western) evangelicalism.

However, as Christians, even as we wait, we do experience the presence of Christ. Even as we long for the full bodily presence of Christ when he returns or when we go to be with him, we are not left as orphans. Although his presence is mediated, it remains a genuine presence. Because of Christ's relationship with the Spirit, he is genuinely with us through the Spirit. Our experience is not like being separated from a relative on the other side of the world. Jesus' promise to the disciples still stands: he will never leave us or forsake us; he is in us, he is with us and we are not alone (Matt. 28:20).

As with many things in the Christian life, as we think about where Jesus is we need to hold things in tension. We need to remember the absence of Christ: he is not here; we long for his coming; we long to be with him in body as well as in Spirit for that will be better by far. But we also need to remember the presence of Christ: through the Spirit he really is with us.

The activity of Christ

What is Jesus doing now? He is sitting at the right hand of the Father appearing on our behalf. His work of redemption is complete. Nothing more needs to be done – by him or by us – to reconcile us to God. But although the work of redemption is complete, the work of the gospel progressing to the ends of the earth and the work of

---

[2] See e.g. Wright 2007: 160.

Christians continuing steadfast in Christ needs to continue. And Christ (with the Father and the Spirit) is involved in this work. We have seen that he undertakes to ensure that the gospel continues to progress and he is involved in ensuring that Christians persevere to the end.

When we sin, we can remember that Jesus is sitting down, that his work is finished and that he is appearing in heaven on our behalf – that full atonement has been made. When we struggle to persevere and are tempted to give up, we can remember that someone is always praying for us. And not just anyone but the risen and exalted Lord Jesus. Jesus is the one who is continually interceding that we will be saved to the uttermost.

Thus Christian hope, Christian life, Christian faith and Christian theology are all inextricably bound up with the exalted Christ.

Bibliography

Adams, E. (2009), 'The Cosmology of Hebrews', in R. Bauckham, D. R. Driver, T. A. Hart and N. Macdonald (eds.), *The Epistle to the Hebrews and Christian Theology*, Grand Rapids: Eerdmans, 122–139.

Allison Jr, D. C. (2008), 'The Historians' Jesus and the Church', in B. R. Gaventa and R. B. Hays (eds.), *Seeking the Identity of Jesus: A Pilgrimage*, Grand Rapids: Eerdmans, 79–95.

Arnold, C. E. (2010), *Ephesians*, ZECNT, Grand Rapids: Zondervan.

Asher, J. R. (2000), *Polarity and Change in 1 Corinthians 15: A Study of Metaphysics, Rhetoric, and Resurrection*, HUT 42, Tübingen: Mohr Siebeck.

Attridge, H. W. (1989), *The Epistle to the Hebrews: A Commentary on the Epistle to the Hebrews*, Hermeneia, Philadelphia: Fortress.

Back, F. (2002), *Verwandlung durch Offenbarung bei Paulus: Eine religionsgeschichtlich-exegetische Untersuchung zu 2 Kor 2,14–4,6*, WUNT 2.153, Tübingen: Mohr Siebeck.

Ballentine, S. E. (1984), 'The Prophet as Intercessor: A Reassessment', *JBL* 103.2: 161–173.

Baltzer, K. (2001), *Deutero-Isaiah: A Commentary on Isaiah 40–5*, tr. Margaret Kohl, Hermeneia, Minneapolis: Fortress.

Balz, H. R. (1971), *Heilsvertrauen und Welterfahrung: Strukturen der paulinischen Eschatologie nach Römer 8,18–39*, Munich: Chr. Kaiser.

Barclay, J. M. G. (2011), 'Stoic Physics and the Christ-event: A Review of Troels Engberg-Pedersen, Cosmology and the Self in the Apostle Paul: The Material Spirit', *JSNT* 33.4: 406–414.

——— (2015), *Paul and the Gift*, Grand Rapids: Eerdmans.

Barnard, J. (2012), *The Mysticism of Hebrews: Exploring the Role of Jewish Apocalyptic Mysticism in the Epistle to the Hebrews*, WUNT 2.331, Tübingen: Mohr Siebeck.

Barrett, C. K. (1973), *A Commentary on the Second Epistle to the Corinthians*, 2nd edn, BNTC, London: A&C Black.

——— (1994), *A Critical and Exegetical Commentary on the Acts of the Apostles*, vol. 1: *Preliminary Introduction and Commentary on Acts I–XIV*, ICC, Edinburgh: T&T Clark.

Bates, M. W. (2015), 'A Christology of Incarnation and Enthronement: Romans 1:3–4 as Unified, Nonadoptionist, and Nonconciliatory', *CBQ* 77: 107–127.

Bauckham, R. (1993), *The Climax of Prophecy: Studies on the Book of Revelation*, Edinburgh: T&T Clark.

—— (2001), 'The Future of Jesus Christ', in M. Bockmuehl (ed.), *The Cambridge Companion to Jesus*, Cambridge Companions to Religion, Cambridge: Cambridge University Press, 265–280.

—— (2008), *Jesus and the God of Israel: 'God Crucified' and Other Studies on the New Testament's Christology of Divine Identity*, Milton Keynes: Paternoster.

Bauernfeind, O. (1972), '*entynchanō*', in *TDNT* 8: 242–244.

Beale, G. R. (1999), *The Book of Revelation: A Commentary on the Greek Text*, NIGTC, Grand Rapids: Eerdmans.

Belleville, L. L. (1991), *Reflections of Glory: Paul's Polemical Use of the Moses–Doxa Tradition in 2 Corinthians 3.1–18*, JSNTSup 52, Sheffield: Sheffield Academic Press.

Benjamin, W. (1999), 'The Work of Art in the Age of Mechanical Reproduction', in H. Arendt (ed.), *Illuminations*, New York: Schocken, 223–234.

Berkhof, H. (1977), *The Doctrine of the Holy Spirit*, Atlanta: John Knox.

Bertrams, H. (1913), *Das Wesen des Geistes nach der Anschauung des Apostels Paulus*, NTA 4.4, Münster: Aschendorff.

Best, E. (1972), *A Commentary on the First and Second Epistles to the Thessalonians*, BNTC, London: A&C Black.

—— (1988), *Ephesians*, ICC, Edinburgh: T&T Clark.

Betz, H. D. (2000), 'The Concept of the "Inner Human Being" (*ho esō anthrōpos*) in the Anthropology of Paul', *NTS* 46.3: 315–341.

Bock, D. (1996), *Luke 9:51–24:53*, BECNT, Grand Rapids: Eerdmans.

Bockmuehl, M. (1997), *A Commentary on the Epistle to the Philippians*, BNTC, London: Continuum.

Boring, M. E. (1989), *Revelation*, Interpretation, Louisville: John Knox.

—— (1992), 'Narrative Christology in the Apocalypse', *CBQ* 54.4: 702–723.

Boxall, I. (2006), *The Revelation of St John*, BNTC, Peabody: Hendrickson.

Brown, R. E (1970), *The Gospel According to John XIII–XXI*, AB 29A, New York: Doubleday.

Bruce, F. F. (1965), *Commentary on the Epistle to the Hebrews: The English Text with Introduction, Exposition and Notes*, New London Commentaries, London: Marshall, Morgan & Scott.

Buch-Hansen, G. (2010), *'It Is the Spirit That Gives Life': A Stoic Understanding of Pneuma in John's Gospel*, BZNW 173, Berlin: de Gruyter.

Bultmann, R. (1969), 'The Significance of the Historical Jesus for the Theology of Paul', in *Faith and Understanding*, London: SCM, 220–246.

——— (2007), *Theology of the New Testament*, 2 vols., tr. Kendrick Grobel, Waco: Baylor.

Burge, G. M. (1987), *The Anointed Community: The Holy Spirit in the Johannine Tradition*, Grand Rapids: Eerdmans.

Byrne, B. (1996), *Romans*, SP 6, Collegeville: Liturgical Press.

Calvin, J. (1989), *Institutes of the Christian Religion*, 4 vols., tr. Henry Beveridge, Grand Rapids: Eerdmans.

——— (1998a), 'Commentary on 1 John', in *The John Calvin Collection on CD-ROM*, tr. John Owen, Ages Software.

——— (1998b), 'Romans', in *The John Calvin Collection on CD-ROM*, tr. John Owen, Ages Software.

——— (1998c), '1 Corinthians', in *The John Calvin Collection on CD-ROM*, tr. John Owen, Ages Software.

Campbell, C. R. (2012), *Paul and Union with Christ: An Exegetical and Theological Study*, Grand Rapids: Zondervan.

Carson, D. A. (1991), *The Gospel According to John*, Leicester: Inter-Varsity Press.

——— (2002), *Love in Hard Places*, Carlisle: Paternoster.

Chilton, B. D. (1987), *The Isaiah Targum: Introduction, Translation, Apparatus and Notes*, ArBib 11, Edinburgh: T&T Clark.

Chrysostom, J. (1841), *The Homilies of S. John Chrysostom, Archbishop of Constantinople, on the Epistle of St. Paul the Apostle to the Romans*, tr. J. B. Morris, A Library of Fathers of the Holy Catholic Church Anterior to the Division of the East and West vol. 7, London: J. G. F. & J. Rivington.

Church, P. (2017), *Hebrews and the Temple: Attitudes to the Temple in Second Temple Judaism and in Hebrews*, SNTSMS 171, Leiden: Brill.

Ciampa, R. E., and Rosner, B. S. (2010), *The First Letter to the Corinthians*, PNTC, Grand Rapids: Eerdmans.

Clines, D. J. A. (1976), *I, He, We and They: A Literary Approach to Isaiah 53*, Sheffield: Sheffield University Press.

Coakley, S. (2008), 'The Identity of the Risen Jesus: Finding Jesus Christ in the Poor', in B. R. Gaventa and R. B. Hays (eds.), *Seeking the Identity of Jesus: A Pilgrimage*, Grand Rapids: Eerdmans, 301–319.

Cody, A. (1960), *Heavenly Sanctuary and Liturgy in the Epistle to the Hebrews: The Achievement of Salvation in the Epistle's Perspectives*, St Meinrad, Ind.: Grail.

Collange, J. F. (1972), *Enigmes de la deuxième épître de Paul aux Corinthiens: Étude exégétique de 2 Cor. 2,14–7,4*, SNTSMS 18, Cambridge: Cambridge University Press.

—— (1979), *The Epistle of Saint Paul to the Philippians*, London: Epworth.

Conzelmann, H. (1960), *The Theology of St Luke*, London: Faber & Faber.

—— (1967), *Grundriß der Theologie des Neuen Testaments*, Munich: Chr. Kaiser.

—— (1975), *1 Corinthians: A Commentary on the First Epistle to the Corinthians*, Hermeneia, Philadelphia: Fortress.

Cranfield, C. E. B. (1975), *Romans*, 2 vols., ICC, Edinburgh: T&T Clark.

Croy, N. C. (2003), '"To Die Is Gain" (Philippians 1:19–26): Does Paul Contemplate Suicide?', *JBL* 122.3: 517–531.

Crump, D. (1992), *Jesus the Intercessor: Prayer and Christology in Luke-Acts*, Biblical Studies Library, Grand Rapids: Baker.

Dahl, M. E. (1962), *The Resurrection of the Body: A Study of 1 Corinthians 15*, SBT 36, London: SCM.

Deissmann, A. (1892), *Die neutestamentliche Formel 'in Christo Jesu'*, Marburg: N. G. Elwert.

Deissner, K. (1912), *Auferstehungshoffnung und Pneumagedanke bei Paulus*, Naumburg a. d. Saale: Lippert.

Delling, G. (1972), '*panteles*', *TDNT* 8: 66–67.

Duff, P. B. (2008), 'Transformed "from Glory to Glory": Paul's Appeal to the Experience of His Readers in 2 Corinthians 3:18', *JBL* 127.4: 759–780.

Dunn, J. D. G. (1970), '2 Corinthians 3:17: The Lord Is the Spirit', *JTS* 21.2: 309–320.

—— (1973), 'Jesus—Flesh and Spirit: An Exposition of Romans 1:3–4', *JTS* 24: 40–68.

—— (1988a), *Romans 1–8*, WBC 38a, Dallas: Word.

—— (1988b), *Romans 9–16*, WBC 38b, Dallas: Word.

—— (1989), *Christology in the Making: A New Testament Inquiry into the Origins of the Doctrine of the Incarnation*, 2nd edn, London: SCM.

—— (1998), *The Theology of Paul the Apostle*, Grand Rapids: Eerdmans.

—— (2001), 'The Ascension of Jesus: A Test Case for Hermeneutics', in F. Avemarie and H. Lichtenberger (eds.), *Auferstehung–Resurrection: The Fourth Durham–Tübingen Research Symposium; Resurrection, Transfiguration and Exaltation in Old Testament, Ancient Judaism and Early Christianity*, Tübingen: Mohr Siebeck, 301–322.

Eichholz, G. (1983), *Die Theologie des Paulus im Umriß*, 4th edn, Neukirchen-Vluyn: Neukirchener Verlag.

Ellingworth, P. (1993), *The Epistle to the Hebrews*, NIGTC, Grand Rapids: Eerdmans.

Engberg-Pedersen, T. (2009), 'The Material Spirit: Cosmology and Ethics in Paul', *NTS* 55.2: 179–197.

—— (2010), *Cosmology and Self in the Apostle Paul: The Material Spirit*, Oxford: Oxford University Press.

—— (2011), 'Paul's Body: A Response to Barclay and Levison', *JSNT* 33.4: 433–443.

—— (2017), *John and Philosophy: A New Reading of the Fourth Gospel*, Oxford: Oxford University Press.

Epp, E. J. (1981), 'The Ascension in the Textual Tradition of Luke-Acts', in E. J. Epp and G. D. Fee (eds.), *New Testament Textual Criticism: Its Significance for Exegesis: Essays in Honor of Bruce M. Metzger*, Oxford: Clarenden, 131–145.

Eskola, T. (2001), *Messiah and the Throne: Jewish Merkabah Mysticism and Early Christian Exaltation Discourse*, WUNT 2.142, Tübingen: Mohr Siebeck.

Farrow, D. (1999), *Ascension and Ecclesia: On the Significance of the Ascension for Ecclesiology and Christian Cosmology*, Grand Rapids: Eerdmans.

—— (2011), *Ascension Theology*, London: T&T Clark.

Fatehi, M. (2000), *The Spirit's Relation to the Risen Lord in Paul: An Examination of Its Christological Implications*, WUNT 2.128, Tübingen: Mohr Siebeck.

Fay, R. C. (2006), 'Was Paul a Trinitarian? A Look at Romans 8', in S. E. Porter (ed.), *Paul and His Theology*, Leiden: Brill, 327–345.

Fee, G. D. (1987), *The First Epistle to the Corinthians*, NICNT, Grand Rapids: Eerdmans.

—— (1994), *God's Empowering Presence: The Holy Spirit in the Letters of Paul*, Peabody: Hendrickson.

—— (1995), *Paul's Letter to the Philippians*, NICNT, Grand Rapids: Eerdmans.

―――― (2007), *Pauline Christology: An Exegetical-Theological Study*, Peabody: Hendrickson.

―――― (2009), *The First and Second Letter to the Thessalonians*, NICNT, Grand Rapids: Eerdmans.

Feuillet, A. (1956), 'La demeure céleste et la destinée des chrétiens: Exégèse de 2 Co 5,1–10 et contribution à l'étude des fondements de l'eschatologie paulinienne', *RSR* 44: 161–192.

Fitzgerald, J. T. (1988), *Cracks in an Earthen Vessel: An Examination of the Catalogues of Hardships in the Corinthian Correspondence*, SBLDS 99, Atlanta: Scholars Press.

Fitzmyer, J. A. (1993), *Romans: A New Translation with Introduction and Commentary*, AB 33, New York: Doubleday.

―――― (2008), *First Corinthians: A New Translation with Introduction and Commentary*, AB 32, New Haven: Yale University Press.

Fowl, S. (2012), *Ephesians: A Commentary*, NTL, Louisville: Westminster John Knox.

Frei, H. (1997), *The Identity of Jesus Christ: The Hermeneutical Bases of Dogmatic Theology*, Eugene: Wipf & Stock.

Furnish, V. P. (1984), *II Corinthians*, AB 32A, Garden City, N.Y.: Doubleday.

Gaventa, B. R. (2008), 'Learning and Relearning the Identity of Jesus from Luke-Acts', in B. R. Gaventa and R. B. Hays (eds.), *Seeking the Identity of Jesus: A Pilgrimage*, Grand Rapids: Eerdmans, 148–165.

Gieniusz, A. (1999), *Romans 8:18–30: Suffering Does Not Thwart the Future Glory*, Atlanta: Scholars Press.

Gillman, J. (1988), 'A Thematic Comparison: 1 Cor 15:50–57 and 2 Cor 5:1–5', *JBL* 107.3: 439–454.

Gnilka, J. (1976), *Der Philipperbrief*, 2nd edn, HTKNT 10.3, Freiburg: Herder.

Goldingay, J., and Payne, D. (2006), *A Critical and Exegetical Commentary on Isaiah 40–55 Volume II*, ICC, London: T&T Clark.

Goldsworthy, G. (2012), *Christ-Centred Biblical Theology: Hermeneutical Foundations and Principles*, Nottingham: Apollos.

―――― (2015), *The Son of God and the New Creation*, Short Studies in Biblical Theology, Wheaton: Crossway.

Gore, C. (1901), *The Body of Christ: An Enquiry into the Institution and Doctrine of Holy Communion*, London: John Murray.

Gräbe, P. J. (2000), *The Power of God in Paul's Letters*, WUNT 2.123, Tübingen: Mohr Siebeck.

Green, J. (1997), *The Gospel of Luke*, NICNT, Grand Rapids: Eerdmans.

Grieb, K. (2008), '"Time Would Fail Me to Tell . . .": The Identity of Jesus Christ in Hebrews', in B. R. Gaventa and R. B. Hays (eds.), *Seeking the Identity of Jesus: A Pilgrimage*, Grand Rapids: Eerdmans, 200–214.

Groves, J. A. (2004), 'Atonement in Isaiah 53', in C. E. Hill and F. A. James III (eds.), *The Glory of the Atonement: Essays in Honor of Roger Nicole*, Downers Grove: InterVarsity Press; Leicester: Apollos, 61–89.

Gundry-Volf, J. M. (1990), *Paul and Perseverance: Staying in and Falling Away*, WUNT 2.37, Tübingen: Mohr Siebeck.

Gunton, C. E. (2001), '"Until He Comes": Towards an Eschatology of Church Membership', *IJST* 3.2: 187–200.

Guthrie, G. (1994), *The Structure of Hebrews: A Text-Linguistic Analysis*, Grand Rapids: Baker.

——— (2007), 'Hebrews', in D. A. Carson and G. R. Beale (eds.), *Commentary on the New Testament Use of the Old Testament*, Grand Rapids: Baker, 919–996.

Hafemann, S. J. (1990), *Suffering and Ministry in the Spirit: Paul's Defence of His Ministry in II Corinthians 2:14–3:3*, Grand Rapids: Eerdmans.

——— (1995), *Paul, Moses, and the History of Israel: The Letter/ Spirit Contrast and the Argument from Scripture in 2 Corinthians 3*, WUNT 81, Tübingen: Mohr Siebeck.

Hagner, D. A. (1998), *Matthew 14–28*, WBC 33B, Dallas: Word.

Hamilton, N. Q. (1957), *The Holy Spirit and Eschatology in Paul*, Edinburgh: Oliver & Boyd.

Harris, M. (2014), 'The Comings and Goings of the Son of Man: Is Matthew's Risen Jesus "Present" or "Absent"? A Narrative-Critical Response', *BI* 22: 51–70.

Harris, M. J. (2005), *Second Epistle to the Corinthians: A Commentary on the Greek Text*, NIGTC, Grand Rapids: Eerdmans.

Harris III, W. H. (1996), *The Descent of Christ: Ephesians 4:7–11 and Traditional Hebrew Imagery*, AGJU 32, Leiden: Brill.

Harvey, J. D. (1992), 'The "With Christ" Motif in Paul's Thought', *JETS* 35.3: 329–340.

Hawthorne, G. F. (1983), *Philippians*, WBC 43, Waco: Word.

Hay, D. M. (1973), *Glory at the Right Hand: Psalm 110 in Early Christianity*, Nashville: Abingdon.

Hays, R. B. (1993), *Echoes of Scripture in the Letters of Paul*, New Haven: Yale University Press.

——— (1997), *First Corinthians*, Interpretation, Louisville: John Knox.

——— (2008), 'The Story of God's Son: The Identity of Jesus in the Letters of Paul', in B. R. Gaventa and R. B. Hays (eds.), *Seeking the Identity of Jesus: A Pilgrimage*, Grand Rapids: Eerdmans, 180–199.

——— (2016), *Echoes of Scripture in the Gospels*, Waco: Baylor.

Heath, J. (2008), 'Corinth, a Crucible for Byzantine Iconoclastic Debates? Viewing Paul as an Icon of Christ in 2 Cor 4,7–12', in H. Görgemanns, M. von Albrecht, R. Hirsch-Luipold and T. Thum (eds.), *Religiöse Philosophie und philosophische Religion der frühen Kaiserzeit*, Tübingen: Mohr Siebeck, 271–284.

——— (2013), *Paul's Visual Piety: The Metamorphosis of the Beholder*, Oxford: Oxford University Press.

Hengel, M. (1995), *Studies in Early Christology*, Edinburgh: T&T Clark.

Hermann, I. (1961), *Kyrios und Pneuma: Studien zur Christologie der paulinischen Hauptbriefe*, Munich: Kösel.

Hoehner, H. W. (2002), *Ephesians: An Exegetical Commentary*, Grand Rapids: Baker.

Hoffmann, P. (1978), *Die Toten in Christus: Eine religionsgeschichtliche und exegetische Untersuchung zur paulinischen Eschatologie*, Münster: Aschendorff.

Hofius, O. (1993), 'The Lord's Supper and the Lord's Supper Tradition: Reflections on 1 Corinthians 11:23b–25', in B. F. Meyer (ed.), *One Loaf, One Cup: Ecumenical Studies of 1 Cor 11 and Other Eucharistic Texts. The Cambridge Conference on the Eucharist August 1988*, Macon: Mercer University Press, 75–115.

Holdsworth, B. (2004), 'The Other Intercessor: The Holy Spirit as Familia-Petitioner for the Father's Filiusfamilia in Romans 8:26–27', *AUSS* 42.2: 325–346.

Horn, F. W. (1992), *Das Angeld des Geistes: Studien zur paulinischen Pneumatologie*, Göttingen: Vandenhoeck & Ruprecht.

——— (2000), 'Kyrios und Pneuma bei Paulus', in U. Schnelle (ed.), *Paulinische Christologie: Exegetische Beiträge; Hans Hübner zum 70. Geburtstag*, Göttingen: Vandenhoeck & Ruprecht, 59–75.

Horst, P. W. van der (2000), '"Only Then Will All Israel Be Saved": A Short Note on the Meaning of καὶ οὕτως in Romans 11:26', *JBL* 119.3: 521–525.

Hughes, P. E. (1977), *A Commentary on the Epistle to the Hebrews*, Grand Rapids: Eerdmans.

Jamir, L. (2017), *Exclusion and Judgment in Fellowship Meals: The Socio-Historical Background of 1 Corinthians 11:17–34*, Eugene: Pickwick.

Jenson, R. W. (1997), *Systematic Theology*, vol. 1: *The Triune God*, Oxford: Oxford University Press.

Jewett, R. (1971), *Paul's Anthropological Terms*, Leiden: Brill.

—— (2007), *Romans: A Commentary*, Hermeneia, Minneapolis: Fortress.

Jipp, J. W. (2016), '"For David Did Not Ascend into Heaven . . ." (Acts 2:34a): Reprogramming Royal Psalms to Proclaim the Enthroned-in-Heaven King', in D. K. Bryan and D. W. Pao (eds.), *Ascent into Heaven in Luke-Acts: New Explorations of Luke's Narrative Hinge*, Minneapolis: Fortress, 42–61.

Jobes, K. H. (2011), Review of Gitte Buch-Hansen: *'It Is the Spirit That Gives Life': A Stoic Understanding of Pneuma in John's Gospel*, Berlin: de Gruyter, 2010; in *BBR* 21.4: 564–567.

Johnson, L. T. (2012), 'The Body in Question: The Social Complexities of the Resurrection', in C. Skinner and K. Iverson (eds.), *Unity and Diversity in the Gospels and Paul: Essays in Honor of Frank J. Matera*, Atlanta: SBL, 225–247.

Johnson, N. C. (2017), 'Romans 1:3–4: Beyond Antithetical Parallelism', *JBL* 136.2: 467–490.

Jonge, H. J. de (2013), 'The Chronology of the Ascension Stories in Luke and Acts', *NTS* 59: 151–171.

Käsemann, E. (1942), 'Die Legitimität des Apostels: Eine Untersuchung zu II Korinther 10–13', *ZNW* 41: 33–71.

—— (1969), 'Blind Alleys in the "Jesus of History" Controversy', in *New Testament Questions of Today*, London: SCM, 23–65.

—— (1980), *Commentary on Romans*, tr. G. W. Bromiley, Grand Rapids: Eerdmans.

Keefer, A. J. (2016), 'The Use of the Book of Proverbs in Systematic Theology', *BBR* 46.1: 35–44.

Keener, C. S. (2003), *The Gospel of John: A Commentary*, 2 vols., Peabody: Hendrickson.

—— (2005), *1–2 Corinthians*, The New Cambridge Bible Commentary, Cambridge: Cambridge University Press.

Kelly, A. J. (2014), *Upward: Faith, Church, and the Ascension of Christ*, Collegeville: Liturgical Press.

Kim, S. (1982), *The Origin of Paul's Gospel*, Grand Rapids: Eerdmans.

—— (2002), *Paul and the New Perspective: Second Thoughts on the Origin of Paul's Gospel*, Grand Rapids: Eerdmans.

Kirk, J. D. (2016), *A Man Attested by God: The Human Jesus of the Synoptic Gospels*, Grand Rapids: Eerdmans.

Klauck, H.-J. (1982), *Herrenmahl und hellenistischer Kult: Eine religionsgeschichtliche Untersuchung zum ersten Korintherbrief*, NTA 15, Münster: Aschendorff.

———— (1987), 'Erleuchtung und Verkündigung: Auslegungsskizze zu 2 Kor 4,1–6', in L. de Lorenzi (ed.), *Paolo: Ministro del Nuovo Testamento (2 Co 2,14–4,6)*, Rome: Abbazia di S. Paolo, 267–316.

———— (1989), 'Präsenz im Herrenmahl: 1 Kor 11:23–26 im Kontext hellenistischer Religionsgeschichte', in H.-J. Klauck (ed.), *Gemeinde, Amt, Sakrament: Neutestamentliche Perspektiven*, Würzburg: Echter, 313–330.

———— (2006), *Ancient Letters and the New Testament: A Guide to Context and Exegesis*, Waco: Baylor University Press.

Koester, C. R. (2001), *Hebrews: A New Translation with Commentary*, AB 36, New York: Doubleday.

———— (2005), 'God's Purposes and Christ's Saving Work According to Hebrews', in J. G. van der Watt (ed.), *Salvation in the New Testament: Perspectives on Soteriology*, Leiden: Brill, 361–387.

———— (2014), *Revelation: A New Translation with Introduction and Commentary*, AB 38A, New Haven: Yale University Press.

Kollmann, B. (2000), 'Paulus als Wundertäter', in U. Schnelle, T. Söding and M. Labahn (eds.), *Paulinische Christologie: Exegetische Beiträge; Hans Hübner zum 70. Geburtstag*, Göttingen: Vandenhoeck & Ruprecht, 76–96.

König, A. (1989), *The Eclipse of Christ in Eschatology: Toward a Christ-Centered Approach*, Grand Rapids: Eerdmans.

Koole, J. L. (1998), *Isaiah Part 3 Volume 2: Isaiah 49–55*, tr. Anthony P. Runia, Leuven: Peeters.

Kreitzer, L. J. (1987), *Jesus and God in Paul's Eschatology*, JSNTSup 19, Sheffield: JSOT Press.

Kurianal, J. (2000), *Jesus Our High Priest: Ps 110,4 As Substructure of Heb 5,1–7,28*, European University Studies 693, Frankfurt: Peter Lang.

Kürzinger, J. (1958), 'Σύμμόρφους τῆς εἰκόνος τοῦ υἱοῦ αὐτοῦ (Röm 8,29)', *BZ* 2: 294–299.

Kuschnerus, B. (2002), *Die Gemeinde als Brief Christi: Die kommunikative Funktion der Metapher bei Paulus am Beispiel von 2 Kor 2–5*, FRLANT 197, Göttingen: Vandenhoeck & Ruprecht.

214

Kuss, O. (1963–78), *Der Römerbrief*, 3 vols., Regensburg: F. Pustet.

Ladd, G. E. (1968), *The Pattern of New Testament Truth*, Grand Rapids: Eerdmans.

Lambrecht, J. (1983a), 'Transformation in 2 Cor 3,18', *Bib* 64: 243–254.

—— (1983b), 'Structure and Line of Thought in 2 Cor 2:14–4:6', *Bib* 64: 344–380.

—— (1985), 'Philological and Exegetical Notes on 2 Cor 13,4', *Bijdragen* 46.3: 261–269.

—— (2006), *Second Corinthians*, SP 8, Collegeville: Liturgical Press.

—— (2009), 'From Glory to Glory (2 Corinthians 3,18): A Reply to Paul B. Duff', *ETL* 85.1: 143–146.

Lampe, G. W. H. (1977), *God as Spirit*, Oxford: Clarendon.

Lane, W. L. (1991), *Hebrews 1–8*, WBC 47a, Waco: Word.

Levison, J. R. (2012), Review of Troels Engberg-Pedersen, *Cosmology & Self in the Apostle Paul: The Material Spirit*, Oxford: Oxford University Press, 2010; and Gitte Buch-Hansen, *'It Is the Spirit That Gives Life': A Stoic Understanding of Pneuma in John's Gospel*, Berlin: de Gruyter, 2010, in *Pneuma* 34.1: 117–119.

Lim, K. Y. (2009), *'The Sufferings of Christ Are Abundant in Us' (2 Corinthians 1.5): A Narrative Dynamics Investigation of Paul's Sufferings in 2 Corinthians*, LNTS, London: T&T Clark.

Lincoln, A. (1990), *Ephesians*, WBC 42, Dallas: Word.

—— (1991), *Paradise Now and Not Yet: Studies in the Role of the Heavenly Dimension in Paul's Thought with Special Reference to His Eschatology*, SNTSMS 43, Cambridge: Cambridge University Press.

—— (2006), *Hebrews: A Guide*, London: T&T Clark.

Lindgård, F. (2005), *Paul's Line of Thought in 2 Corinthians 4:16–5:10*, WUNT 2.189, Tübingen: Mohr Siebeck.

Lofhink, G. (1971), *Die Himmelfahrt Jesu*, Munich: Kösel.

Lohse, E. (2003), *Der Brief an die Römer*, KEK 4, Göttingen: Vandenhoeck & Ruprecht.

Luckensmeyer, D. (2009), *The Eschatology of First Thessalonians*, NTOA/SUNT 71, Göttingen: Vandenhoeck & Ruprecht.

Luther, M. (1961), *Luther's Works Volume 37: Word and Sacrament Vol. 3*, ed. and tr. R. Fisher, Philadelphia: Fortress.

—— (1967), *Luther's Works Volume 30: The Catholic Epistles*, ed. Jaroslav Pelikan, tr. W. A. Hansen, St Louis: Concordia.

Luz, U. (2005), *Matthew 21–28*, tr. J. E. Crouch, Hermeneia, Minneapolis: Fortress.

McDonald, J. I. H. (1983), 'Paul and the Preaching Ministry: A Reconsideration of 2 Cor.2:14–17 in Its Context', *JSNT* 5: 35–50.

Marcel, G. (1950), *The Mystery of Being I: Reflection and Mystery*, tr. G. S. Fraser, Chicago: Henry Regnery.

Markschies, C. (1993), 'Sessio ad Dexteram: Bemerkungen zu einem altchristlichen Bekenntnismotiv in der christologischen Diskussion der altkirchlichen Theologen', in M. Philonenko (ed.), *Le Trône de Dieu*, WUNT 69, Tübingen: Mohr Siebeck, 252–317.

Marshall, I. H. (2007), 'Acts', in D. A. Carson and G. R. Beale (eds.), *Commentary on the New Testament Use of the Old Testament*, Grand Rapids: Baker, 515–606.

Martin, D. B. (1995), *The Corinthian Body*, New Haven: Yale University Press.

Martin, R. P. (1986), *2 Corinthians*, WBC 40, Waco: Thomas Nelson.

——— (1997), *A Hymn of Christ: Philippians 2:5–11 in Recent Interpretation and in the Setting of Early Worship*, Downers Grove: InterVarsity Press.

——— (2004), *Philippians*, WBC 43, Waco: Thomas Nelson.

Martyn, J. L. (2003), *History and Theology in the Fourth Gospel*, 3rd edn, Lousiville: Westminster John Knox.

May, A. S. (2004), *The Body for the Lord: Sex and Identity in 1 Corinthians 5–7*, JSNTSup 278, London: T&T Clark.

Meeks, W. (1972), 'The Man from Heaven in Johannine Sectarianism', *JBL* 91.1: 44–72.

Meier, J. P. (2001), *A Marginal Jew: Rethinking the Historical Jesus*, vol. 3: *Companions and Competitors*, New York: Doubleday.

Menzies, A. (ed.) (1896), 'The Testament of Abraham', in W. A. Craigie (tr.), K. Knight (rev.), *Ante-Nicene Fathers Volume 9*, Buffalo, N.Y.: Christian Literature Publishing. Cited 25 July 2018. Online <http://www.newadvent.org/fathers/1007.htm>.

Metzger, B. M. (1994), *A Textual Commentary on the Greek New Testament*, 2nd edn, Stuttgart: Deutsche Bibelgesellschaft.

Michaelis, W. (1968), '*prōtotokos*', in *TDNT* 6: 871–881.

Miligan, W. (1898), *The Ascension and Heavenly Priesthood of Our Lord*, London: Macmillan.

Miller, P. D. (1994), *They Cried to the Lord: The Form and Theology of Biblical Prayer*, Minneapolis: Fortress.

Mitchell, M. M. (2004), 'Epiphanic Evolutions in Earliest Christianity', *Illinois Classical Studies* 29: 183–204.

Moffitt, D. M. (2016), 'Serving in the Tabernacle in Heaven: Sacred Space, Jesus's High-Priestly Sacrifice, and Hebrews' Analogical Theology', in G. Gelardini and H. W. Attridge (eds.), *Hebrews in Contexts*, Leiden: Brill, 259–279.

Moo, D. J. (1996), *The Epistle to the Romans*, NICNT, Grand Rapids: Eerdmans.

Moritz, T. (1996), *A Profound Mystery: The Use of the Old Testament in Ephesians*, NovTSup, Leiden: Brill.

Moule, C. F. D. (1966), 'The Christology of Acts', in L. E. Keck and J. L. Martyn (eds.), *Studies in Luke-Acts: Essays Presented in Honor of Paul Schubert*, Nashville: Abingdon, 159–185.

Mounce, R. H. (1998), *The Book of Revelation*, NICNT, Grand Rapids: Eerdmans.

Murphy-O'Connor, J. (1977), 'Eucharist and Community in First Corinthians', *Worship* 50: 370–385.

——— (1986), '"Being at Home in the Body We Are in Exile from the Lord" (2 Cor. 5:6b)', *RB* 93.2: 212–241.

——— (1991), 'Christ and Ministry', *Pacifica* 4: 121–136.

——— (1999), 'The Whole Christ', *Liber annuus Studii biblici franciscani (LASBF)* 49: 181–194.

Murray, J. (1960), *The Epistle to the Romans: The English Text with Exposition and Notes*, London: Marshall, Morgan & Scott.

Nolland, J. (1989), *Luke 1–9:20*, WBC 35A, Dallas: Word.

Norman, R. (2001), 'Beyond the Ultimate Sphere: The Ascension and Eschatology', *Modern Believing* 42.2: 3–15.

Novakovic, L. (2012), *Raised from the Dead According to Scripture: The Role of Israel's Scripture in the Early Christian Interpretations of Jesus' Resurrection*, JCTS 12, London: T&T Clark.

Novenson, M. W. (2012), *Christ Among the Messiahs: Christ Language in Paul and Messiah Language in Ancient Judaism*, Oxford: Oxford University Press.

O'Brien, P. T. (1987), 'Romans 8:26, 27: A Revolutionary Approach to Prayer?', *RTR* 46.3: 65–73.

O'Collins, G. (2009), *Christology: A Biblical, Historical, and Systematic Study of Jesus*, Oxford: Oxford University Press.

Oliveira, A. de (1990), *Die Diakonie der Gerechtigkeit und der Versöhnung in der Apologie des 2. Korintherbriefes: Analyse und Auslegung von 2 Kor 2,14–4,6; 5,11–6,10*, Münster: Aschendorff.

Orr, P. C. (2014), *Christ Absent and Present: A Study in Pauline Christology*, WUNT 2.354, Tübingen: Mohr Siebeck.

—— (2018), 'Paul and Pastors in Ephesians: The Pastor as Teacher', in A. S. Malone, T. J. Burke and B. S. Rosner (eds.), *Paul as Pastor*, London: Bloomsbury T&T Clark, 83–94.

Osborne, G. R. (2002), *Revelation*, BECNT, Grand Rapids: Baker Academic.

Osei-Bonsu, J. (1986), 'Does 2 Cor. 5.1–10 Teach the Reception of the Resurrection Body at the Moment of Death?', *JSNT* 28.9: 81–101.

Paige, T. (2002), 'Who Believes in "Spirit"? *Pneuma* in Pagan Usage and Implications for the Gentile Christian Mission', *HTR* 95: 417–436.

Palmer, D. W. (1975), 'To Die Is Gain (Philippians 1:21)', *NovT* 17: 203–218.

—— (1987), 'The Literary Background of Acts 1:1–14', *NTS* 43.3: 427–438.

Pascut, B. (2017), *Redescribing Jesus' Divinity Through a Social Science Theory: An Interdisciplinary Analysis of Forgiveness and Divine Identity in Ancient Judaism and Mark 2:1–12*, WUNT 2.438, Tübingen: Mohr Siebeck.

Perriman, A. (2005), *The Coming Son of Man: New Testament Eschatology*, Milton Keynes: Paternoster.

Peterson, D. G. (1982), *Hebrews and Perfection: An Examination of the Concept of Perfection in the Epistle to the Hebrews*, SNTSMS 47, Cambridge: Cambridge University Press.

—— (2009), *The Acts of the Apostles*, PNTC, Nottingham: Apollos.

Plummer, A. (1915), *A Critical and Exegetical Commentary on the Second Epistle of Paul to the Corinthians*, ICC, Edinburgh: T&T Clark.

Porter, S. E. (2016), 'The Unity of Luke-Acts and the Ascension Narratives', in D. K. Bryan and D. W. Pao (eds.), *Ascent into Heaven in Luke-Acts: New Explorations of Luke's Narrative Hinge*, Minneapolis: Fortress, 111–136.

Powers, D. G. (2001), *Salvation Through Participation: An Examination of the Notion of the Believers' Corporate Unity with Christ in Early Christian Soteriology*, Leuven: Peeters.

Prince, D. T. (2007), 'The "Ghost" of Jesus: Luke 24 in Light of Ancient Narratives of Post-Mortem Apparitions', *JSNT* 29: 287–301.

Proudfoot, M. (1963), 'Imitation or Realistic Participation: A Study of Paul's Concept of "Suffering with Christ"', *Int* 17.2: 140–160.

Rabens, V. (1999), 'The Development of Pauline Pneumatology: A Response to F. W. Horn', *BZ* 43: 161–179.

—— (2010), *The Holy Spirit and Ethics in Paul: Transformation and Empowering for Religious-Ethical Life*, WUNT 2.283, Tübingen: Mohr Siebeck.

Reischl, W. C., and Rupp, J. (1848–60), *Cyrilli Hierosolymarum archiepiscopi opera quae supersunt Omnia*, 2 vols., Munich: Lentner.

Ricoeur, P. (1992), *Oneself as Another*, tr. K. Blamey, Chicago: University of Chicago Press.

Ridderbos, H. N. (1975), *Paul: An Outline of His Theology*, Grand Rapids: Eerdmans.

Robinson, J. A. T. (1952), *The Body: A Study in Pauline Theology*, SBT 1, London: SCM.

Rosner, B. S. (1994), *Paul, Scripture and Ethics: A Study of 1 Corinthians 5–7*, Leiden: Brill.

Rowe, J. K. (2007), 'Acts 2.36 and the Continuity of Lukan Christology', *NTS* 53: 37–56.

Schmisek, B. (2011), 'Paul's Vision of the Risen Lord', *BTB* 41: 76–83.

Schmithals, W. (1988), *Der Römerbrief: Ein Kommentar*, Gütersloh: G. Mohn.

Schneiders, S. M. (2008), 'Touching the Risen Jesus: Mary Magdalene and Thomas the Twin in John 20', in C. Koester and R. Bieringer (eds.), *The Resurrection of Jesus in the Gospel of John*, WUNT 222, Tübingen: Mohr Siebeck, 153–176.

—— (2013), *Jesus Risen in Our Midst: Essays on the Resurrection of Jesus in the Fourth Gospel*, Collegeville: Liturgical Press.

Schreiber, S. (1996), *Paulus als Wundertäter: Redaktionsgeschichtliche Untersuchungen zur Apostelgeschichte und den authentischen Paulusbriefen*, Berlin: de Gruyter.

—— (2003), 'Paulus im "Zwischenzustand": Phil 1.23 und die Ambivalenz des Sterbens als Provokation', *NTS* 49.3: 336–359.

Schreiner, T. (1998), *Romans*, BECNT, Grand Rapids: Baker.

—— (2015), *Hebrews*, BTCP, Nashville: B&H.

Schreiner, T., and Caneday A. (2001), *The Race Set Before Us: A Biblical Theology of Perseverance and Assurance*, Downers Grove: InterVarsity Press; Leicester: Inter-Varsity Press.

Schröter, J. (1998), 'Schriftauslegung und Hermeneutik in 2 Korinther 3: Ein Beitrag zur Frage der Schriftbenutzung des Paulus', *NovT* 40: 231–275.

Schwartz, E., and Straub, J. (1971), *Acta conciliorum oecumenicorum*, vol. 4.1, Berlin: de Gruyter.

Schweitzer, A. (1998), *The Mysticism of Paul the Apostle*, tr. William Montgomery, Baltimore: Johns Hopkins University Press.

Seeligman, I. L. (2004), *The Septuagint Version of Isaiah and Cognate Studies*, ed. R. Hanhart and H. Spiekermann, FAT 40, Tübingen: Mohr Siebeck.

Shum, S.-L. (2002), *Paul's Use of Isaiah in Romans: A Comparative Study of Paul's Letter to the Romans and the Sibylline and Qumran Sectarian Texts*, WUNT 2.156, Tübingen: Mohr Siebeck.

Silva, M. (2005), *Philippians*, BECNT, Grand Rapids: Eerdmans.

Singer, P. (1975), *Animal Liberation*, London: Harper Collins.

Sleeman, M. (2009), *Geography and the Ascension Narrative in Acts*, SNTSMS 146, Cambridge: Cambridge University Press.

——— (2016), 'The Ascension and Spatial Theory', in D. K. Bryan and D. W. Pao (eds.), *Ascent into Heaven in Luke-Acts: New Explorations of Luke's Narrative Hinge*, Minneapolis: Fortress, 157–173.

Smalley, S. S. (1998), *John: Evangelist & Interpreter*, 2nd edn, Downers Grove: InterVarsity Press.

Smith, D. (2010), 'Seeing a Pneuma(tic Body): The Apologetic Interests of Luke 24:36–43', *CBQ* 72: 752–772.

Smith, G. (1998), 'The Function of "Likewise" (ὡσαύτως) in Romans 8:26', *TynB* 49.1: 29–38.

Snyman, A. H. (2005), 'A Rhetorical Analysis of Philippians 1:12–26', *AcT* 25.1: 89–111.

Son, S.-W. A. (2009), 'The Church as "One New Man": Ecclesiology and Anthropology in Ephesians', *SwJT* 52.1: 18–31.

Soskice, J. M. (1985), *Metaphor and Religious Language*, Oxford: Clarendon.

Spicq, C. (1952), *L'Epitre Aux Hébreux*, Paris: J. Gabalda.

Stegman, T. D. (2005), *The Character of Jesus: The Linchpin to Paul's Argument in 2 Corinthians*, AnBib 158, Rome: Editrice Pontificio Istituto Biblico.

Stenning, J. F. (1949), *The Targum of Isaiah*, Oxford: Clarendon.

Strauss, M. L. (1995), *The Davidic Messiah: The Promise and Its Fulfillment in Lukan Christology*, JSNTSup 110, Sheffield: Sheffield Academic Press.

Svendsen, S. N. (2009), *Allegory Transformed: The Appropriation of Philonic Hermeneutics in the Letter to the Hebrews*, WUNT 2.269, Tübingen: Mohr Siebeck.

Tait, A. (1912), *The Heavenly Session of Our Lord: An Introduction to the History of the Doctrine*, London: Robert Scott.

Talbert, C. H. (2002), *Romans*, Smith & Helwys Bible Commentary, Macon, Ga.: Smyth & Helwys.

Thielman, F. (2010), *Ephesians*, BECNT, Grand Rapids: Baker.

Thiselton, A. C. (2000), *The First Epistle to the Corinthians: A Commentary on the Greek Text*, NIGTC, Grand Rapids: Eerdmans.

Thompson, M. M. (2001), *The God of the Gospel of John*, Grand Rapids: Eerdmans.

—— (2015), *John: A Commentary*, Louisville: Westminster John Knox.

Thrall, M. E. (1994), *A Critical and Exegetical Commentary on the Second Epistle to the Corinthians*, vol. 1: *Introduction and Commentary on II Corinthians I–VII*, ICC, Edinburgh: T&T Clark.

—— (2000), *A Critical and Exegetical Commentary on the Second Epistle to the Corinthians*, vol. 2: *Commentary on II Corinthians VIII–XII*, ICC, Edinburgh: T&T Clark.

Tilling, C. (2012), *Paul's Divine Christology*, WUNT 2.323, Tübingen: Mohr Siebeck.

Torrance, T. F. (1976), *Space, Time and Resurrection*, Edinburgh: T&T Clark.

Unnik, W. C. van (1963), '"With Unveiled Face", an Exegesis of 2 Corinthians iii 12–18', *NovT* 6: 153–169.

Waard, J. de (1997), *A Handbook on Isaiah*, Winona Lake: Eisenbrauns.

Wagner, J. R. (2002), *Heralds of the Good News: Isaiah and Paul 'In Concert' in the Letter to the Romans*, Leiden: Brill.

Wallace, D. B. (1996), *Greek Grammar Beyond the Basics*, Grand Rapids: Zondervan.

Walton, S. (2016), 'Jesus, Present And/Or Absent? The Presence and Presentation of Jesus as a Character in the Book of Acts', in F. Dicken and J. Snyder (eds.), *Characters and Characterization in Luke-Acts*, LNTS 548, London: Bloomsbury, 123–140.

Wanamaker, C. A. (1990), *The Epistles to the Thessalonians*, NIGTC, Grand Rapids: Eerdmans.

Ward, G. (1999), 'Bodies: The Displaced Body of Jesus Christ', in J. Milbank, C. Pickstock and G. Ward (eds.), *Radical Orthodoxy: A New Theology*, London: Routledge, 163–181.

Ware, J. (2014), 'Paul's Understanding of the Resurrection in 1 Corinthians 15:36–54', *JBL* 133.4: 809–835.

Watson, F. (2004), *Paul and the Hermeneutics of Faith*, London: T&T Clark.

Weima, J. A. D. (2014), *1–2 Thessalonians*, BECNT, Grand Rapids: Baker Academic.

Westcott, B. F. (1892), *The Epistle to the Hebrews: The Greek Text with Notes and Essays*, London: Macmillan.

Westermann, C. (1969), *Isaiah 40–66: A Commentary*, London: SCM.

Whybray, R. N. (1978), *Thanksgiving for a Liberated Prophet: An Interpretation of Isaiah Chapter 53*, JSOTSup 4, Sheffield: Sheffield University Press.

Wilk, F. (1998), *Die Bedeutung des Jesajabuches für Paulus*, Göttingen: Vandenhoeck & Ruprecht.

Windisch, H. (1968), *The Spirit-Paraclete in the Fourth Gospel*, tr. J. W. Cox, Philadelphia: Fortress.

Windsor, L. J. (2017), *Reading Ephesians and Colossians After Supersessionism: Christ's Mission Through Israel to the Nations*, Eugene: Cascade.

Witherington III, B. (1998), *The Acts of the Apostles: A Socio-Rhetorical Commentary*, Grand Rapids: Eerdmans.

Woll, D. B. (1981), *Johannine Christianity in Conflict: Authority, Rank, and Succession in the First Farewell Discourse*, SBLDS 60, Chico: Scholars Press.

Wong, E. (1985), 'The Lord Is the Spirit (2 Cor 3:17a)', *ETL* 61.1: 48–72.

Wrede, W. (1971), *The Messianic Secret*, tr. J. C. G. Grieg, London: James Clarke.

Wright, N. T. (1991), *The Climax of the Covenant: Christ and the Law in Pauline Theology*, Edinburgh: T&T Clark.

––––––– (2003), *The Resurrection of the Son of God*, Christian Origins and the Question of God 3, London: SPCK.

––––––– (2007), *Surprised by Hope*, London: SPCK.

Ziesler, J. A. (1983), *Pauline Christianity*, Oxford: Oxford University Press.

Zumstein, J. (2008), 'Jesus' Resurrection in the Farewell Discourses', in C. R. Koester and R. Bieringer (eds.), *The Resurrection of Jesus in the Gospel of John*, WUNT 2:222, Tübingen: Mohr Siebeck, 103–126.

Zwiep, A. W. (1997), *The Ascension of the Messiah in Lukan Christology*, NovTSup 87, Leiden: Brill.

––––––– (2001), 'Assumptus est in caelum: Rapture and Heavenly Exaltation in Early Judaism and Luke-Acts', in F. Avemarie and H. Lichtenberger (eds.), *Auferstehung–Resurrection: The Fourth Durham-Tübingen Research Symposium; Resurrection, Transfiguration and Exaltation in Old Testament, Ancient Judaism and Early Christianity*, Tübingen: Mohr Siebeck, 323–439.

———— (2010), *Christ, the Spirit and the Community of God*, WUNT 2.293, Tübingen: Mohr Siebeck.

———— (2016), 'Ascension Scholarship: Past, Present and Future', in D. K. Bryan and D. W. Pao (eds.), *Ascent into Heaven in Luke-Acts: New Explorations of Luke's Narrative Hinge*, Minneapolis: Fortress, 7–26.

Index of authors

INDEX OF AUTHORS

Index of Scripture references

231

INDEX OF SCRIPTURE REFERENCES

Titles in this series:

An index of Scripture references for all the volumes may be found at
http://www.thegospelcoalition.org/resources/nsbt

Lightning Source UK Ltd.
Milton Keynes UK
UKHW020659191121
394250UK00010B/821

9 781783 597482